THE COMPLETE
ASIAN
COOKBOOK

THE COMPLETE
ASIAN
COOKBOOK

Terry Tan

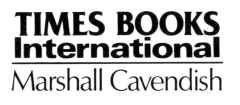

TIMES BOOKS
International
Marshall Cavendish

UK edition jointly published
1984 by Times Books International, Singapore
and Marshall Cavendish Books Limited, London

© Times Books International 1982
No 1 New Industrial Road
Singapore 1953

Cover copyright: Marshall Cavendish Limited 1984

Printed in Yugoslavia

ISBN 0 86307 226 7

INTRODUCTION

More than one overseas visitor has remarked on Singapore's national pastime — shopping. Urban development and a more than buoyant economy have, naturally, thrown up veritable emporiums of consumer goods and what's the good of having money if you can't buy? But this wry observation is only half right. The real Singapore pastime, the one that visitors who stay briefly and have less opportunity to notice, is eating.

When Stamford Raffles, farsighted though he must have been to envision Singapore as a colonial trading post, bar none, first set foot on the swampy island of 1819 he could not have known he laid the foundation for one of the world's most mouth-watering culinary heritages. And he had some two thousand years of help.

Way back before the Christian era ships flying Indian, Chinese and Arabian flags plied the area with their cargo holds laden to the beam with precious tea, ginger and spices. The Sri Vijaya empire with its royal seat in Sumatra also embraced this far-flung sea town then known as Temasek.

In the ensuing centuries wars were fought and territorial rights asserted and in time Temasek became part of the Javanese empire ruled by the Majapahit. More power struggles resulted when the Siamese cast their eyes on this spice-rich region and Singapura, as Temasek came to be named, was utterly destroyed.

The vicious grip of jungle growth became the true victor and the island slumbered in the tropical humidity.

When Raffles came in 1819 he was eyed with suspicion by several hundred Malays. These were believed to be descendants of outlawed princelings, assorted cutthroats and pirates who plundered the region during the slumbering years.

The pungence in the air that greeted this East Indian Company clerk came from the pepper and gambier plants cultivated by the handful of Chinese who found their way here from other migrant settlements in the Malay Peninsula.

Melaka, or Malacca, was already the fount of the Straitsborn community and had been so for over 300 years. Malaccan traders made a bee-line for the new colonial outpost to be joined by other fortune hunters from the Celebes, Java, Sumatra, India and of course South China.

Our wonderful culinary heritage really began in earnest then. In the holds of graceful Indiamen, Javanese prahus and Chinese junks were such exotic goods as peacock feathers, exotic plumes from tropical birds, porcelain from China, bolts of silk, and tea, sugar, sago, pepper, nutmeg, cloves, cinnamon and coriander.

As Singapore flourished under the British administration more migrants came with the gleam of gold in their eyes. From the different villages in the province of Guangdong came Cantonese with their sweet and sour dishes, spring rolls and fried rice.

From this greatest school of cooking — some say the best in the world with more than 50,000 dishes — came a no-holds-barred menu of pig's stomach in pepper, chicken claws in oyster sauce, duck's webs, snakes, sea cucumbers and myriad ways of cooking pork.

The Hokkiens came with their clear soups, soy sauce, red-cooked meats and braised seafood dishes. The Fujian province has a long sea coast and seafood that could not be finished at one sitting would be dried, salted or preserved. Though Swatow cooking is not a school by itself — the five major schools of Chinese cooking being Cantonese, Shangtung, Szechuan, Fujian and Hunan and two minor ones of Yang Zhou and Vegetarian — it contributed to Singapore its steamed dishes and classical desserts.

Indian traders, the cornerstone of the community in Singapore, never ate a meal that was not authentically Indian till today. Whether

5

they came as indentured labourers, rubber tappers, clerks, entrepreneurs from Madras (capital of Tamil Nadu), Kerala, Sri Lanka, Pakistan, the Punjab and even Persia (the few Parsis were Zoroastrians who originated from Persia), they clung fiercely to their cuisine.

Transplanted by force of circumstances or a desire to make fortunes, this tenacious love for home-grown food was natural enough. The Malay sea-faring folk had already developed their own style of cooking from which the Straits Chinese borrowed heavily to develop and refine their unique cuisine.

To Westerners there might seem little difference between a Malay curry and a Straitsborn curry, a Hainanese steamed chicken and a Swatow boiled hen or Cantonese stewed duck and the Hokkien variety. But the differences were more than subtle with later modification by Singaporeans hard pressed for time. It is the Chinese propensity to borrow, and adapt that the cuisine is such a vast one.

I am all for this developmental and experimental school if, for nothing else, cooking will continue to be an art to be enjoyed and savoured rather than a chore. I have myself shamelessly conned friends to part with this recipe or that and adapted them to suit my tastes.

FOOD — MANY CULTURES IN ONE POT

Growing up as I did in an extended family that often sat down 20 to a meal, it was a marvellous childhood that grew fat on food. Ours was a rambling pre-war bungalow and had a huge kitchen that looked more like a factory. Actually for a time after the war, it was turned into a factory of sorts when my father decided he wanted to go into the record-pressing industry.

I vaguely recall machinery and lots of workers who also ate off the boss. There was always someone cooking, peeling vegetables or stirring huge cauldrons of soup or porridge.

My father's people were of Amoy or Hokkien stock and when he married my mother, who was of Swatow stock, our cuisine was an ever-changing one.

You see, my mother was my father's second official wife, the first being a Hokkien lady whose people hailed from Penang and Malacca. Both my father and mother and his first wife were all Straitsborn Singaporeans with the added bonus that my father also spent some years in Indonesia and had a penchant for Indonesian food.

Then there were the innumerable family retainers — we were rather better off before the old man died — assorted visitors from Penang, Malacca, Indonesia and Shanghai. My father was some kind of civil engineer who dabbled in anything that made money and had business associates from such far-flung places as Beijing, Taiping, America and England.

There was always someone or other who dined in the house and my poor mother, good cook though she was, had to prepare some of the strangest dishes. But like a good wife she never complained and my culinary heritage was richer for it. We often ate Shanghainese food, Penang food, Thai food, Malay food and Indonesian food.

Our neighbours contributed to the melting pot as well. My mother, in her later years, had some kind of a resident masseuse, a Malay woman who would sit and yarn with us while my mother was getting ready for her nightly rubdown. She imparted her cooking skills and taught us how to make good satay, serondeng, ketupat and Malay cakes. We had the privilege of having Indian, Eurasian, Punjabi and a few Arab neighbours who often came bearing trays laden with food on their festive New Years.

Hari Raya Puasa, the Malay New Year and the last day of the Ramadan Month, was especially splendid. My mother's masseuse and a few other neighbours would bring ketupat (rice parcels) that went with mutton and chicken

curry, serondeng (fried coconut), sambal prawns and an assortment of sweetmeats. It was no trouble at all to coax the recipes out of Mak Siti or Mrs Maniam.

This was the time before urban bulldozers mowed down village attap houses to make way for skyrise flats. We were living in a Chinese-style bungalow surrounded by several Malay villages. These villagers were an enterprising lot making use of their spare time to cook little tidbits for sale.

Often the sale counter was an extension of Aminah's kitchen worktop area that also doubled as a bed for afternoon naps. This "baleh-baleh" as we called it was the nurturing ground for some of my childhood's most mouthwatering memories.

From it came trays of rich, red spicy Mee Siam, Lontong and Nasi Lemak (curry noodles, rice cakes with vegetable curry and coconut rice eaten with a compote of fried fish, cucumber and sambal).

Even in later years when I was much older, and visiting my grandparents' home along the coast, this memory was rekindled. Behind my grandfather's rambling house were several similar villages where not only Malay seagoing folk made ends more than meet by selling the same tidbits, there were also Hainanese fishermen who introduced us to a whole new range of food.

Hainanese cooking reaches its glory in Hainanese chicken rice, a culinary classic, but there's much more to the cuisine than we care to think. There used to be makeshift hawker stalls all over Singapore selling specifically Hainanese "karly png" or "curry rice" and with the passage of time and urbanisation, these stalls vanished but not their food.

I remember the dishes and have had on many occasions entertained with their delicious pork chops with onions, beancurd soup, salted vegetable and pork and chicken curry.

The Hainanese too must be singled out as talented cooks by virtue of two factors. In the golden age of the Straits Chinese who were wealthy, Hainanese men were hired as cooks. They had come from their native Hainan island knowing only kitchen skills and had no trouble getting employment with the well-heeled Straitsborn families.

The British colonials later cottoned on to the same kitchen wizards and there was born a generation of Hainanese cooks who excelled in cooking Western dishes. These were the fore-runners of the restaurant chefs who till this day hold court in hallowed English pub-like eating establishments.

They could, and still can, outcook the most Mrs Beeton when it came to steak and kidney pies, oxtail, roast beef and yorkshire pudding and trifles of the most sinful beauty.

My father too had a Hainanese chauffeur-cum-secretary who loved nothing more than cooking on his off days. But he did have a taste for some barbaric combinations like monkey meat in wine and roast dog. I have tasted his monkey meat but chewing on Fido's bones was something I eschewed vehemently.

RECIPES

Nothing quite reflects our multi-cultural character as Singapore home-cooking. Few, if any family, practices the homogeneity in cooking styles as, say, a German or Italian family would. For the Singapore family is as likely to sit down to a meal composed of a Cantonese soup, a Malay curry, a Western salad or Indian dessert as go out for a pizza.

Our cosmopolitanism is taken to its nth degree at the dinner table (since most Singaporeans work, lunch is invariably a hawker food affair), something that foreign visitors never fail to be mildly astonished at.

Thus it is on this premise that this Singapore cookbook has been written because it would be difficult to define what makes a typical Singapore-home-cooked meal. A dish, or two perhaps but a whole meal is apt to be regional, international or a mixture of both!

It is equally pointless to categorise because restaurant dishes are well within the range of Singapore cooks and hawker fare is often whipped up when one can't be bothered to go out.

For the benefit of those who are beginner-cooks, I have simplified and modified where I think it will not alter the taste too much. I am totally unashamed of admitting that I very often cannot be bothered to spend more than half an hour in the kitchen.

Besides, I subscribe to the philosophy that to entice novice cooks to develop a liking for cooking, one must first show him or her the simplest way. After this, you can go and spend two hours grinding spices if you think it's worth the effort.

People the world over are getting more urbanised each day and until they become instinctive cooks, are unlikely to be won over by some purist admonition that you must stew beef for six hours over the stove because pressure-cooking for 30 minutes is simply not the same.

By the same token few are going to hark back to yesterday's age-old method of dicing vegetables when an electric processor does the job three times as fast. The difference in taste, texture or whatever is far outweighed by the time saved for learning yet another dish.

One kitchen implement of old that still provokes heated arguments about its efficacy or lumbering uselessness is the pestle and mortar or batu lesong as it is called in Malay. This is nothing more than a hollowed-out granite bowl with a granite pestle. Wet or dry spices are placed in the hollow and ground by hand till they are fine.

The belief persists that curry spices ground thus are finer and taste better. There is some truth in this as onions, garlic and other fresh root spices release their pungent oils more effectively than they would if ground in an electric blender. On the other hand a pestle and mortar can be messy to use and does not allow more than so much to be ground at one go. It also takes a lot more time and for this reason alone most people would give it a miss.

My mother, till the day she passed on, simply refused to use my blender preferring to grind her spices in multiple lots when she cooked large amounts. No amount of coaxing or persuasion would make her change her mind and I must admit it made sense (with hindsight) that time is of no consequence if one is proud of one's culinary heritage. Today I suggest using short cuts simply because advocating the use of a pestle and mortar would merely fall on deaf ears.

This is neither "selling out" nor cocking a snook at veteran cooks who can afford to be singular purists. I say if you have the time by all means stretch the task. If you don't, taking short cuts is the only sensible way to learn. And learn you can as I have learnt these past 25 years that my mother's methods were not necessarily the best.

Harking back to an earlier time, my family used to have an even more lumbering implement called the batu giling. This was a large slab of granite too heavy to be moved anywhere — it used to sit on a raised platform so users did not have to squat — and came with a granite roller that weighed a ton. Spices and even meats would be first cut up and distributed evenly in the centre of the slab. The roller would be manipulated back and forth with a rolling-pin action and everything would be ground to a remarkable fineness.

Many Indian families still use this implement as spices figure in just about every one of their dishes. And no implement yet invented can process chillies to the same degree of fineness. This I can vouch for but I'm not about to lug my mother's batu giling to my apartment kitchen!

CONTENTS

Fish and other seafood

USEFUL TIPS

ABALONE
This is the edible muscle of a large sea mollusc and resembles a giant sea scallop. Canned abalone are available at most Chinese supermarkets. Cook simply with chicken in a clear broth for abalone soup. Very tasty stewed in oyster sauce.

ALMONDS
Whole almonds keep better while ground almonds are best used up within a few weeks of being opened. Slivered almonds lightly toasted make a nice garnish for saffron rice.

ALUMINIUM FOIL
Food wrapped in foil keeps much better for refrigeration as no ice crystals can form on meat or fish. Charcoal-grilled food wrapped in foil also seals in flavours and prevents drying up from evaporation.

BACON
Bacon deserves more than its breakfast-appearance-only reputation. Chopped bacon imparts a lovely flavour when fried to whatever else is tossed into the wok. As a substitute for Chinese sausages in clay pot rice, bacon is perfectly respectable.

BAMBOO SHOOTS
Canned bamboo shoots are available from some supermarkets and Chinese grocers and taste just as good as fresh ones, which are not only hard to come by, but take a lot of work to pre-prepare. As a vegetable it has a chameleon quality to blend with chicken, mushrooms and beef. Particularly important in Chinese spring rolls, bamboo shoots can be kept for up to two weeks if immersed in water and refrigerated.

BANANA LEAVES
One of the most indispensable leaves used in Asian cooking, banana leaves are used not only to wrap all manner of meats and seafood for grilling they are also used as dinner plates in Indian meals. Use aluminium foil to the same effect.

BEANCURD (TOFU)
Beancurd is generally available from health food shops and Chinese grocers. Ordinary beancurd is usually sold in 225g (8oz) blocks, and silken beancurd (which is much softer), is sold in vacuum-packed cardboard containers. Both types usually need to be drained on kitchen paper before use. Some recipes refer to dried beancurd, and this can sometimes be found in Chinese grocers.

BEANSPROUTS
Grown from green mung beans and sold in most supermarkets and western health food stores either fresh or canned. Fresh beansprouts can be kept refrigerated for up to a week if sealed in a plastic bag.

BLACK BEANS, SALTED
Heavily salted soy beans sold in Chinese supermarkets in cans and jars. They have to be rinsed in water before being added to meat or seafood dishes. Use sparingly as a little goes a long way.

CASHEW NUTS
Kidney-shaped beans that make a crunchy topping to stir-fried vegetables. If you buy raw cashews dry-fry them in a wok with salt until slightly oily fragrance exudes. Keep in air-tight jars or they turn soft very fast.

CELLOPHANE (TRANSPARENT) NOODLES
Another mung bean by-product available from most Chinese grocers. These transparent noodles must be first soaked in water before being added to soups or stir-fried dishes. They need only minutes of simmering.

CHINESE SAUSAGES
Thin sausages filled with raw, lean and fat pork sold at most Chinese and speciality food

stores. Steam or fry and cut into diagonal slices before adding to clay pot rice or fried rice.

COCONUTS
Another beautiful ingredient in Singapore cooking, the coconut is used fresh in most Asian countries. However, coconut creams either in blocks or cans, make perfect substitutes if used in curries. The processed product lacks the subtle flavour so important in the preparation of Singapore desserts but can be used all the same. Desiccated coconut when reconstituted with hot water renders a milk that is thin and watery and suitable for mild curries. It is well worth the trouble to grate a fresh coconut to be squeezed for milk if you can find one.

CORNFLOUR or CORN STARCH
An especially useful thickener in Cantonese dishes. Cornflour should be mixed with a little cold water (never use hot or you'll get lumps) and then added to simmering or boiling liquid. 1 tablespoon cornflour will thicken about 500 ml (16 fl oz) of stock for gravy consistency required in most Chinese dishes.

CURRY POWDER
There is no mystique in curry powder. Curry paste is curry powder moistened with a little water to facilitate frying. Dry powder tends to burn quickly in hot oil. Each seasoned cook has his or her individual blend, the balance of which depends on personal taste. The spices used are generally unvarying but curry powder or paste needs the added fillip of sliced onions, ginger or whole spices to give curries characteristic flavour. Commercially prepared curry powders are convenient and save you the bother of mixing fiddly amounts. For those who wish to mix their own here are two suggestions. As a rule, 2 tbsp of curry powder or paste is sufficient for 500 g (1 lb) of meat or fish for a mild curry and 4 tbsp for a stronger curry. Mix spices well and store in airtight bottles. If you are using

coconut milk or tamarind juice for your curry use 1 or 2 tbsp of either to moisten your curry powder before frying.

DEEP-FRYING
This means cooking foods, especially batter-coated seafood and vegetables, in enough oil to completely cover them. The result of deep-frying is vastly different from shallow pan-frying because the high heat quickly cooks the food, sealing in all the natural juices and cooking the inside without it coming in contact with the oil. Typical examples are batter-coated items which, when properly deep-fried, are crisp outside and succulent inside. Only vegetable, peanut or corn oil must be used. Solid animal fats like butter or ghee burn easily. A good investment is a deep-fryer with a fryer basket.

MEAT CURRY POWDER
400 g (13 oz) ground coriander
150 g (5 oz) ground aniseed
100 g (3 oz) ground cumin
100 g (3 oz) ground pepper
150 g (5 oz) ground chilli
60 g (2 oz) ground turmeric
30 g (1 oz) ground cinnamon
1 tsp ground cardamom
1 tsp ground cloves

FISH CURRY POWDER
400 g (13 oz) ground coriander
150 g (5 oz) ground fennel
150 g (5 oz) ground cumin
100 g (3 oz) ground pepper
150 g (5 oz) ground chilli
70 g (2½ oz) ground turmeric
50 g (1¾ oz) ground cardamom

TO BE LEFT WHOLE AND FRIED WITH PASTE
4 star anise (available from Chinese grocers)
6 cloves
2 cinnamon sticks 5 cm (2 in) long
1 tbsp fenugreek (available from health food shops or seed merchants).

DOUBLE-BOILING

If you have a traditional double-boiler it's ideal for long, slow cooking processes. Food is placed in one boiler which is in turn placed in a larger boiler filled with boiling water. Thus it is the action of the slow simmering water that cooks the food instead of direct heat. Herby chicken soups and birds' nests are usually double-boiled for several hours.

FISH

All types of dried fish, including cuttlefish, shrimps, prawns, anchovies and silver fish, can be bought from Chinese supermarkets. King, and other large prawns, are kept frozen or in the chiller cabinet. Canned abalone, and strongly flavoured shrimp paste are also usually available from Chinese supermarkets.

RICE FLOUR

Sold ready ground rice flour is used mainly for making desserts and for adding to other flours for dumpling skins. Sold in packets of 250 g (½ lb) and 500 g (1 lb) ready for use. Makes a light batter with water and when added to mashed bananas or other root vegetables gives bulk without making fritters heavy.

GARLIC

This strong-smelling bulb of the leek family is as important to stir-fried vegetables as cream is to strawberries. A few cloves crushed and tossed in hot oil "starts" the wok and prepares the cooking fat for whatever food is cooked in it. The pungence is transformed into fragrance without which most stir-fried vegetables are colourless. Fried crushed garlic makes a beautiful garnish for seafood soups and dumpling stews.

GIBLETS

Enough cannot be said about the treatment of giblets. They certainly deserve more attention than being thrown away. Cleaned properly and fried with pineapple or any sharp vegetable, giblets make a rich and nourishing dish. Contrary to popular belief giblets do not smell any more than beef does.

GINGER

Ginger has a remarkable affinity with chicken, mushrooms and curries. Shredded green ginger (grated from peeled fresh root ginger) tossed in oil, adds a new dimension to stir-fried beef or chicken and tempers richness. Ginger *juice* is obtained by squeezing out the finely grated ginger.

GINGKO NUTS

These are available in cans from some Chinese grocers and Japanese food suppliers. As they are already peeled and simmered, they may be used straight away.

HONEY

Nature's own nectar that even Asian cooks have adopted as a star item in marinades and basting liquids. Certainly a lot healthier than processed sugar and more fragrant especially when rubbed on fowls for roasting or grilling. Makes a good substitute for palm sugar in certain Asian or Singapore dishes which call for sweetness.

LEMON

Where a dish calls for lime juice, the equivalent amount of lemon juice will do just as well. Though less sharp than lime juice it serves exactly the same purpose. Grated lemon peel also makes a good substitute for fragrant lime leaves or lemon grass.

LEMON GRASS

Grown in tropical countries, lemon grass is used in a wide range of tamarind-based curries and makes an unforgettable dish when sliced and ground with curry spices: tossed into gravies or used as a basting brush, it has a special affinity with seafood. If difficult to obtain, however, grated lemon rind may be substituted, or a thin strip of lemon rind if the lemon grass is to be left whole.

MACADAMIA NUTS

Macadamia nuts are indispensable as thickening agents in curry paste for Singapore curries. Simply grind or pound into a thick paste and add to curry spices. Skinned almonds may be used if macadamias are not easily available.

MUSHROOMS

Of the many types available I find Chinese dried mushroom caps have the most flavour. These have to be soaked in hot water first and are excellent simply stewed, tossed into soup or stuffed with meat or seafood and grilled. Button, straw and fresh western mushrooms are all excellent with stir-fried vegetables.

PANDAN LEAVES OR SCREWPINE LEAVES

An indispensable flavouring and colouring ingredient in Asian desserts and a few curries. The leaves are crushed or tied into knots and flavour extracted by boiling or squeezing. Use a vanilla pod as substitute.

PLUM SAUCE

The base of sweet-sour sauce, plum sauce can be bought in jars or loose amounts from Chinese Supermarkets. Equal amounts of this and tomato sauce make a basic sweet-sour mix that has the right combination of flavours.

SAFFRON

Incredibly expensive stamens of the crocus plant, saffron comes in dark-red strands with a strong perfume. Used mainly in biryani it is far superior to turmeric which is often used as a substitute. Apart from yielding the same yellow colouring the latter is nowhere near as fragrant as saffron.

SESAME OIL

This is not a cooking medium but rather a flavouring. A few drops of sesame oil in oil used for deep-frying will impart a lovely fragrance to food like tempura and prawns or seafood in batter.

SOY SAUCE

Three types of soy sauce are generally available from most supermarkets; ordinary, which can be used for any purpose, light, and heavy, (also known as black soy sauce). Oyster, fish and Hoi Sin sauce can be obtained from Chinese supermarkets.

TAMARIND

Dried tamarind and pressed tamarind pods are widely available from Indian and Chinese grocers. Instructions for use are on the packets. Tamarind paste is also available, although sometimes it tends to ferment in storage. If unobtainable, use lemon juice diluted with water.

VEGETABLES

Fresh bean shoots, mustard greens and Chinese cabbage are sold in most Chinese supermarkets. Mustard greens and salted or preserved vegetables are also obtainable canned.

WATER CHESTNUTS

Available canned; water chestnuts chopped up and added to minced pork or prawns for spring rolls give a delightful crunch.

WOK

Possibly the mostly versatile cooking implement ever invented. The wok can be used for frying, braising, boiling, steaming with great effect. Cast iron is the best material for a wok but aluminium and stainless steel are just as good if kept dry or oiled after every cooking session. Electric and non-stick woks with lids are very handy for braising, when stir-frying, always use a wooden spoon to avoid chipping the wok's non-stick coating.

THE STORY OF SPICES

Allspice
Dried berry of the allspice plant with fragrance not unlike a mixture of nutmeg, cloves and cinnamon (hence the name). Good with meat dishes, pickled vegetables and fruits and rich egg-based cakes like the Indonesian layer cake.

Aniseed
Faintly liquorice flavour and one of the trio that make up basic curry powder. The other two are coriander and cumin. Rather bland flavour used on its own but good with meat casseroles, mild curries and sambals.

Caraway
A whole seed that is sharp and pppery and credited with some reputation as an antacid. Used mainly in western cooking as flavouring for pickled vegetables and cakes and breads.

Cardamom
Pale white dried seed capsules that are slightly lemony and bitter-sweet. Indispensable in Indian lamb and mutton curries. Also good with stewed fruit and gingerbread.

Chillies
Ground from whole dried pods and the hottest of all peppery spices. A little goes a long way so use sparingly. On average and even for the uninitiated one teaspoon of chilli powder would be sufficient for a curry paste or mix for one chicken.

Cinnamon
Dried inner bark of the cinnamon plant usually sold in curled sticks or powder form. Sweet and slightly musky flavour ideal for curries and hot toddies. When using whole sticks for infusion remove before serving.

Cloves
Dried unopened buds with strong and tangy flavour. Used whole in beef stews, chicken pies and pineapple cakes and tarts. Usually goes with cinnamon and delightful in mulled wines.

Coriander
Dried seed or powder form of the aromatic coriander plant. Pungent and slightly sweet and the basis of all Asian curries. Very good on its own with duck and chicken and combines extremely well with soy sauce and sugar.

Cumin
Dried seed or ground with aromatic flavour not unlike aniseed. Indispensable to curry powder and good with pickles and fruit pies.

Curry Powder
A blend of ground spices: turmeric, coriander, aniseed, cumin, ginger and onion depending on type of curry. Basis is mixture of 2 parts coriander to one part each of aniseed and cumin, one large onion and 1 tbsp ginger shreds or powder.

Fennel
Also known in Asia as "sweet cumin", it has much the same flavour as aniseed.

Fenugreek
Small brownish seeds with a slightly bitter flavour, they must be used judiciously. Particularly good in fish curries where the whole seeds are dry fried before being mixed with other spices.

Garam Masala
A spice blend that contains any of the following: cumin, black pepper, cloves, cardamom ground together. Not a hot spice mix and usually added towards the end of cooking.

Laos Root
Also known as galangal or galingale, it has a delicate flavour that is often not noticed. Largely an optional ingredient and can be substituted with ordinary green ginger.

Mustard Seed
Sweet musky flavour and used grated in mild curries. Used more in desserts and confectionery.

Paprika
Dried, ground sweet red peppers that are not at all hot. Ideal for curries for those who prefer them mild.

Pepper (black or white)
Whole dried inner peppercorns or ground to a powder. Largely used as a condiment in Asian cooking.

Saffron
The world's most expensive spice, it comes in whole dried strands or ground. Exotic golden colour and a pungent aroma transform long grain rice into the princely biryani. Use sparingly.

Sesame
Whole seed, dried or toasted with a sweet nutty flavour. Used largely as a condiment in Asian sweetmeats and a topping for snacks.

Turmeric
Yellow root, sold fresh or in powder form. Bright yellow colour that stains permanently and with a slightly bitter taste. Important ingredient in yellow curries and sometimes used as a cheap substitute for saffron.

A Selection of Ingredients for Asian Cooking

1	*Yow char kway*	12	Soaked cuttlefish	23	Fried egg noodles (fine)
2	Dried soybean cakes	13	Dried cuttlefish	24	Black shrimp paste
3	Small dried soybean cakes	14	Fried egg noodles	25	Rice vermicelli
4	Chinese sausages	15	Century eggs	26	Sesame oil
5	Salt fish	16	Salted duck's eggs	27	Preserved soy beans
6	Rice malt sauce	17	Thick yellow noodles		(light variety)
7	Black soy sauce	18	*Wonton* skin	28	Oyster sauce
8	Light soy sauce	19	Quail's eggs	29	Dried egg noodles
9	Mushroom sauce	20	Dried prawns	30	*Tow-see*
10	Fish sauce	21	Dried young anchovies	31	*Hoi sin* sauce
11	Chinese rice wine	22	Green pea flour	32	Macaroni

33	Thick rice vermicelli	44	Sharksfin
34	*Wonton* egg noodles	45	Fine rice vermicelli
35	Firm soybean cake	46	Dried radish
36	Soft soybean cake	47	Young corn cobs
37	Flat rice noodles	48	Tamarind
38	Soybean skin *(fu chok)*	49	Dried lily flowers
39	*Teem chok*	50	Black sweet malt
40	Plum sauce	51	Dried anchovies
41	Spring roll skin	52	Dried shrimp paste
42	Spring roll skin	53	Transparent noodles
43	Fresh Hokkien mee	54	Dried tamarind skin

Asian Vegetables, Herbs and Fruits

1 Screwpine leaves	17 Tomatoes	32 Cucumber	45 Chinese chives (with flowers)	59 Coriander leaves
2 Banana flower	18 Bird chillies	33 Carrot	46 Young ginger	60 Curry leaves
3 Pumpkin	19 Yam	34 Cauliflower	47 Ginger	61 Watercress
4 Winter melon	20 Bamboo shoot	35 Mustard green (*kai choy*, Chinese)	48 Small sour starfruit	62 Celery
5 Long bottle gourd	21 Yam bean	36 Radish	49 Chinese spinach (*tong hoe*)	63 Lettuce
6 *Pisang mas*	22 Lady's fingers	37 Red & green chillies	50 Water chestnuts	64 *Kiamchye* (salted *kuakchye*)
7 *Pisang rajah*	23 Capsicum	38 Sweet potato leaves	51 Cabbage	65 *Daun kadeok*
8 *Pisang tandok*	24 Bittergourd	39 Chinese white cabbage	52 Basil (*Daun selaseh*)	66 Turmeric leaf
9 *Pisang hijau*	25 Vegetable marrow	40 Leek	53 Basil (*Daun kemangi*)	67 Long beans
10 *Petai*	26 Pineapple	41 Potatoes	54 Mint leaves	68 Chinese chives (without flowers)
11 Drumsticks	27 Limes (large), local limes (small)	42 *Bunga kantan*	55 Soybean sprouts	69 *Daun kessom*
12 Lemon grass	28 Lemons	43 French beans	56 Beansprouts	70 Mustard green (*kai choy*, local)
13 Tapioca	29 Angled loofah	44 Chinese mustard greens (white stalk variety)	57 Spring onion	71 Mustard green (*choy sum*)
14 Onions	30 Green eggplant		58 Galingale	
15 Garlic	31 Purple eggplant			
16 Shallots				

FISH AND OTHER SEAFOOD

I have the most endearing and enduring memories of my childhood when I romped the muggy days and balmy nights away by the sea. Even as a child of six, the sea's bounty was an endless fascination. My grandparents' home was a sprawling Chinese-style home with wide verandahs that faced the sea barely 10 metres away. There for the taking were catfish, clams, razor-sharp molluscs, squid, prawns and the occasional washed-ashore sea cucumber.

In the backyard were the herbs so loved by the Straits Chinese and the two came together something beautiful and fragrant. Lemon grass with fish, turmeric leaves with prawns and tamarind, banana leaves used to wrap all manner of seafood and the dozens of other unidentifiable greens that went into the innumerable spicy salads we ate.

In later years, when I was much older, my father had a small bungalow that not only was by the sea we had the waves lapping at our front gate. It was marvellous holding a fishing rod with a line that dangled a fat worm at its extreme end while I leaned along the railings of the patio. If I got lucky, I could virtually swing my catch along a graceful arc and right into our kitchen. Alas, it wasn't so easy and the fish were too wily to rise to my bait. The real fish came from the dozens of sampans and large fishing boats that crunched up to shore in the early hours.

I did not need much coaxing to follow my mother and several aunties and neighbours to buy the freshest seafood straight from the boat. Fresh anchovies, still pearly white and breathing, enormous green-tinged prawns that had a lot of jumping life in them, slumberous ray fish, snappers, garoupas and the rare silvery-skinned wolf herring that is still my favourite.

We kids would linger in the hope the fishermen would spare a handful or two of tiny squid black with ejected ink as a protest against their ignominious fate. Sometimes a few cents would part hands and off we would go to the village behind my grandparents' home. I would seek out the itinerant hawker who sold his fried rice cakes (chye tow kway) for 10 cents a plate all rich and oily with lard, sweet black sauce and egg.

With some persuasion he would toss in our squid and fry up the most delicious breakfast. And for lunch there would always be fish on the table. Fish fresh and leaping just minutes ago. I learnt to gut fish and treat them with respect long before I learnt to climb my first tree.

Barbecued Fish

Cooking time: 15 minutes

1 whole mackerel about 650 g (1¼ lbs)
1 tsp vinegar
1 tsp salt
1 tsp turmeric powder
1 tsp chilli powder
2 pieces banana leaf about 35 cm (14 in)
   squared or foil of the same size
3 tbsp oil

SPICES
1 large onion
3 cloves garlic
1 stalk lemon grass or grated lemon rind
½ tsp grated lemon rind
1 tbsp coriander powder
1 tsp chilli powder

Wash and clean fish. Make diagonal slits along both sides of body about 1 cm (½ in) deep. Rub fish with vinegar, salt, turmeric and chilli powder. Set aside for 15 minutes.

Pound or blend spices till fine. Scald banana leaves with hot water until pliant and place fish on double layer. Smear fish all over with pounded spices and spoon remaining inside stomach cavity.

Dribble oil all over. Wrap banana leaves round fish until completely covered. Place under hot grill or over hot charcoal and cook for 8 minutes on each side. Open up leaf or foil in the last 3 minutes of grilling to sizzle fish surface. This also allows excess moisture to evaporate so you don't get a steamed fish instead.

Stuffed Hake (illustrated on p. 32)

Cooking time: 10 minutes

I had the marvellous opportunity of learning some exotic dishes from the Indo-Chinese countries when my family home was a boarding house for foreign students. At various times I had to cook for Laotians, Thais, Koreans and Cambodians. One of the Cambodians, I forget his name now, taught me this recipe. Actually the word "stuff" is somewhat a misnomer as no stuffing is involved. Rather, a compote of spices, whether fried or boiled, is poured over the previously fried fish.

1 hake (or small cod steaks may be used) about
   450 g (14 oz)
6 tbsp oil

SPICES
2 stalks lemon grass or grated lemon rind
2 fresh red chillies
¾ tsp grated lemon rind
1 tsp salt
2 cloves garlic

Wash and clean hake and cut into steaks about 2 cm (¾ in) thick. Fry in hot oil until light brown and cooked through. Leave aside. Pound spices together until fine and stir fry in the remaining oil

Fry until oil seeps out again and sprinkle a little water over if it looks too dry. Put back pieces of hake and give the whole a good stir. Serve garnished with fresh coriander leaves.

Grilled Spiced Fish (illustrated on p. 44)

Cooking time: 15 minutes

1 kilo (2 lbs) fish (any meaty kind)
2 tbsp soy sauce
Juice of 2 limes
1 red chilli, sliced
3 tbsp oil

SPICES
1 tbsp coriander powder
1 tsp cumin powder
½ tsp turmeric powder
3 cloves garlic
1 tsp chilli powder
1 large onion
1 tsp salt

Pound spices until fine. If you are using powder, grate the other ingredients first and then stir in the powdered spices. Wash and clean fish and make a deep slit in stomach and along sides.

Rub pounded spices all over fish and stuff remaining spices inside stomach cavity. Secure with thread or toothpicks.

Mix oil, soy sauce and lime juice and pour over stuffed fish. Place on a wire rack and grill for about 8 minutes on each side. Serve garnished with sliced red chillis.

How long your fish takes to cook depends on the thickness of the fish.

Sambal Fish

Cooking time: 13 minutes

500 g (1 lb) grey mullet without bone
½ coconut, grated
Juice of 2 limes
1 tsp grated lemon rind
250 ml (9 fl oz) water
4 tbsp oil

SPICES
5 red chillies, seeded
2 stalks lemon grass or grated lemon rind
10 almonds
1 large onion
2 cloves garlic

Wash and clean fish and cut into pieces 4 cm x 2 cm (1 ½ in x ¾ in). Pound spices till fine and rub about 2 tsp all over fish. Leave aside. Fry remaining spices in hot oil until fragrant. Squeeze coconut for water for milk.

Add half to spices and bring to the boil. Add fish and simmer for 4 minutes. Add the remaining milk and finish cooking for about 3 minutes. Oil should have risen to the top by now.

Steamed Plaice with Ginger

Cooking time: 8 minutes

1 large plaice
3 slices green ginger
1 tsp salt
2 sour plums (optional)
1 tbsp lard strips or
1 tbsp lard
2 stalks spring onions
1 tsp pepper

Wash plaice and score a cross-cut on either side. Place in a deep metal dish. Shred ginger and spread evenly all over fish. Lightly mash sour plums and place at the centre of the crosscut.

Arrange lard strips to cover fish or dribble lard all over to keep fish moist. Lay spring onions whole across fish and steam for about 8 minutes. Sprinkle with salt and pepper just before serving. It is important to use a little oil when steaming fish else the fish meat becomes rather dry.

Gulai Fish (Curry Fish) (illustrated on p. 34)

Cooking time: 15 minutes

300 g (10 oz) cod fillets
3 tbsp oil
1 tbsp tamarind paste
600 ml (1 pint) water
1 tbsp pepper
1 tsp salt
2 red chillies

SPICES
2 cloves garlic
2 large onions
1 tbsp shrimp paste powder
4 slices ginger
4 red chillies
2 stalks lemon grass or grated lemon rind

Pound spices until fine. Fry in hot oil for three minutes and until oil seeps out again. Add water mixed with tamarind and bring to the boil. Add pepper, salt and whole chillies and fish left either whole or cut into large chunks. Simmer for about 4 minutes.

Whole Snapper in Hot Sauce

Cooking time: 20 minutes

1 whole red snapper about 500 g (1 lb)
1 stalk spring onions, chopped
1 large knob ginger, chopped
3 cloves garlic, chopped
2 tsp pepper
1 tsp chilli powder
2 tbsp preserved soy beans, washed and mashed
1 tsp black soy sauce
1 tsp sugar
2 tbsp cornflour
250 ml (8 fl oz) water
1 tsp vinegar
Oil for frying

Wash and clean fish and trim off a little of the fins and tail for easier frying. Make diagonal slits on both sides and pat dry. Deep fry in hot oil until crisp and remove to serving dish.

Remove all but 4 tbsp oil and fry chopped ginger, garlic, pepper and chilli powder for 1 minute. Add soy beans, soy sauce, sugar, and water mixed with cornflour. Simmer until sauce thickens and add chopped spring onions. Add vinegar and pour sauce over fish to serve.

Fried Fish with Broccoli

Cooking time: 5 minute

300 g (10 oz) cod fillets
150 g (5 oz) broccoli
2 cloves garlic
200 ml (7 fl oz) water
1 tbsp cornflour
4 tbsp oil
2 tbsp sesame oil
1 tsp salt
2 tbsp Chinese wine or sherry
1 tsp light soy sauce
1 tsp peper

Cut cod fillets into bite-sized pieces and marinate in Chinese wine, soy sauce, sesame oil and salt and pepper for 10 minutes. Heat oil and fry garlic until brown. Break broccoli into florets and toss with garlic for 1 minute.

Add fish and fry for another minute or so. Dissolve cornflour with water and add to fish. Put in marinade as well and simmer for 30 seconds. Serve hot.

Stuffed Hake (recipe on p. 30)

Grilled Mackerel

Cooking time: 8 minutes

This is a rather unusual fish in that it does not take well to frying at all. It is best steamed or baked but must be eaten hot or it takes on a rather oily pungence. It also has the peculiar feature of shingled scales that can be removed in one whole piece once the hardtail is cooked.

2 medium-sized mackerel
1 tsp salt
1 tbsp oil

INGREDIENTS FOR SAUCE
3 tbsp black soy sauce
1 tbsp shrimp paste
4 fresh red chillies
1 tsp sugar

Wash and clean mackerel and remove entrails. Rub with salt and grill on a wire rack for 6 minutes on each side. Turn off grill and leave fish to keep warm.

Toast the shrimp paste for 2 minutes on each side over naked flame and pound with chillies. Mix with black soy sauce and sugar and use as dip for grilled mackerel.

Sambal Ikan Bilis (Anchovies)

Cooking time: 15 minutes

10 dried chillies
2 large onions
6 skinned almonds
2 tsp shrimp paste
1 tbsp tamarind powder (or paste)
200 ml (7 fl oz) water
5 tbsp oil
250 g (½ lb) anchovies
1 tsp salt
1 tsp sugar

Pound together chillies, previously soaked in hot water until soft, with onions, almonds and shrimp paste until fine. Dissolve tamarind powder (or paste) in water.

Heat oil and stir-fry anchovies until crisp and brown.

Leave aside to drain on absorbent paper. Fry pounded ingredients in remaining oil for about 3 minutes. Add tamarind water, salt and sugar and simmer for 5 minutes. Add fried anchovies and give it a quick stir. Serve on a bed of plain boiled rice.

Fried Sprats (Tamban)

Cooking time: 5 minutes

400 g (13 oz) sprats
2 tbsp cornflour
1 tsp salt
Oil for deep frying

Wash and clean sprats. Remove heads and entrails. Dust with flour and salt and fry in hot oil for 2 minutes until golden brown.

The recipe can be adapted to use a tamarind paste instead of cornflour. Mix 3 tbsp tamarind paste with 250 ml (8 fl oz) water and marinate fish for 5 minutes. Drain but do not wash and fry in hot oil for 2 minutes. Drain on absorbent paper.

Gulai Fish (left, recipe on p. 33),
Prawns Fried with Pineapple and Chillies (right, recipe on p. 85).

Spicy Fish Soup

Cooking time: 10 minutes

750 ml (1¼ pints) water
1 tsp shrimp paste, toasted
5 fresh red chillies
1 stalk lemon grass, bruised or grated lemon
   rind
4 slices green ginger
3 shallots, sliced
3 cloves garlic, chopped
400 g (13 oz) snapper or boneless fish fillets
2 tsp fish or light soy sauce
1 tsp pepper

Bring water to the boil. Pound shrimp paste with chillies and add to boiling water. Cut fish into thick chunks and add to water. Add all other ingredients and simmer for 5 minutes. This soup has a peculiarly pungent taste that has as many aficionados as enemies so check with friends if they like shrimp paste before you serve it.

Sweet-sour Fish (illustrated opposite)

Cooking time: 15 minutes

1 tbsp oil
1 large onion, sliced
2 tomatoes, quartered
2 tbsp canned pineapple chunks
1 large grey mullet about 600 g (1½ lbs)
5 tbsp cornflour
500 ml (16 fl oz) oil for frying fish
1 stalk spring onion, cut into 4 cm (1½ in)
   lengths
1 bunch fresh coriander leaves, shredded
   roughly
SWEET SOUR SAUCE
2 tbsp plum sauce
6 tbsp pineapple syrup from canned pineapple
4 tbsp tomato sauce
1 tsp cornflour
350 ml (11 fl oz) water

Fry onion in 1 tbsp oil for 1 minute and add quartered tomatoes and pineapple chunks. Mix all sauce ingredients and add to onions, tomatoes and pineapples. Bring to the boil and remove from heat. Keep warm.

Score deep diagonal cuts in mullet and dry thoroughly. Dust with cornflour and fry in hot oil for about 8 minutes until crisp, cooked and brown. Place fish in a large deep dish and pour sauce over. Garnish with spring onions and fresh coriander leaves.

Fish Java

Cooking time: 15 minutes

4 tbsp oil
2 large onions, chopped
2 cloves garlic, pounded
2 tbsp melted palm sugar or golden syrup
3 tbsp lemon juice
3 tbsp black soy sauce
1 tsp salt
1 large plaice about 500 g (1 lb)
Oil for deep frying

SPICES
5 red chillies
1 tbsp shrimp paste powder
1 tsp lemon grass powder or grated lemon rind
1 tsp ginger powder

Heat oil and fry onions and garlic for 2 minutes. Add pounded spices and continue frying for another 4 minutes. Add lemon juice, salt, sugar and soy sauce and bring to the boil.

Simmer for 2 minutes and remove from fire. Wash and clean fish and deep fry until brown. To serve, place fish on an oval platter and pour gravy over. Garnish with fresh coriander leaves or whatever greens you fancy.

Fish Croquettes

Cooking time: 15 minutes

600 g (1¼ lbs) fish meat
250 g (8 oz) canned, boiled potatoes
1 tbsp butter
1 tsp salt
1 tsp pepper
3 tbsp cornflour
1 stalk spring onion, chopped
1 egg, lightly beaten
Golden breadcrumbs
Oil for deep frying

Steam fish meat for about 5 minutes. Remove to cool. Mix cooled fish meat with mashed potatoes, butter, salt, pepper, cornflour and chopped spring onion. Shape into cutlets and dip each into beaten egg. Roll in breadcrumbs and fry until golden brown.

Steamed Seabass with Ham and Mushrooms

Cooking time: 12 minutes

1 large seabass about 750 g (1½ lbs)
3 slices lean ham
5 Chinese mushrooms, soaked in hot water for
    5 minutes
1 stalk spring onion
3 slices of green ginger
3 tbsp oil
3 tbsp sliced shallots

SAUCE
1 tsp light soy sauce
1 tsp sesame oil
1 tsp pepper
1 tbsp Chinese wine or sherry

Mix sauce ingredients and leave aside. Wash and clean seabass and make diagonal slits along both sides about 5 cm (2 in) apart. Slits may be as deep as the bone.

Cut ham into six slices and insert one slice in each slit together with one mushroom cap. Lay spring onions whole and ginger slices on a large, deep plate.

Place seabass on top and steam over high heat for 10 minutes. Just before fish is ready, heat a wok with 3 tbsp oil and fry shallots until brown. Add sauce and once it sizzles, pour over the whole steamed fish.

Grilled Whole Fish with Soy Sauce (top, recipe on p. 43),
Sliced Fish with Tree Fungus and Crab Sauce (recipe on p. 55).

Fish Soup with Beancurd, Salted Vegetable (illustrated opposite)

Cooking time: 6 minutes

1 tsp oil
1 tsp salt
250 g (½ lb) cod fillet
150 g (5 oz) salted vegetable, soaked in water
**   for 10 minutes**
1 square beancurd or tofu about 150 g (5 oz)
600 ml (1 pint) water
2 cloves garlic
1 bunch fresh coriander
½ fish stock cube or Japanese bonito seasoning

Cut fish fillets into bite-sized pieces and marinate in 1 tsp oil and a little salt. Bring water to boil. Cut beancurd into 3 cm (1¼ in) cubes. Cut salted vegetable into bite-sized pieces and wash once again squeezing out moisture.

This is to render it less salty. Add to boiling water together with beancurd and fish. Add seasoning and taste for saltiness. It does not usually require salt as the salted vegetable provides enough. Simmer for 4 minutes.

Meanwhile fry crushed garlic until light brown. Serve soup garnished with fresh coriander and fried garlic.

Fish with Lemon Grass

Cooking time: 8 minutes

1 red snapper about 500 g (1 lb)
2 stalks lemon grass or grated lemon rind
2 fresh red chillies
1 small onion
2 cloves garlic
1 tsp salt
2 slices green ginger
2 tbsp oil

Wash and clean fish and make slits on both sides. Pound together lemon grass, chillies, garlic, ginger, onion and salt. Liberally coat fish with this mixture making sure all the slits are anointed. Put fish on rack and brush with oil. Grill for 4 minutes on each side.

To test if fish is ready, use a metal skewer and poke into deepest part of fish. If it comes out clean, the fish is done.

Another way is to see if the eyes have popped out of their sockets. If they have, the fish is cooked. Serve this grilled fish with a pungent chilli sauce (see below).

PUNGENT CHILLI SAUCE
Pound together 4 chillies, 1 clove garlic and 1 slice ginger. Mix with 1 tsp vinegar, 1 tsp sugar and 1 tsp soy sauce.

Chilli Stuffed Fish

Cooking time: 8 minutes

1 small red snapper or trout about 350 g (¾ lb)
3 fresh red chillies
2 tsp ground turmeric
1 tsp salt
1 clove garlic
Oil for deep frying

Wash and clean fish and remove entrails. Slit the stomach further down towards the tail to accommodate the spices. Score deep 2-cm (¾ in) cuts diagonally along both sides of fish.

Pound chillies, turmeric, salt and garlic until very fine. Stuff all cavities of fish with the mixture. Fry until brown and crisp.

Prawn Omelette (left, recipe on p.95),
Fish Soup with Beancurd and Salted Vegetable.

Fish Acar

Cooking time: 25 minutes

500 g (1 lb) herring or mackerel
4 red chillies
4 green chillies
5 tbsp (malt) vinegar
400 ml (13 fl oz) water
2 tbsp sugar
1 tsp salt
400 ml (13 fl oz) oil
Large knob ginger, sliced
4 cloves garlic, sliced
6 shallots, sliced

SPICES
5 red chillies
6 skinned almonds
10 shallots
4 cloves garlic
1 tbsp ginger shreds
1 tsp turmeric powder

Cut fish into large chunks, wash and pat dry. Deseed chillies and cut into long strips or in halves. Wipe dry with paper napkins. Boil malt vinegar with water for a few minutes and add salt and sugar. Remove and allow to cool

Heat half of the oil and fry fish until crisp and cooked through. Remove fish to serving plate or casserole. In remaining oil fry pounded spices until fragrant. This should take about 6 minutes. Mix fried spices with fish and stir gently until well mixed. Pour in vinegar and water mixture to let steep.

Heat remaining oil and fry sliced shallots, garlic and ginger until light brown. Add to fish and top up with sliced red and green chillies. Let steep for 24 hours before serving.

NOTE: Do not use aluminium pot for boiling vinegar. Use enamel-based utensils.

Pickled Fish

If you can find absolutely fresh snapper or mackerel fillets, this makes a delightful appetiser.

400 g (13 oz) fish fillets
2 tbsp vinegar
1 tbsp sugar
1 tbsp black soy sauce
2 tbsp peanuts
1 bunch fresh coriander leaves

Wash fish and wipe dry thoroughly. Using a sharp knife, slice fish as thin as possible. Remove fish skin if you don't like its taste. Bring vinegar to a gentle boil and allow to cool completely. Remove peanut skins and pound till grainy but not too fine. Mix with cooled vinegar, sugar and soy sauce and stir till sugar melts. Pour over fish in a glass or enamel dish and steep for half an hour. Serve on a lettuce leaf garnished with coriander leaves.

Braised Fish

Cooking time: 15 minutes

1 red snapper or sea bream about 400 g (13 oz)
2 tbsp Chinese wine or sherry
2 tbsp black soy sauce
2 tbsp shredded ginger
2 stalks spring onions
1 tsp salt
1 tsp sugar
1 tbsp oil or lard
400 ml (13 fl oz) water

Clean snapper and remove sharp fins. Mix other ingredients and bring to the boil. Lower heat and put whole snapper in. If snapper is too large cut into two but this dish looks much better when fish is presented whole. Simmer for 10 minutes and turn off heat. Residual heat will finish the cooking process.

Steamed Fish with Ginger

Cooking time: 8 minutes

2 medium-sized white pomfret or any white
   meat fish
4 slices ginger cut into shreds
1 fresh red chilli, sliced
1 tbsp lard or vegetable oil
1 tsp salt
1 tsp light soy sauce

Wash and clean fish and make a cross cut on each side so fish will cook through easily. Place in a steaming plate (not plastic) and put shredded ginger and red chilli all over fish. Mix oil, salt and soy sauce and pour over fish. Steam for about 8 minutes or until fish eyes pop out.

Grilled Whole Fish with Soy Sauce (illustrated on p. 38)

Cooking time: 10 minutes

1 large pomfret, snapper or mackerel
1 tsp salt
2 tbsp oil
2 tbsp black soy sauce

SAUCE DIP
4 tbsp black soy sauce
2 fresh red chillies, sliced
2 limes
1 tsp sugar

Clean and wash fish and leave whole. Score along the sides about 1 cm (½ in) deep. Rub with salt and place on a rack under hot grill. Brush with oil mixed with black soy sauce and grill for 5 minutes on each side.

Fish should be cooked when parts of the skin are charred. Squeeze juice of 2 limes and mix with all other sauce ingredients. Serve fish with this sauce dip.

Fish Masak Pedas (Fish in Tamarind and Turmeric)

Cooking time: 10 minutes

4 tbsp oil
2 stalks lemon grass, bruised or grated lemon rind
3 tbsp tamarind paste
1 litre (1¾ pints) water
2 whole seabass
2 tsp salt
2 tsp sugar
1 tsp black soy sauce

SPICES
10 almonds
5 red chillies or
1 tsp chilli powder
1 large onion
1 tsp turmeric powder
1 tbsp shrimp paste powder

Fry-pounded spices in hot oil until fragrant. Add lemon grass (or rind) and stir fry for 2 minutes. Mix tamarind paste with water and add to fried spices. While gravy is simmering, clean and gut fish and cut into large chunks. Add to gravy and simmer for 5 minutes. Add salt, sugar and soy sauce and simmer for 2 minutes more.

Fried Fish with Hot Sambal

Cooking time: 15 minutes

1 500 g (1 lb) fish (any firm-fleshed white or
  dark fish)
4 tbsp oil
2 tbsp preserved soy beans, drained and
  mashed
1 tbsp sugar
1 tbsp tamarind paste
300 ml (½ pint) water
SPICES
1 tsp chilli powder
1 large onion
2 cloves garlic
1 stalk lemon grass or grated lemon rind
1 tbsp shrimp paste powder

Clean and gut fish. Cut into two if too large for frying pan. Heat oil and fry fish until brown. Leave aside Put in pounded spices and fry until oil seeps out again.

Add preserved soy beans, sugar and tamarind mixed with water. Bring to a boil and scoop up immediately to cover fried fish. Served garnished with slices of cucumber.

Otak (Baked Fish in Spices)

Cooking time: 8 minutes

1 kg (2 lbs) fish meat (any firm white fish)
2 coconuts, grated or
10 tbsp desiccated coconut
100 ml (3½ fl oz) water
5 tbsp coconut (to be fried and pounded
  separately)
1 turmeric leaf, sliced fine
3 fragrant lime leaves, sliced fine, or ¾ tsp
  grated lemon rind
1 tsp salt
1 tsp sugar
4 eggs, beaten
2 tbsp cornflour
20 pieces banana leaf, each 10 cm (4 in)
  square. (Use foil as an alternative).

SPICES
12 skinned almonds
4 large onions
15 dried chillies or
1 tbsp chilli powder
2 tbsp coriander powder
1 tsp turmeric powder
2 tbsp shrimp paste powder
1 tbsp lemon grass powder or grated lemon
  rind

Shape fish meat into rectangular cakes to soak in a little water. Knead coconut in water for milk. In a dry pan fry the 5 tbsp coconut until light brown. Pound or blend till fine.

Mix pounded spices with coconut milk, sliced aromatic leaves, salt, sugar, beaten eggs and cornflour with fish and ground coconut and shape into small cakes to be wrapped in banana leaves or foil.

Consistency should be like soft butter. To make the banana leaves more pliable, scald them in hot water. Fold each otak parcel securely with toothpicks and grill for 5 minutes on each side.

Grilled Spiced Fish (recipe on p. 31).

Fish Curry with Tomatoes

Cooking time: 10 minutes

500 g (1 lb) firm-fleshed fish like mackerel,
   snapper or mullet
1 tsp turmeric powder
1 tsp salt
6 tbsp oil
2 tomatoes, sliced into two each
1 tbsp curry powder
1 tsp salt
½ fresh coconut, grated
500 ml (16 fl oz) water
2 tsp salt

SPICES
1 large onion
4 cloves garlic
1 tbsp shredded ginger

Wash and dry fish and cut into bite-sized pieces. Rub all over with salt and turmeric powder. Heat oil and fry pieces, a batch at a time until golden brown. Drain and set aside. In remaining oil fry spices until oil seeps out again. Add curry powder moistened with 2 tbsp of coconut milk and continue frying for a few minutes more.

Squeeze coconut with water and add to spices. Bring to the boil and add fish, tomatoes and salt. Simmer for 5 minutes or until tomatoes turn slightly mushy.

Fish Curry with Okra (Lady's Fingers) (illustrated opposite)

Cooking time: 10 minutes

6 lady's fingers
4 tbsp oil
1 large onion, sliced
3 green chillies, deseeded and sliced lengthwise
1 thumb-sized piece ginger, pounded
2 cloves garlic, pounded
½ coconut, grated
250 ml (8 fl oz) water
3 tbsp tamarind paste
400 ml (13 fl oz) water
400 g (13 oz) snapper fillets or any
   firm-fleshed fish
2 tsp salt
SPICES
2 tbsp corinander powder
2 tsp cumin powder
2 tsp aniseed powder
1 tsp chilli powder

Cut stalks off lady's fingers and cut each into two. Heat oil and fry onion and chillies until soft but not brown. Add pounded garlic and ginger and fry until mixture is fragrant. Add pounded spices and fry for 2 minutes until fragrant.

Squeeze coconut with 250 ml (8 fl oz) water and mix tamarind with 400 ml (13 fl oz) water. Combine both liquids and add to spices. Bring to the boil. Add fish, lady's fingers and salt and simmer for about 5 minutes.

Fish with Fried Shallots

Cooking time: 20 minutes

1 large plaice about 400 g (13 oz)
12 shallots
8 tbsp oil
1 tsp pepper
1 tsp salt

Wash and clean fish, removing entrails. Make deep slits on both sides of fish till the bone. Pat dry and fry in oil until brown and crisp. Slice shallots fine and fry in remaining oil until crisp and brown. Drain off all but 1 tbsp of oil and sprinkle pepper and salt all over. Pour over fried fish and serve hot.

Boiled Fish Soup

Cooking time: 10 minutes

400 g (13 oz) firm white fish
2 stalks lemon grass or grated lemon rind
1 large onion
1 tomato
2 red chillies, deseed and slit into two
1 tsp salt
1 tsp pepper
500 ml (16 fl oz) water
2 tbsp tamarind paste
1 tbsp sugar

Cut fish into large chunks. Slice lemon grass, onion and tomato. Mix water with tamarind paste and strain off pith. Put all ingredients in pot, except fish, and bring to the boil. Simmer for 5 minutes until flavours are well incorporated. Add fish and simmer for 5 minutes more. Adjust seasoning to taste and serve hot.

Deep-fried Fish in Batter

Cooking time: 10 minutes

500 g (1 lb) fish fillets (snapper or mackerel)
1 tsp salt
3 lemon wedges
4 tbsp tartare sauce

FOR THE BATTER
5 tbsp plain flour
1 tbsp cornflour
1 can beer
1 tsp salt
1 tsp pepper
1 tbsp sesame oil
Oil for deep-frying

Cut fish into 2-cm (¾ in) slices and rub with salt. Mix plain flour with cornflour and sift into a bowl. Make a well in the centre and pour beer in. You can use water but beer makes a much lighter batter. Adjust the amount of liquid to make batter that just coats fish without flowing off completely. Add salt, pepper and sesame oil and allow to stand in refrigerator for 30 minutes. Heat oil and dip each piece of fish completely in batter. Deep-fry until golden brown and drain on absorbent paper. Serve with lemon wedges and tartare sauce.

Kuah Lada (Peppery Fish Curry)

Cooking time: 10 minutes

1 whole mackerel, about 500 g (1 lb)
2 small aubergines or courgettes
4 tbsp oil
1 stalk lemon grass, bruised or grated lemon
   rind
4 tbsp tamarind paste
750 ml (1¼ pints) water
1 tsp salt
1 tsp sugar

SPICES
2 red chillies
8 almonds
2 cloves garlic
1 large onion
1 tsp turmeric powder
2 tbsp black pepper powder

Cut fish into large pieces. Halve aubergines lengthwise and make a cut down two-thirds of each half. Fry spices in oil until fragrant. Add lemon grass or rind. Blend tamarind paste with water and add to spices. Bring to a boil and add fish, and sugar. Simmer for 2 minutes and add aubergines and salt. Simmer for 5 minutes more and serve with plain boiled rice.

Fish Curry with Salted Vegetable

Cooking time: 15 minutes

3 mackerel or snapper fillets
3 tbsp tamarind paste
750 ml (1¼ pints)
150 g (5 oz) salted vegetable
3 tbsp oil
1 tbsp shredded ginger
1 tbsp curry powder
3 tbsp water
1 stalk curry leaf or
1 tsp curry leaf powder
1 tbsp shredded ginger
1 tbsp sugar

Wash fish and cut into large chunks. Soak salted vegetable in plenty of water and leave to stand while you prepare other ingredients. Heat oil and fry shredded ginger until light brown. Add curry powder previously moistened with 3 tbsp water.

Drain salted vegetable and squeeze liquid out. Add to frying spices and continue to stir fry for three or four minutes. Mix tamarind with water and add to pan. Bring to the boil and add fish and curry leaf.

Simmer 5 minutes and add sugar. You do not need to add salt as the vegetable has enough saltiness. However, taste and adjust with a sprinkle of salt if you find it too bland for your taste.

Placian Thai-style Fried Fish (illustrated opposite)

Cooking time: 12 minutes

Being rather impoverished can add a great deal to your culinary library as I found out. I was newly married and living in a rented house somewhat beyond my wife's and my meagre means. A friend knew some Thai students who were looking for a place to stay that didn't cost them hostel rates and that also had a kitchen.

These two Thai girls, Nik and Wan, turned out not only to be charming students of English but excellent cooks. In the 14 months they lived with us they taught us some mouth-watering savoury dishes and desserts that we never knew existed — that is until we visited Thailand many years later.

1 large seabass or seabream about 650 g
  (1 ¼ lbs)
Oil for deep frying
1 stalk spring onions, cut into 4 cm (1 ¼ in) pieces
3 cloves garlic, crushed
3 tbsp shredded green ginger
2 tbsp fish sauce
1 tbsp palm sugar or brown sugar
2 tbsp tamarind juice or
lemon juice
1 tsp pepper
1 bunch fresh coriander leaves, chopped
2 red chillies, seeded and sliced

Deep fry fish in hot oil until crisp. In 3 tbsp oil fry spring onions till soft, add garlic and ginger and continue frying until light brown. Add fish sauce, sugar, tamarind or lemon juice and simmer for 2 minutes. Add a little water if it is too dry. Pour over fish and serve garnished with pepper, chilli and coriander.

Fish in Thick Coconut Milk

Cooking time: 12 minutes

4 mackerel steaks each about 2 cm (¾ in)
  thick
1 coconut grated or
300 g (10 oz) desiccated coconut
400 ml (13 fl oz) water
1 tsp salt
2 pieces dried tamarind
1 stalk lemon grass, bruised or grated lemon
  rind
3 tbsp oil
SPICES
5 red chillies
4 dried chillies (soaked in water for
  10 minutes)
3 cloves garlic
1 large onion
1 tsp turmeric

Squeeze coconut with water for thick milk. Add 1 tsp salt. Pound spices till fine and fry in hot oil until fragrant. Add dried tamarind, lemon grass and stir for 1 minute. Add fish and coconut milk and simmer for 5 minutes. Adjust taste with a little more salt if necessary.

Another way of cooking this tasty fish curry is to first fry the fish until golden brown before adding it to the gravy. This method also prevents the fish from falling apart should you need to reheat leftovers.

Sumatran Spiced Fish

Cooking time: 20 minutes

I ate this delicious dish once during Hari Raya (Malay New Year) at a friend's home and she told me it comes from the Batak culinary heritage in North Sumatra. You can use any meaty fish steaks.

600 g (1 lb 2 oz) cod steaks
1 coconut, grated
400 ml (13 fl oz) water
4 stalks lemon grass or grated lemon rind
2 tomatoes
6 French beans
1 tsp salt
1 tsp sugar
Juice of 2 limes
2 red chillies, deseeded and sliced

SPICES
1 large onion
4 cloves garlic
2 tsp chilli powder or paste
1 tbsp shredded ginger
4 fragrant lime leaves or
1 tsp grated lemon peel

Blend or grind spices till fine. Squeeze coconut with water and extract milk. Mix with spices and bring to the boil. Simmer over gentle heat for 10 minutes until thick and fragrant.

Clean fish and cut into bite-sized pieces. Bruise lemon grass or slice fine as you like. The latter method will impart more flavour to the gravy. Quarter tomatoes and cut French beans into 4-cm (1½ in) lengths. Add all these ingredients and seasoning to the simmering coconut milk gravy and simmer for 5 minutes more. Serve garnished with sliced red chillies.

Fried Fish in Wine

Cooking time: 20 minutes

1 snapper or meaty fish about 500 g (1 lb)
Oil for deep frying
4 slices ginger
1 large onion
1 tbsp malt vinegar
2 tbsp Chinese wine or white wine
1 tbsp light soy sauce
1 tsp sugar
1 tsp cornflour
2 tbsp water
2 stalks spring onions, chopped

Clean fish and cut into bite-sized pieces. Bruise lemon grass or slice fine as you like. The latter method will impart more flavour to the gravy. Quarter tomatoes and cut French beans into 4-cm (1½ in) lengths. Add all these ingredients and seasoning to the simmering coconut milk gravy and simmer for 5 minutes more. Serve garnished with sliced red chillies.

Mixed Seafood in Tamarind Gravy (illustrated on p. 54)

Cooking time: 7 minutes

Not even the classic French bouillabaise has anything on this! The sharpness of tamarind has remarkable afinity with seafood and does not in any way mask the flavour of prawns, fish or shellfish. One thing you must insist on in cooking this dish is absolutely fresh produce. Anything less would result in a dish that might as well be last night's stew because the acidity of tamarind demands the firmest flesh else they (the fish or prawn) will disintegrate.

**10 King prawns or cod and prawn mixture
   of equivalent weight**
2 red chillies
3 green chillies
3 tbsp tamarind paste
500 ml (16 fl oz) water
1 tbsp shrimp paste powder
2 tsp sugar
1 tsp salt
1 large onion, sliced
2 stalks lemon grass or grated lemon rind
2 fragrant lime leaves

Clean prawns and cut off whiskers and hard bristles at the head. If using fish, cut into manageable portions to fit into pot.

Mix water with tamarind, shrimp paste, salt, onions, lemon grass and bring to the boil. Boil it good for three minutes and add seafood and chillies.

Finish cooking for two minutes and add lime leaves. Do not overboil or prawns will become hard.

NOTE: If you can't get hold of lemon grass and tamarind the equivalent amounts of lemon juice — 1 lemon to 300 ml (½ pint) water — and 1 tsp of grated lemon rind in place of 1 stalk lemon grass will produce a decent substitute dish that won't have your reputation ruined.

Mild Fish Curry

Cooking time: 10 minutes

2 tbsp tamarind paste
1 tbsp lemon juice
600 ml (1 pint) water
4 mackerel steaks or any thick meaty fish
1 tsp salt
1 tsp sugar
2 stalks lemon grass or grated lemon rind
2 green chillies

CURRY PASTE
1 tsp chilli powder
1 tsp turmeric powder
1 large onion
1 stalk lemon grass or grated lemon rind
1 tbsp shrimp paste powder

Blend curry paste in a blender or pestle and mortar if you have one. Mix tamarind paste and lemon juice with water and bring to the boil. Add spice paste and simmer for one minute. Add fish, salt, sugar, whole lemon grass and green chillies. If you want a milder taste, slice the chillies into two lengthwise and deseed. Simmer for another three minutes.

Seafood and Beancurd Croquette

Cooking time: 4 minutes

1 large square beancurd or tofu
150 g (5 oz) prawns, shelled
150 g (5 oz) fish meat
1 tbsp cornflour
1 egg
1 tsp salt
1 tsp sugar
1 tbsp chopped spring onions
Breadcrumbs for coating
1 egg for coating liquid
Oil for deep frying

Mash beancurd or tofu fine. Mince prawns with fish meat and mix well either in a pestle and mortar or a deep bowl. Do this with a vigorous beating action so as to induce air into the mixture which, when fried, will be light and crunchy.

Add cornflour, lightly beaten egg, salt, sugar and spring onions. Beat the second egg lightly and leave aside. Shape mixture into croquette about 5 cm x 3 cm x 1 cm (2 in x 1 ¼ in x ½ in). You should get about 12 croquettes.

Dust your hands with a little cornflour and shape them so mixture won't stick to fingers. Dip each croquette in beaten egg and roll in breadcrumbs. Deep fry for 3 to 4 minutes or until light brown. Serve with a side dip of chilli sauce.

NOTE: One way to economise on bread crumbs is to use up left-over cream crackers, saltines or toasted old bread. Crumble with a rolling pin or any heavy object and store in airtight jar.

Sliced Fish with Tree Fungus, Crab Sauce (illustrated on p. 38)

Cooking time: 10 minutes

3 tbsp lard
2 cloves garlic, crushed
4 tbsp crab meat
3 tbsp tree fungus, soaked till soft
400 ml (13 fl oz) water
1 tbsp cornflour
1 tbsp Chinese wine or sherry
1 tsp salt
1 tbsp pepper
300 g (10 oz) fish fillets, cod, huss or haddock
1 tbsp oil

Heat lard and fry crushed garlic until light brown. Wash and drain fungus and add to pan. Fry for 1 minute and add crab meat. Stir for 1 minute. Mix water with cornflour, wine, salt and pepper and add in.

Bring to the boil and while it's simmering to reduce a little, slice fish into bite-sized pieces. Marinate in 1 tbsp oil for a few minutes. Add to crab sauce and simmer for 2 minutes or until fish turns completely white. Serve hot.

Fried Fish Slices with Straw Mushrooms

Cooking time: 5 minutes

400 g (13 oz) white fish fillets
1 can straw mushrooms
15 mange tout
4 tbsp oil
2 cloves garlic
2 tbsp sesame oil
1 tsp salt
200 ml (7 fl oz) water
1 tbsp cornflour
1 tbsp Chinese wine or sherry
1 tsp pepper

Clean fish and cut into bite-sized pieces. Wash and drain mange tout. Drain straw mushrooms. Crush garlic. Heat oil and fry garlic until brown.

Add mange tout and fry for 2 minutes. Add fish and straw mushrooms and continue frying for 1 minute more. Dissolve cornflour in water and add to pan together with wine, pepper, salt and sesame oil. Stir for 1 more minute and serve hot.

Deep-fried Fish Fillets

Cooking time: 10 minutes

400 g (13 oz) white fish fillets

MARINADE INGREDIENTS
1 tbsp sesame oil
2 tbsp rice wine or sherry
1 tsp salt
1 tbsp chopped ginger

INGREDIENTS FOR BATTER
5 egg whites
3 tbsp cornflour
1 tbsp plain flour
Oil for deep frying

Cut fish into bite-sized pieces and marinate for 10 minutes. Beat egg whites until stiff peaks form and blend in flours to make batter.

Heat oil until smoking. Dip one piece at a time in the batter and gently drop into hot oil. Fry for about five minutes or until golden brown and drain on absorbent paper. Serve on a bed of lettuce leaves.

Asam Pedas (Fish in Tamarind)

Cooking time: 15 minutes

500 g (1 lb) mackerel
1 tsp salt
5 red chillies
2 large onions
1 tsp turmeric powder
3 stalks lemon grass or grated lemon rind
1 tbsp shrimp paste powder
2 tbsp tamarind paste
650 ml (1¼ pints) water

Clean fish and rub a little salt all over. Cut into two steaks if fish is too large. Pound together chillies, onions, turmeric, shrimp paste and 2 stalks of lemon grass.

Bruise the other stalk and leave aside. Stir pounded ingredients in water mixed with tamarind and simmer for 10 minutes to blend the spices. Add fish and bruised lemon grass and simmer for 5 minutes. Add salt and serve with sambal belacan (see page 288).

Fried Fish Cakes in Chilli

Cooking time: 15 minutes

Oil for deep frying
3 fish cakes, available from Chinese grocers,
    each about 250 g (½ lb)
200 ml (7 fl oz) water
1 tbsp lime juice
2 tsp sugar
1 tsp salt
SPICES
2 large onions
2 tsp chilli powder
1 tsp turmeric powder
2 cloves garlic
6 almonds

Blend or pound spices till fine. Deep fry fish cakes until light brown and slightly wrinkled outside. It should take about 5 minutes. Remove to cool and slice or leave whole as you wish.

Heat oil and fry spices until fragrant. Add water and lime juice and bring to the boil. Add fried fish cakes, sugar and salt and simmer for 2 minutes.

Whole Sea Perch in Tamarind Curry

Cooking time: 10 minutes

This tasty fish is also known as the barramundi in Australia and very much in demand in Hong Kong. It can grow to more than a metre (3 feet) in length but the ones found here and in Malaysia are about half this size. The Malays call this golden-brown and silvery skinned fish ikan siakap.

4 tbsp oil
2 tbsp tamarind paste
500 ml (16 fl oz) water
½ coconut, grated
100 ml (3½ fl oz) water
1 tsp salt
1 tsp sugar
1 whole sea perch, (or any firm white fish),
    cut into 3-cm (1¼ in) thick steaks.
1 stalk curry leaves
SPICES
1 large onion
3 cloves garlic
2 tbsp shredded ginger
3 tbsp coriander powder
2 tsp cumin powder
2 tsp fennel powder or seeds, crushed
2 tsp chilli powder
1 tsp turmeric powder

Mix tamarind with 500 ml (16 fl oz) water. Squeeze coconut with 100 ml (3½ fl oz) water. Mix both liquids with salt and sugar. Heat oil and fry blended or pounded spices until fragrant.

Add tamarind and coconut milk and bring to the boil. Add fish and simmer for 5 minutes. Add curry leaves and adjust seasoning. Simmer for 5 minutes more or until fish is cooked.

Fish and Bamboo Shoot Curry

Cooking time: 10 minutes

3 tbsp oil
250 g (½ lb) mackerel steaks
small can bamboo shoots
1 tsp salt
1 tsp sugar
1 coconut, grated
400 ml (13 fl oz) water

SPICES
1 large onion
4 slices stem ginger
2 tsp chilli powder
1 tsp turmeric powder
2 cloves garlic

Pound slices until fine. Cut mackerel into 3-cm (1¼ in) square cubes or larger if you like. Squeeze coconut with water for milk. Heat oil and fry spices till fragrant. Add coconut milk and bring to the boil. Add fish and bamboo shoots, salt and sugar and simmer for 5 minutes. Adjust seasoning.

Pike Fried with Salted Vegetable

Cooking time: 10 minutes

2 tbsp oil
200 g (7 oz) salted vegetable, soaked in water
   for ½ hour
400 g (13 oz) pike or monkfish cut into
   bite-sized pieces
2 cloves garlic, sliced
2 tbsp shredded ginger
2 red chillies
1 tsp sugar
300 ml (½ pint) water
2 tbsp sesame oil

Wash pike, drain and set aside. Cut salted vegetables into 2-cm (¾ in) wide strips and squeeze out moisture. Heat oil and fry garlic and ginger until light brown.

Add pike and sliced chillies and fry for 3 minutes. Add water, seasoning and sesame oil and simmer for 2 minutes. It may be necessary to adjust seasoning with a little salt if the vegetable does not impart too much of its saltiness.

Squid Curry

Cooking time: 20 minutes

3 tbsp oil
3 green chillies, deseeded and sliced
6 shallots, sliced
½ coconut, grated
400 ml (13 fl oz) water
2 tsp salt
500 g (1 lb) cleaned and sliced squid
2 tomatoes, halved

SPICES
2 tbsp curry paste
1 stalk curry leaves

Heat oil and fry sliced green chillies for 1 minute. Dish up and set aside. Fry sliced shallots until brown and crisp. Remove and drain. Squeeze coconut with water for milk.

Heat oil and fry curry paste until fragrant. Add curry leaves and fry for 1 minute more. Add coconut milk and salt and simmer for 2 minutes. Add squid and simmer for 5 minutes. Add tomatoes and simmer for 2 minutes more. Serve garnished with fried chillies and shallots.

Fried Crayfish in Black Bean Sauce (illustrated on p. 82)

Cooking time: 10 minutes

6 crayfish tails
4 tbsp oil
1 tbsp shredded ginger
1 tbsp preserved black beans
2 red chillies, sliced
300 ml (½ pint) water
2 stalks spring onions

With a sharp twist, remove crayfish heads. There's really very little meat in the heads and not worth the trouble to cut them open. Cut down the belly with kitchen scissors and remove tail meat in one piece

Cut into thick rounds. Heat oil and fry ginger for 1 minute. Add preserved black beans and fry for 1 minute more. Add crayfish and sliced chillies and fry for 2 minutes.

Add water and bring to the boil Simmer for 5 minutes. Garnish with spring onions cut into 5 cm (2 in) lengths.

Fried Cockles in Spices (illustrated on p. 65)

Cooking time: 10 minutes

3 tbsp oil
1 kg (2 lbs) cockles
5 red chillies
4 cloves garlic
1 tsp turmeric powder
1 tsp pepper
1 tsp sugar
200 ml (7 fl oz) water
1 stalk lemon grass, bruised or 1 tsp grated
　　lemon rind
1 tsp salt

Wash cockles in plenty of water and pry each one open to remove meat. Do not wash again. Pound chillies with garlic, turmeric, pepper and sugar. Heat oil and fry spices until fragrant. Add lemon grass and cockles and fry for 1 minute. Add water and bring to the boil. Add salt and serve hot.

Pike in Preserved Soy Beans

Cooking time: 10 minutes

2 tbsp oil
2 cloves garlic, crushed
**2 tbsp preserved soy beans, washed and
    drained**
2 red chillies, sliced
1 stalk spring onions
300 ml (½ pint) water
2 tsp sugar
**300 g (10 oz) pike or monkfish cut into bite-
    sized cubes**
1 bunch fresh coriander leaves

Heat oil and fry garlic until brown. Add soy beans and fry for a minute or so. Add chillies, spring onions cut into 4 cm (1½ in) lengths and water and bring to the boil. Add the rest of the ingredients and simmer for 5 minutes. Garnish with coriander leaves.

Crab Curry (illustrated on p. 62)

Cooking time: 15 minutes

I have had a 20-year love affair with crab curry though these crustaceans are the very devil to teeth cavities. Still, for the sake of good food, I soldier, or should I say, solder on and try not to crack porcelain crowns in the attempt to get at crab meat.

3 large crabs
5 tbsp oil
15 shallots, chopped
5 slices ginger
3 red chillies, chopped
1 stalk curry leaves
2 tsp chilli powder
1 tsp turmeric powder
½ coconut, shredded
300 ml (½ pint) water
2 tsp salt
2 tbsp lemon juice

Remove large shells of crabs and fibrous tissue. Cut each crab into four and remove each large claw. Crack the claws with a sharp tap to enable easy breaking for diners. Reserve any coral in a small bowl.

Heat oil and fry shallots, ginger, curry leaves and chopped chillies for 2 minutes. Add chilli and turmeric powder and fry for 1 minute more. Add crab pieces and fry until they turn a deep pink. Add coconut milk (½ coconut squeezed with 300 ml (½ pint) water), salt and lemon juice and simmer for 5 minutes until crab turns bright red. Add coral last.

Thai Stuffed Squid

Cooking time: 15 minutes

Oil for deep-frying
6 large squid
500 g (1 lb) minced pork
6 Chinese mushrooms
4 cloves garlic, crushed
1 large onion, finely chopped
1 stalk fresh coriander leaves, chopped
1 tsp pepper
1 tsp salt
2 red chillies, chopped
2 tbsp black soy sauce

PEANUT SAUCE
4 red chillies
2 pieces peanut brittle
2 tsp sugar
Juice of 2 limes
1 tbsp light soy sauce

Wash and clean squid. Remove eyes from tentacles. Mix minced pork with all other ingredients except black sauce and stuff each squid three-quarters full. Do not stuff full or filling will be forced out when squid shrinks during frying. Rub each stuffed squid with black soy sauce and deep-fry a few at a time for 2 minutes each.

You could, alternatively, boil squid first before stuffing them. To make the sauce, simply pound chillies with garlic until fine. Pound peanut brittle separately and mix all ingredients.

Sweet Squids

Cooking time: 15 minutes

The key ingredient in this dish is the sweet, black sauce that is available from some Indonesian restaurants. It's sold as "Kecap Manis".

500 g (1 lb) squid
1 tbsp tamarind paste
4 tbsp water
1 tsp salt
2 tbsp kecap manis
Oil for deep frying

Clean squid and remove stomach. Discard tentacles if you don't like them but cut away the eyes if you are using them. Cut squid into rings and marinate in tamarind paste, water, salt and sweet sauce for 20 minutes. Drain well and deep-fry in hot oil for 1 or 2 minutes until squid pieces are crisp and deep brown.

Boiled Cockles

Cooking time: 1 minute

This very humble cockle or blood clam can provoke the most enthusiastic response among Singaporeans. Many a time during my youth have I sat down with friends and polished off kilos of this clam which were barely cooked in fast and furious boiling water. But like most seafood, this clam can also result in some fast and furious reaction in the stomach.

But if your system can take it, go to town and sit down to a feast without the slightest fear. I prefer to eat "see hum" as it is fondly called in Singapore, judiciously, perhaps half a kilo (one pound) or so at a time. What's most important is good chilli and vinegar sauce, the lack of which reduces the cockle to merely another shellfish.

3 kg (6 lbs) cockles
Plenty of hot boiling water

SAUCE
10 red chillies
4 cloves garlic
5 tbsp rice or salt vinegar
1 tbsp black soy sauce

Wash cockles in many changes of water until every trace of mud is removed. Drain and scald in boiling water for no more than 30 seconds. Do a batch at a time so you get to eat them freshly cooked.

Actually they are about half-cooked done this way. Some people like them almost raw and others boiled to death — there's no accounting for taste.

To open each cockle, place middle and forefingers of both hands at the bottom where the hinge is. Using the edge of your thumb or thumbnail, gently pry open. But do not forget to remove that tiny fleck of mud that invariably clings to where the cockle is attached by a ligament.

Fried Small Squid in Pepper and Soy Sauce

Cooking time: 5 minutes

Those who find squid unpalatable never cease to wonder why others can bear to eat them, ink and all. I had one aunt who wouldn't eat squid unless the ink sac was cooked as well rendering the dish a midnight black. I have the same sentiment with certain squid dishes but when it comes to eating squid Japanese sashimi style, the ink has to go.

2 tbsp oil
1 clove garlic, crushed
400 g (14 oz) small squid each no more than
4 cm (1½ in) in length
1 tsp salt
2 tbsp black soy sauce
2 tsp pepper

Wash squid and do not remove any part of squid. Drain well. Heat oil and fry crushed garlic until brown. Add squid, salt, soy sauce and pepper and stir over high heat for 3 or 4 minutes.

It is important that you drain squid well or the dish becomes mushy. The result of well-fried squid should be a dry, peppery and salty dish.

Stir-fried Mussels (below, recipe on p. 73),
Fried Cockles in Spices (recipe on p. 60).

Deep-fried Stuffed Crabs (illustrated on p. 58)

Cooking time: 15 minutes

Oil for deep frying
4 large crabs each about 300 g (10 oz)
200 g (7 oz) minced pork
1 tbsp cornflour
1 stalk spring onions
1 tsp salt
1 tsp fish sauce
1 tsp pepper
Fresh coriander leaves for garnish

Wash crabs and remove fibrous matter. The best way to kill a crab is to insert a sharp knife into the centre cleft covered by the flap of soft shell. One sharp knock will do but you will also find the crab reacts to this sudden demise by shedding a few of its claws.

It doesn't matter as you will be breaking them off anyway. Put crabs whole in a deep pan with a little water and salt and bake covered for 5 minutes. When crabs turn a bright red they are cooked.

Remove and pry off shells. Crack large claws and remove meat. Do the same with small claws and remove cooked coral as well. Unfortunately, no instrument invented is able to remove crab meat successfully, so there's no alternative but to dig in with the fingers.

Wash shells and set aside. Mix crab meat and coral with minced pork, cornflour, chopped spring onions, salt, fish sauce and pepper and stuff back into shells. Deep fry in hot oil for 3 minutes each and garnish with coriander leaves.

Spicy Dried Prawns

Cooking time: 5 minutes

We used to have a backyard where grew wild lemon grass and all manner of greens that invariably found their way into our capacious kitchen and onto the dining table. One such green was the Sayur Paki, a thin-stalked vegetable with dark green or pale yellow, waxy leaves. The dark green ones were discarded and only the tender pale yellow ones used. My mother called this dish kerabu the reason and meaning of which I have not been able to find out. Since this vegetable is all but gone from the scene I suggest you use watercress raw.

4 tbsp small dried prawns soaked in hot water
    and pounded roughly
Handful of paki or watercress, washed and
    dried
4 tbsp coconut, grated and fried till brown
6 bird chillies or red chillies
1 coconut, grated
1 tsp salt
2 tbsp lime juice
1 tbsp sugar

Squeeze coconut without water for thick coconut creme. Add a few drops of warm water to facilitate squeezing. Leave in the fridge to chill with a little salt from the 1 tsp allowance. When ready to serve combine all ingredients but leave sugar till last or the kerabu will become watery.

Baked Crab

Cooking time: 5 minutes

4 large crabs, any variety
2 tsp salt
5 tbsp water

SAUCE
3 tbsp preserved soy beans
2 red chillies
3 limes
1 tbsp sugar
1 bunch coriander leaves

Wash crabs and remove fibrous matter. Heat wok and dry fry whole crabs and salt for 1 minute. You can put them in live and cover. When the resultant racket dies down, remove cover and add water to steam-bake for 5 minutes. Serve crabs whole with sauce dip.

Wash preserved soy beans and drain. Roughly pound chillies and mix with soy beans. Squeeze juice of limes into mixture and add sugar. Remove lime pith and slice lime skins into fine strips. Mix with dip and chopped coriander leaves.

Fried Crabs in Preserved Soy Beans

Cooking time: 18 minutes

2 large crabs
3 tbsp oil
2 cloves garlic, crushed
2 red chillies, sliced
1 tbsp preserved soy beans, washed and
  mashed
200 ml (7 fl oz) water
1 tsp salt
1 tsp sugar
1 stalk spring onions

Wash and cut crabs into four pieces. Reserve coral. Heat oil and fry crushed garlic until brown. Add sliced chillies and fry for 1 minute. Add soy beans and fry for 1 minute. Add crabs and stir-fry until they turn a bright pink. Add water, salt and sugar and simmer for 3 minutes. Add coral and simmer for 1 minute. Garnish with spring onions.

Salt and Pepper Crab

Cooking time: 10 minutes

3 crabs
4 tbsp oil
2 tsp salt
2 tsp good black pepper
4 tbsp water

Prepare crabs the usual way and cut into four pieces. Wash and drain. Heat wok and dry fry crabs quickly for 2 minutes. Remove crabs and wash wok. When wok is hot again, add oil and fry salt and pepper for 30 seconds. Add fried crab and toss around until all pieces are well coated with salt and pepper mixture. Serve hot.

Squid in Chilli Oil (illustrated opposite)

Cooking Time: 10 minutes

2 tbsp oil
10 large squid about 8-cm (3 in) each
1 tbsp tarmarind paste
1 tsp salt
2 tsp sugar
4 tbsp water

SPICES
2 large onions
4 dried chillies, soaked till soft
4 red chillies
2 cloves garlic
1 tbsp tomato puree

Pound or blend spices except tomato puree. Add puree afterwards.Wash squid and remove entrails and ink sac. Cut each into two. Mix tamarind with water, sugar and salt.

Heat oil and fry spices until fragrant. Add tamarind liquid and bring to the boil. There should be the barest amount of liquid and a thick fragrant paste. Add squid and fry for 3 minutes. Shred a few fragrant lime leaves over squid for added zest.

Squid in Tamarind and Lemon Grass Sauce

Cooking time: 10 minutes

1 tbsp lard
500 ml (16 fl oz) water
2 tbsp tamarind paste
2 stalks lemon grass or tsp grated lemon rind
1 tsp salt
1 tsp sugar
400 g (13 oz) squid

Mix tamarind paste with water and lard and bring to the boil. Add salt and lemon grass sliced into diagonal pieces about 1-cm (½ in) thick. Add sugar and squid (whole) and simmer for 5 minutes. The gravy should be inky black, sour and lemony.

Crab in the Basket

Cooking time: 20 minutes

This is a variation on Prawns in Yam Basket (see page 96) and uses crab in a milk sauce.

1 prepared yam basket
3 tbsp oil
2 cloves garlic, crushed
2 egg whites
1 tbsp cornflour
400 ml (13 fl oz) milk
1 tsp salt
1 stalk spring onions, cut into 4-cm (1 ½ in) lengths
1 bunch coriander leaves
250 g (½ lb) crab meat

Heat oil and fry crushed garlic until brown. Beat egg whites until stiff peaks form and mix with cornflour. Mix with milk and add to pan after frying garlic and stir over low heat.

Add crab and salt and continue stirring until soft white balls form. Be careful heat is not too high or milk will burn. When solidified, dish out onto yam basket and garnish with spring onions and coriander leaves.

Fried Chilli Crabs (illustrated on p. 58)

Cooking time: 10 minutes

This is a hot favourite of many visitors to Singapore and can be the bane or boon of restaurants. I have often heard it being said that if a restaurant cannot prepare decent chilli crabs it ought not to be in business. Perhaps a little unfair because chilli crabs, before the exodus of tourists, were never a main item on restaurant menus.

By some quirk, it endeared itself to foreigners and it was only a crawl away to becoming the raison d'etre for anyone visiting a seafood place. Quite the best way to eat chilli crabs is to cook it yourself because you don't pay astronomical prices and because it is very easy to do.

5 tbsp oil
2 large crabs
4 red chillies
3 cloves garlic, crushed
100 ml (3½ oz) tomato ketchup (about half
  a bottle)
1 tsp salt
1 tsp pepper
100 ml (3½ fl oz) water
1 egg

Remove crab shells and scoop out coral. Put coral aside and wash shells. Remove fibrous matter and cut each crab into four pieces. Crack large claws just slightly to facilitate eating. Wash and drain.

Heat oil and fry crushed garlic until brown. Roughly pound chillies and add to hot oil to fry to 1 minute. Add crab and stir fry for 2 minutes. Add ketchup, salt and pepper and bring to a fast boil. Add water to the consistency of gravy you like and adjust seasoning. When gravy boils crack in the egg and give the whole a good stir. Serve with chunks of bread.

Braised Sea Cucumber (illustrated on p. 72)

Cooking time: 30 minutes

An uglier creature never crawled along the sea bottom. This delicacy among Cantonese cooks is also called a Sea Slug and slug is what it looks like. Its reputation for being somewhat of an aphrodisiac may have something to do with its frequent appearance at Chinese meals but I suspect it comes more from the fact that it has a vaguely phallic shape. Whatever, it makes good eating and a perfect foil for rich sauces as it has a rather bland, gelatinous flavour. They usually come pre-boiled and cleaned and you need only slice them and toss into the pot.

2 tbsp lard
2 cloves garlic, crushed
2 tbsp Chinese wine
1 tsp light soy sauce
1 tsp salt
400 ml (13 fl oz) water
1 tbsp cornflour
6 sea cucumbers

Heat lard and fry garlic until brown. Add all ingredients except sea cucumbers and simmer for 5 minutes. Slice sea cucumbers into thick pieces and simmer for 25 minutes.

Sea Cucumber and Minced Pork Soup

Cooking time: 15 minutes

Actually this is more a loose stew than a soup and makes a hearty meal in itself.

4 tbsp oil
3 cloves garlic, crushed
4 sea cucumbers, sliced thickly
200 g (7 oz) minced pork
1 tsp cornflour
1 tsp salt
2 tbsp chopped spring onions
1 tsp pepper
2 litres (3½ pints) water
1 chicken stock cube
Fresh coriander leaves

Heat oil and fry crushed garlic until brown. Scoop up all but one tbsp and set aside for garnish. Mix minced pork with cornflour, salt, spring onions and pepper and shape into small balls.

Reheat pan and fry sliced sea cucumbers for 2 minutes. Add water and stock cube and bring to the boil. Add minced pork balls and simmer for 6 minutes. Garnish with fried garlic and coriander leaves.

Grilled Squid with Orange Sauce

Cooking time: 10 minutes

2 large squid about 150 g (5 oz) each
½ tsp salt
2 tbsp orange sauce, available at most Chinese emporiums
1 tbsp black soy sauce

Wash squid and rub with salt to remove slime. Remove tentacles and entrails. Do not remove the mottled skin. Cut off squid eyes being careful not to separate tentacle stump.

Fix tentacles back to squid with toothpick. Rub squid all over with black soy sauce and stand for 5 minutes. Grill under high heat for 8-10 minutes. In the last 2 minutes of grilling pour orange sauce all over. Serve with a sweet pickle.

Fried Dried Prawns with Pickled Olives

Cooking time: 5 minutes

3 tbsp dried shrimps, soaked till soft
2 large black pickled olives
2 red chillies, sliced
2 tsp sugar
2 tbsp fried lard (chee yeow char) optional
4 tbsp sugar
½ tsp salt

If you have rendered lard into fat for the fried lard chips, use the remaining oil. Otherwise use ordinary peanut oil. Heat oil and fry soaked dried shrimps until brown. Add pickled olives and chillies and fry till chillies turn brown. Dish up to cool and mix with all other ingredients. Serve as a condiment or with plain boiled porridge.

Stir-fried Mussels (illustrated on p. 65)

Cooking time: 5 minutes

2 tbsp oil
2 cloves garlic, crushed
2 tbsp shredded ginger
500 g (1 lb) mussels
300 ml (½ pint) water
1 tbsp black soy sauce
1 tsp salt
2 tsp pepper

Wash mussels in plenty of water to remove all dirt and mud. Heat oil and fry garlic and ginger until brown. Add mussels and fry for 3 minutes until half open. Add water and seasoning and simmer until mussels open completely. Garnish with Chinese parsley.

Fried Oyster Omelette

Cooking time: 5 minutes

This famous Singapore hawker dish known as "or chien" (Hokkien) or "or luak" (Teochew) is not easy to recreate at home unless you have the huge flat pan the hawker uses. It is in this instance that the wok pales in comparison.

However, the flat frying pan used in western cooking is a decent substitute — and one that I had to resort to during extended stays in London and when the desire for or luak consumed me. You also need a special flour made from water chestnuts but ordinary cornflour will do if you can't find this.

5 tbsp lard
4 tbsp water chestnut flour or cornflour
300 ml (½ pint) water
3 eggs
10 to 15 fresh oysters
2 tsp fish sauce
1 tsp chilli powder (mix with a little water)
1 bunch fresh coriander leaves
4 tbsp chopped spring onions

Heat flat frying pan with 2 tbsp lard until smoking. Mix flour with water to a thin liquid. Pour into pan and swivel around. Allow to brown lightly. Crack eggs onto this batter and spread around.

Turn up heat and fry until brown on one side. Flip over to brown other side. Add more lard or all of 5 tbsp if necessary. The characteristic of this dish is its greasiness, cholesterol be damned. When omelette is brown, cut into pieces and add oysters. Add sauce and chilli and give it all a good stir. Serve with coriander leaves and spring onions.

Braised Sea Cucumber (recipe on p. 70).

Abalone Dip

Cooking time: 5 minutes

2 cans abalone

CHILLI AND PEANUT SAUCE
4 red chillies
2 cloves garlic
3 pieces peanut brittle or 4 tbsp chunky
   peanut butter
1 tbsp black soy sauce
1 tbsp vinegar
1 tbsp sugar

Pound chillies and garlic till fine. Pound peanut brittle until grainy. Mix all ingredients and serve as a dip for abalone.

Deep-fried Oysters

Cooking time: 5 minutes

Oil for deep frying
5 tbsp plain flour
2 tbsp cornflour
200 ml (7 fl oz) water
1 tsp salt
20 fresh oysters

Mix flours and water to make a thick batter. Add salt. Heat oil till smoking. Dip each oyster in batter and fry a few at a time until golden brown. Serve on a bed of lettuce and with a chilli or tomato ketchup dip.

Abalone with Mushrooms and Bamboo Shoots

Cooking time: 8 minutes

4 tbsp oil
2 cloves garlic, crushed
1 can abalone, sliced
8 Chinese mushrooms soaked until soft
2 wedges bamboo shoots, sliced
2 tbsp Chinese wine or sherry
1 tsp salt
2 tbsp oyster sauce
1 tsp pepper
300 ml (½ pint) water

Heat oil and fry crushed garlic until brown. Add bamboo shoots, mushrooms and abalone and fry for 2 minutes. Add wine, salt, oyster sauce and pepper and stir for 2 more minutes. Add water and simmer for 5 minutes. Serve hot.

Pickled Bean Clam

As a barefoot waif who romped the seashore at my grandparents' home in Siglap, where now tower blocks of government houses, I used to spend hours scraping in the warm sand for these small shells called remis in Malay. Reclamation has largely driven the remis back into the sea but with new beaches being sculptured from reclaimed land the remis seems to be making a comeback. They are the size of shirt buttons but make delicious morsels when pickled.

500 g (1 lb) bean clam
4 tbsp black soy sauce
2 tbsp sugar
4 red chillies

Place bean clams in a deep earthenware jar or glass bottle.

Add soy sauce, sugar and whole chillies and pickle for 4 days. Take an occasional peep and when the clams open a fraction they should be ready. I must warn you they make compulsive eating. Open one and you're likely to finish off the whole lot.

Stewed Abalone (illustrated on p. 76)

Cooking time: 60 minutes

Of all the crustacea in warm oceans this remains the most princely in taste though others may argue it is plebian compared with some other rarer molluscs in Hong Kong. I would not dare argue with anyone who has lived for any length of time in this British colony for who knows what Hong Kong people do not eat?

The abalone, being less spectacularly expensive in Singapore — some dried ones in Hong Kong fetch practically their weight in gold — has to be my favourite for this reason. It has a rich flavour all its own and need but the barest touch of seasoning be it boiled, stewed or eaten straight from its can.

1 can abalone
2 tbsp oyster sauce
2 cloves garlic, crushed
2 tbsp oil
500 ml (16 fl oz) water

Slice abalone into fairly thick pieces. Heat oil and fry chopped garlic until brown. Add oyster sauce and water and bring to the boil. Add abalone and transfer to pot with tight-fitting lid. Stew for an hour or more.

Cold Lobster Salad

Cooking time: 5 minutes

1 whole lobster about 600 g (1 lb 2 oz)
¼ head lettuce
4 tbsp mayonnaise

Boil lobster whole and remove taii meat. Cut into rings and chill slightly in refrigerator. Shred lettuce fine and mix with lobster meat. Pour mayonnaise over and serve as a cocktail.

Spicy Mussel Soup

Cooking time: 10 minutes

3 tbsp oil
500 g (1 lb) mussels
2 cloves garlic
6 peppercorns
3 cloves
1 tsp pepper
600 ml (1 pint) water
1 tsp salt

Wash and scrub mussels well. Crush garlic. Heat oil and fry garlic until brown. Add mussels and fry for 2 minutes. Add peppercorns, cloves and pepper and fry for 1 minute more. Add water and bring to the boil. Simmer for 5 minutes and add salt.

Raw Oysters Thai Style

10 oysters
3 limes
4 shallots, sliced
2 red chillies, sliced
1 tsp sugar

Remove oysters from shell but do not wash. Chill slightly. Squeeze limes for juice and mix with sliced shallots, chillies and sugar. Mix with oysters and serve on a lettuce leaf as an appetiser.

Oyster Stew

Cooking time: 10 minutes

10 oysters
400 ml (13 fl oz) milk
100 ml (3½ fl oz) water
2 cloves
1 stick cinnamon about 4cm (1½ in) long
1 tsp salt
1 tsp pepper
1 boiled potato, diced
1 large onion, sliced
Pinch powdered nutmeg

Put all ingredients, except oysters, to the boil and simmer over gentle heat for 5 minutes. Stir constantly to prevent milk from boiling and add oysters after removing shells. Simmer for 2 minutes and serve hot with buttered toast.

Stewed Abalone (recipe on p. 75).

Deep-fried Squid

Cooking time: 5 minutes

Oil for deep frying
500 g (1 lb) small whole squid
2 tbsp plain flour
1 tsp salt
1 tsp pepper
2 tbsp orange sauce

Wash squid and leave whole. Dry fry in pan until cooked and all liquid has evaporated. Dish up and drain. When cool, dredge in flour, salt and pepper. Heat oil until smoking and deep fry squid.

Squid must be absolutely dry or you're likely to find hot oil splattering onto your face. Drain on absorbent paper and trickle orange sauce over before serving. Leave out orange sauce if you prefer the squid crisp.

Fried Squid and Beancurd

Cooking time: 6 minutes

3 tbsp oil
1 large square beancurd or tofu
2 cloves garlic, crushed
2 tbsp preserved soy beans, washed and
   drained
300 g (10 oz) squid, sliced into bite-sized
   pieces and scored in a criss-cross pattern
300 ml (½ pint) water
1 tsp sugar
1 stalk spring onions
1 stalk celery

Heat oil and fry beancurd until light brown. Remove to cool and cut into bite-sized pieces. Reheat oil and fry crushed garlic until brown. Add preserved beans and fry for 1 minute more.

Add squid and beancurd and fry for 3 minutes. Add water and bring to the boil. Simmer for 2 minutes and add sugar. Serve garnished with spring onions and celery.

Dried Osyters and Mushroom Stew

Cooking time: 40 minutes

I did not have the smacking pleasure of eating dried oysters until introduced to its marvellous smoky flavour by my mother-in-law. Very much a Cantonese ingredient, it is perhaps rather off-putting as it takes quite a while to cook. It also has the distinction of being both an ingredient and a seasoning, and stew containing a handful of these delicious bites needs little else for extra flavour.

1 litre (1 ¾ pints) water
1 large square lard about 6 cm (2 ¼ in) squared
2 tbsp black soy sauce
1 tsp salt
20 dried oysters
10 Chinese mushrooms

Soak oysters and mushrooms for 10 minutes and drain. Combine all ingredients and simmer in a casserole or pot with a tight-fitting lid for 40 minutes. The gravy should be reduced by more than half. This makes a marvellous change when you've had a surfeit of meat.

Prawn Compote

Cooking time: 5 minutes

500 g (1 lb) prawns (uncooked)
3 tbsp oil
**1 tbsp preserved soy beans, washed and
  mashed**
4 tbsp water
1 tbsp sugar

INGREDIENTS TO BE SLICED
1 stalk lemon grass or strip of lemon rind
3 cm (1 ¼ in) piece ginger
1 tsp ground turmeric
1 large onion
3 red chillies
3 cloves garlic
**2 fragrant lime leaves or 2 tsp grated lemon
  rind**

Do not be daunted by the number of ingredients as most need only to be sliced fine. Wash and clean prawns. Leave tails on for better presentation. Heat oil and fry sliced ingredients for one minute.

Add prawns, mashed soy beans and water. Fry for 2 minutes more and then add salt and sugar. Reduce the amount of chillies if you don't like it to too hot.

Prawns, Cashew Nuts and Green Pepper (illustrated on p. 80)

Cooking time: 5 minutes

3 tbsp oil
1 clove garlic, crushed
250 g (9 oz) medium-sized prawns (uncooked)
20 cashew nuts
1 large green pepper
1 tsp salt
1 tsp sugar
250 ml (8 fl oz) water
1 tbsp cornflour
1 stalk spring onions, chopped fine.

Wash and shell prawns and slit down the back of each to remove the vein. Sprinkle sugar over drained prawns and leave aside for 20 minutes or so.

This is to render a crunch to the prawns when cooked. Dice green pepper into pieces 2 cm (¾ in) squared. Heat oil and fry crushed garlic until light brown.

Toss green pepper, prawns and cashew nuts in to stir fry quickly for about 1 minute. Dissolve cornflour in water and add to pan. Bring to boil and serve garnished with spring onions.

Indian Prawn Curry

Cooking time: 20 minutes
½ coconut, shredded
500 ml (16 fl oz) water
2 tbsp lemon juice
1 kg (2 lbs) (uncooked) prawns
3 cloves garlic, chopped
1 large onion, chopped
1 tbsp grated ginger
14 cm (5½ in) stick cinnamon
**2 stalks lemon grass, bruised or 2 tsp grated
  lemon rind**
1 tsp turmeric powder
1 tbsp chilli powder
2 tsp salt
1 tsp sugar
5 tbsp oil

Squeeze coconut with water and add 1 tbsp lemon juice to let milk curdle a little. Wash and clean prawns but leave shells on. Remove about 2 cm (¾ in) of the head if the whiskers are too long.

Fry chopped ginger, garlic, onion, lemon grass, cinnamon in hot oil for 2 minutes. Add turmeric, chilli and salt and fry for 1 minute more. Add slightly curdled coconut milk and bring to the boil. Add prawns and the rest of the ingredients. Simmer for 10 minutes and serve garnished with fresh coriander leaves.

Stir-fried Pepper Prawns

Cooking time: 5 minutes

500 g (1 lb) medium-sized prawns (uncooked)
2 tsp black pepper
2 tsp salt
3 tbsp oil

Wash and dry prawns thoroughly but leave shells intact. Cut off the last 2 cm (¾ in) of the prawn head. In a hot dry pan, dry fry the prawns until they turn pink. Cover for a minute for prawns to cook through and add pepper and salt. Stir-fry quickly and then add oil. Give pan a good shake so prawns are completely coated with oil, salt and pepper. Serve hot.

Prawn Balls

Cooking time: 10 minutes

Oil for deep-frying
1 large onion, finely minced
2 cloves garlic, finely minced
2 tbsp chopped spring onions
1 tsp pepper
1 tsp salt
1 lightly beaten egg
1 tbsp cornflour
750 g (1 ½ lbs) prawns, shelled and minced

Mix all ingredients and form into balls about 3 cm (1 ¼ in) in diameter. You could also form into flat patties for faster cooking. Heat oil until smoking and fry prawn balls a few at a time. Lift pan off the fire if prawn balls turn too brown. Fry for 5 minutes and drain on absorbent paper. Serve with a chilli garlic dip. See below.

CHILLI GARLIC DIP
Pound or blend together 10 fresh red chillies and 4 cloves garlic. Add 1 tbsp vinegar and 1 tsp sugar. If you have some peanut brittle use it instead of processed sugar for a crunchy flavour in the dip.

Sambal Prawns

Cooking time: 10 minutes

500 g (1 lb) prawns
5 tbsp desiccated coconut or
½ coconut, grated
350 ml (11 fl oz) water
5 tbsp oil
1 tbsp salt
1 tbsp sugar

INGREDIENTS TO BE SLICED
1 fresh red chilli
1 stalk lemon grass or tsp grated lemon rind
4 shallots
2 cloves garlic

SPICES
3 red chillies
1 large onion
6 skinned almonds
1 tbsp tomato puree

Pound spices until fine except tomato puree which is to be mixed in after pounding. Wash and clean prawns, leaving tails on if you prefer. Squeeze coconut with water or leave dessicated coconut in same amount of hot water for 10 minutes.

Squeeze for thin milk. Heat 2 tbsp of oil and fry sliced ingredients until light brown. Remove and drain. Fry pounded spices in remaining oil until fragrant. Add coconut milk and bring to a boil. Add prawns, salt and sugar and simmer for 5 minutes. Garnish with fried ingredients.

Prawns, Cashew Nuts and Green Pepper (recipe on p. 79).
Tamarind Eggs (recipe on p. 230).

Blazing Hot Prawns

Cooking time: 10 minutes

Be forewarned that this dish can literally "burn the roof of your mouth." But for chilli afficionados, it's blazing ambrosia.

4 tbsp oil
2 large onions, sliced fine
3 cloves garlic, sliced fine
3 tbsp chilli powder
1 tsp turmeric
1 tbsp shrimp paste powder
350 ml (11 fl oz) water
2 tsp brown sugar
2 tbsp tomato puree
650 g (1¼ lbs) prawns, shelled
1 tsp salt

Heat oil and fry onions and garlic until golden brown. Add chilli and turmeric and fry over low heat for 1 minute. The heat must not be too high or you will have a bitter tasting spice mix. Add shrimp paste powder at this point and continue to fry for 1 more minute. Add water and bring to the boil.

Add prawns, sugar, tomato puree and salt and simmer gently for 5 minutes. The gravy should be a redolent red and of a thick consistency. Serve with rice or as a sambal spread for festive sandwiches. This dish is not unlike the Szechuan chilli prawns which have the same propensity for rendering diners speechless.

Prawns in Batter

Cooking time: 5 minutes

Oil for deep frying
5 tbsp plain flour
1 tbsp cornflour
6 tbsp or ¼ can beer
Pinch of salt
1 egg
500 g (1 lb) medium-sized prawns (uncooked)

You might find it strange to use the good old 'pinta' as liquid for a batter coating but suffice to know that beer makes a marvellous lightening agent and your batter will be fluffier than if you use just plain water.

Mix flour and beer until you get the consistency that will stick to the prawns without too much flowing off. Adjust with more flour or beer if it's too thin.

Lightly beat egg and incorporate into batter. Add salt and leave batter in the refrigerator for about 15 minutes. Wash prawns and shell. Remove thin vein at the spine but keep tails on. Drain and dry.

Heat oil until smoking. Dip each prawn into batter and deep fry for about 3 minutes or until batter is light brown. Drain on absorbent paper and serve immediately. Battered prawns do not wait for anybody.

Quick Prawn and Watercress Salad

Cooking time: 3 minutes

300 g (10 oz) prawns, (cooked)
150 g (5 oz) watercress
2 tbsp French or Thousand Island dressing

Wash watercress and shred coarsely. Mix with prawns and add dressing for a crunchy, nutritious appetiser.

Prawns on Toast (top, recipe on p. 89),
Fried Crayfish in Black Bean Sauce (recipe on p. 60).

Hot and Sour Prawns

Cooking time: 10 minutes

4 tbsp oil
250 g (½ lb) coconut or desiccated coconut
400 ml (13 fl oz) water
1 lemon, squeezed for juice
1 tbsp fish sauce or light soy sauce
500 g (1 lb) prawns (cooked)

SPICES
1 tsp turmeric powder
1 tsp lemon grass powder or grated lemon rind
4 cloves garlic
1 tbsp chilli powder
1 tbsp coriander powder
1 tsp cumin powder
1 tbsp shrimp paste powder
4 shallots

Pound spices together until fine. Squeeze coconut with 400 ml (13 fl oz) water for milk. If you use desiccated coconut, use equivalent amount of hot water and steep desiccated coconut for at least 5 minutes before squeezing out milk.

Alternatively, use a blender. Heat oil and fry pounded spices till fragrant and oil seeps out again. Add coconut milk and lemon juice and bring to the boil.

Add prawns and seasoning and simmer for 4 minutes. Serve with bread or rice. You can stretch this dish by adding sliced French beans, or courgettes.

Gingery Prawns

Cooking time: 8 minutes

4 tbsp oil
2 tbsp minced ginger
1 tbsp minced garlic
1 tsp salt
1 tsp sugar
1 tsp vinegar
500 g (1 lb) prawns, (uncooked)
2 tbsp spring onions, chopped

SPICES
1 tsp chilli powder
1 tsp lemon grass powder or grated lemon rind
1 tsp pepper
3 tbsp sliced shallots

Pound spices together until fine. Heat oil and fry garlic and ginger until light brown. Add pounded ingredients and stir-fry for 1 minute.

Add prawns, sugar, salt and vinegar. Continue frying until prawns turn pink. You may add a few sprinkles of water if you like a moister dish. Serve garnished with spring onions.

NOTE: If you can get hold of some ginger wine, add a tbsp for a delicious tang.

Fried Prawns and Mangoes

Cooking time: 5 minutes

3 tbsp oil
2 cloves garlic, crushed
3 green chillies, sliced
2 green mangoes, sliced with skin
1 tbsp fish sauce
1 tbsp sugar
300 g (10 oz) medium-sized uncooked prawns,
   peeled
1 tbsp cornflour

Slice mangoes into bite-sized pieces and soak in water while you prepare other ingredients. This is to prevent them turning black.

Wash and drain prawns and coat with cornflour. Heat oil and fry crushed garlic until brown. Add drained pieces of mangoes and fry for 2 minutes over high heat. Add green chillies and prawns and stir fry for another 3 minutes until prawns turn pink. Add fish sauce and sugar and give it a quick stir.

You need not add water as there is enough liquid from the mangoes. Serve with plain boiled rice. Drained cling peaches make a sweeter substitute if you don't like the tartness of mangoes.

Prawns Fried with Pineapple and Chillies

Cooking time: 5 minutes

3 tbsp oil
2 cloves garlic, crushed
3 green chillies
1 red chilli
300 g (10 oz) prawns, shelled
2 tsp sugar
10 chunks canned pineapple or
equivalent fresh pineapple
1 tsp salt
1 tbsp cornflour
250 ml (8fl oz) water
1 tsp light soy sauce
1 tsp pepper

Deseed chillies and cut each into two. Leave to soak in a bowl of water to remove pungence if you like a milder dish. Wash prawns and marinate in 2 tbsp sugar for 15 minutes.

This makes the prawns crisp. Heat oil and fry crushed garlic until brown. Add chilli, prawns, pineapple and salt and stir fry over high heat for 3 minutes.

Dissolve cornflour in water and add to prawns together with soy sauce and pepper. Bring to the boil and serve with plain boiled rice.

Spicy Prawn Omelette

Cooking time: 6 minutes

4 eggs, lightly beaten
2 tbsp milk
250 g (½ lb) small prawns or shrimps, shelled
   and roughly chopped
1 tsp salt
1 stalk fresh coriander leaf
1 tsp pepper
2 cloves garlic
3 fresh red chillies
2 shallots
4 tbsp oil

Pound together garlic, chillies, pepper, coriander leaf and shallots. Heat 2 tbsp of oil and fry this spice mix for 3 minutes. Add prawns and stir fry quickly adding a few drops of water if mixture is too dry.

Add salt, scoop up and leave aside. Clean pan and heat remaining oil. Mix egg with milk and make thin, round omelettes about 12 cm in diameter. Spoon some prawn mixture onto each omelette when cool enough to handle and make into rolls. Serve as an appetiser.

Spicy Sour Prawns

Cooking time: 8 minutes

1 coconut
250 ml (8 fl oz) water
1 tbsp tamarind paste
150 ml (5 fl oz) water
4 tbsp oil
500 g (1 lb) prawns, shelled
3 tomatoes, quartered
1 tbsp light soy sauce
2 tbsp sugar

SPICES
1 tsp turmeric powder
1 tsp lemon grass powder or grated lemon rind
2 cloves garlic
1 tsp chilli powder
1 tsp pepper
1 tbsp coriander powder
1 tbsp cumin powder
1 small onion
1 tsp prawn paste powder

Moisten spices with a little water and set aside. Squeeze coconut with 250 ml (8 fl oz) water for milk. Mix tamarind with 150 ml (5 fl oz) water. Fry spices in oil until fragrant.

Add coconut milk and bring to the boil. Add prawn and tomatoes, tamarind water, soy sauce and sugar. Bring to the boil again and serve garnished with strips of fresh red chillies.

Prawn Dumplings (Sui Kow)

Cooking time: 8 minutes

This is one of the myriad dishes that constitute the wonderful culinary tradition that is collectively known as dim sum. Literally it means "food to touch the heart." It sure touches the region below the heart, that is the stomach, and while most dim sum dishes are laborious and impractical to make at home, a few like this are well worth some effort.

20 won ton wrappers, available at most
   Chinese shops
350 g (12 oz) prawns, shelled and chopped
   roughly
6 water chestnuts, peeled and chopped
   roughly
100 g (3 oz) minced pork mixed with 1 tbsp
   cornflour
1 tsp salt
1 tbsp sesame oil
1 tsp pepper
200 g (7 oz) mustard greens

FOR THE SOUP
5 tbsp dried anchovy (ikan bilis)
1.5 litres (2½ pints) water
2 tsp salt
1 tbsp sesame oil
3 tbsp chopped spring onions, for garnish
1 tsp pepper

Mix prawns, pork, chestnuts, salt, sesame oil and pepper. Place a level tbsp on each won ton wrapper and fold opposite corners over. Seal with a little water along the sides. Steam for 5 minutes.

Boil all stock ingredients except spring onions and pepper for 30 minutes. Strain off anchovies. Add cleaned mustard greens whole in last 2 minutes of simmering and when soup boils, pour into deep bowl with dumplings.

Prawn Thom Yam Soup (recipe on p. 93).

Gulai Prawns and Pineapple

Cooking time: 10 minutes

The loveliest thing about being born into an extended family is to have any number of aunts who are excellent cooks. The fact that my father had two official wives made the family pot even richer.

His first wife, whom we kids called First Mother (my mum was number two) hailed from Penang. She had a daughter who married into a Penang Hokkien family and frequently my sister's mother-in-law would treat us to her north Malayan style cooking.

She was also a devout Buddhist and made frequent trips to Thailand, coming back not only with the Thai language which she spoke fluently, but recipes for the most delicious curries and snacks. Though this dish was adopted by the Straitsborn community it remains Penang in character, the Penangites themselves being our Malaysian Straitsborn counterparts.

1 small pineapple, not too ripe
10 large prawns, (uncooked)
5 tbsp oil
600 ml (1 pint) water
3 tbsp tamarind paste
1 tbsp lard
1 tsp salt
1 tsp sugar

SPICES
8 almonds
1 tsp ground turmeric
1 tbsp shrimp paste
5 red chillies
12 shallots
2 stalks lemon grass or 2 tsp grated lemon rind

Pound spices not too fine. Traditionally this dish requires that the spices be a little pithy. You can either bruise the lemon grass and leave whole or pound together with spices.

Cut pineapples into four lengthwise and cut 1-cm (½ in) thick slices from each. Remove the core if you don't like its sharpness. Cut off prawn feelers and leave unshelled. Mix water with tamarind and discard pulp. Fry pounded spices in oil until fragrant. Add all other ingredients and simmer for 4 minutes or until prawns are cooked.

Prawns with French Beans

Cooking time: 5 minutes

3 tbsp oil
2 cloves garlic, sliced
2 red chillies, sliced
10 French beans, sliced diagonally fine
300 g (10 oz) prawns
1 tsp salt
Pinch monosodium glutamate
5 tbsp water

Heat oil and fry sliced garlic until brown. Add sliced chillies and French beans and fry for 1 minute. Add prawns and fry until prawns turn pink. Add seasoning and water and simmer for 1 minute.

Prawn Croquettes

Cooking time: 15 minutes

2 large potatoes, boiled till soft
2 eggs
3 tbsp milk
300 g (10 oz) prawns, shelled
1 tbsp cornflour
1 stalk spring onions, chopped
1 tsp salt
1 tsp oil
2 eggs, lightly beaten
Golden bread crumbs
Oil for deep frying

To save time, cut potatoes into chunks and boil for about 15 minutes. Alternatively, use instant mashed potato but the texture is too powdery.

Mash boiled potatoes. Mince prawns and mix with potatoes, 1 egg, milk, cornflour, chopped spring onions, salt and 1 tsp oil. Shape into croquettes and dip each one in beaten egg. Roll in bread crumbs and deep fry for 3 minutes until golden brown.

Red Prawn Sambal

Cooking time: 8 minutes

5 tbsp oil
3 tbsp tamarind paste
200 ml (7 fl oz) water
1 tsp salt
1 tsp sugar
2 tbsp tomato puree
650 g (1¼ lbs) prawns, shelled and cooked
2 fragrant lime leaves or ½ tsp grated lemon
   rind

SPICES
10 dried chillies, soaked till soft
3 cloves garlic
8 almonds
2 large onions

Pound or blend spices till fine. Heat oil and fry spices till fragrant and oil seeps out again. Mix tamarind with water and remove pulp.

Strain through wire mesh into pan and bring to the boil. Add tomato puree, shredded lime leaves, salt and prawns and stir. There should be a rich layer of red oil on top of dish. Serve with nasi lemak, bread or mee siam.

Prawns on Toast (illustrated on p. 82)

Cooking time: 8 minutes

4 slices white bread
2 eggs, lightly beaten
500 g (1 lb) minced prawns
1 tsp salt
1 tsp pepper
1 stalk spring onions, chopped
1 tsp sesame oil
Oil for deep frying

Cut bread into 4-cm (1½ in) squares. Discard rind. Mix minced prawns with salt, pepper and spring onions. Add 1 tbsp of beaten egg so when mixture is heaped on bread slices they will stick firmly. Heap each slice with mixture and dip in beaten egg. Heat oil and add sesame oil. Fry squares until golden brown. You can also use minced pork for the same recipe but add 2 tsp cornflour to the minced pork as it is inclined to be dry when fried.

Crystal Prawns and Peas

Cooking time: 5 minutes

500 g (1 lb) large prawns (uncooked)
1 tbsp sugar
2 tbsp oil
1 tbsp sesame oil
1 tsp salt
200 ml (7 fl oz) water
1 tbsp cornflour
1 can garden peas
3 large lettuce leaves
Good pinch pepper

You may have eaten this dish at a restaurant and wondered if the prawns were actually cooked! They are very much so and the crispy, slightly translucent texture comes from the prawns being marinaded in sugar for several hours in the refrigerator.

Wash and clean prawns and remove dark vein. Cut a deep slit down the back so when prawns are cooked they curl up nicely into firm rounds. Dry thoroughly and sprinkle sugar all over. Leave in refrigerator for at least 4 hours.

Heat oil and add sesame oil. Put prawns in to fry over high heat for less than 1 minute or until prawns turn an opaque white. Mix water with cornflour and salt and add to prawns. When gravy thickens add peas and dish up immediately. Serve on washed and dried lettuce leaves and garnish with pepper.

Fried Prawn Balls

Cooking time: 5 minutes

500 g (1 lb) prawns, shelled
1 tsp cornflour
1 tsp salt
1 tsp pepper
1 tbsp lard
Golden bread crumbs
2 eggs
2 tbsp sesame oil
Oil for deep frying

Mince prawns roughly. Add salt and pepper and mix well. Lightly beat one egg and add to prawns with cornflour, lard and 1 tsp sesame oil. Lightly beat other egg.

Shape prawn mixture into walnut-size balls and dip in egg. Roll each one in bread crumbs. Heat oil until smoking and add 1 tbsp sesame oil. Fry shrimp balls for 3 to 4 minutes until golden brown.

Skewered Satay Prawns (Prawn Kebab) (illustrated opposite)

Cooking time: 8 minutes

20 medium-sized prawns (uncooked)
1 tbsp coriander powder
2 tsp chilli powder
1 tsp cumin powder
1 tsp aniseed powder
1 tsp sugar
2 tsp salt
¼ coconut
300 ml (10 fl oz) water
4 metal skewers

Peel prawns, wash and dry. Squeeze coconut with water for milk and mix with all ingredients in a deep dish. Leave prawns to marinate for 30 minutes or longer. Put five prawns through each skewer and grill over charcoal or under an electric griller for 4 or 5 minutes, turning once or twice. Baste with marinade to keep prawns moist. Serve with cucumber slices and rice.

Prawn Curry with Okra

Cooking time: 10 minutes

3 tbsp oil
2 tbsp shredded ginger
½ coconut
500 ml (16 fl oz) water
400 g (13 oz) prawns, shelled
4 okra
1 tsp fish sauce
1 tsp sugar

SPICES
1 tbsp coriander powder
1 tsp aniseed powder
1 tsp cumin powder
½ tsp turmeric powder
3 whole cardamoms

Blend all spices except cardamoms. Moisten with 2 tbsp water. Squeeze coconut with water for milk. Cut okra, or lady's finger as they are called in Singapore, into halves, wash and drain.

Heat oil and fry ginger until fragrant. Add spices and fry for 3 minutes until oil seeps out again. Add okra and prawns and stir well. Add coconut milk, salt and sugar and simmer for 5 minutes.

By then okra will still be crunchy so if you want them well cooked, add them in a few minutes before the prawns.

Prawn Otak

Cooking time: 8 minutes

650 g (1¼ lbs) small prawns, chopped roughly
1 coconut, grated
4 tbsp grated coconut without skin
2 tsp salt
10-14 pieces of banana leaves (or foil)
    16 cm x 12 cm (6½ in x 5 in)

SPICES
2 stalks lemon grass or 2 tsp grated lemon rind
10 almonds
1 tsp turmeric powder
2 tsp chilli powder
3 cloves garlic
12 shallots
3 tbsp coriander powder, dry fried for a few
    minutes

PULUT PANGGANG
500 g (1 lb) glutinous rice, washed and soaked
    for a few hours or overnight
300 ml (½ pint) coconut milk
1 tsp salt
Scalded banana leaves 12 cm x 8 cm
    (5 in x 3 in)

Squeeze coconut for milk. Blend or pound spices till fine and mix with coriander powder. Combine spices and coconut milk and bring to the boil. Dry fry 4 tbsp coconut until brown and pound a little.

Add to coconut milk and simmer until thick. Add salt and stir well. Allow to cool. Boil some water and scald banana leaves until they are pliable. Mix prawns with coconut milk mixture and spread about 2 tbsp on each leaf.

Make into a packet by folding ends of banana leaves under firmly. Grill over charcoal or under electric grill for about 5 minutes each side. Prawn Otak can be eaten with steamed, baked glutinous rice called pulut panggang. The recipe follows.

Mix rice with coconut milk and salt and steam for about 15 minutes. The grains should still be firm and just cooked. Allow to cool. Spoon enough rice on each banana leaf to make little rolls about 8 cm x 3 cm (3 in x 1¼ in) diameter. Secure ends with toothpicks. Roast over charcoal or under an electric grill for 5 minutes until banana leaf chars a little.

Prawns in Rich Coconut Milk

Cooking time: 10 minutes

4 tbsp oil
10 shallots, sliced fine
3 green chillies, sliced into two and deseeded
1 coconut, grated
400 g (13 oz) prawns, shelled
2 tomatoes, quartered
400 ml (13 fl oz) water
1 tsp salt

SPICES
2 stalks lemon grass or 2 tsp grated lemon rind
1 large onion
3 red chillies
8 almonds
1 tbsp shrimp paste or powder
2 cloves garlic

Pound spices till fine. Heat oil and fry sliced shallots till brown. Remove and set aside. Fry green chillies until slightly shrivelled. Remove. Squeeze coconut with water for milk.

In remaining oil fry spices until fragrant and add coconut milk. Bring to the boil and add prawns and tomatoes. Simmer for 5 minutes.

Garnish with fried shallots and green chillies.

Prawn Thom Yam Soup (illustrated on p. 86)

Cooking time: 5 minutes

Ever since I had the first taste of this national Thai dish, I have had a passion for any version of it. It is both hard to come by and expensive at genuine Thai restaurants and I make my own which is very easy if you have all the traditional ingredients. Some modification may be necessary if you live in any country other than subtropical or tropical. I have indicated the substitutes.

650 ml (1¼ pints) water
2 tbsp tamarind paste (or 2 tbsp lemon juice)
2 tsp nam pla (or fish or light soy sauce)
2 fragrant lime leaves or 2 tsp grated lemon rind
2 red chillies, slit down ¾ way and deseeded
6 bird chillies (optional)
2 tbsp dried prawns, soaked in water and pounded
2 tsp sugar
400 g (13 oz) large prawns (uncooked)

Mix tamarind with water and discard pulp. Use a fine wire strainer to get a clear soup without residue. Alternatively use powdered tamarind (about 3 tbsp). Put all ingredients except prawns to boil and simmer for 4 minutes. Wash prawns and plunge into boiling soup for as long as it takes prawns to cook. Serve immediately. This hot, sour, sweet and lemony dish is heavenly on a cold night.

Deep-fried Spiced Prawns in Vanilla Pods (illustrated opposite)

Cooking time: 5 minutes

Hunger being the father of innovation and, faced with not much than a few shrimps and left-over vanilla pods, I had this gleam in my eye (and twitch in my stomach) one day. This dish, like so many in this book, is the result of seven parts ingenuity and three parts hunger. The whole, I must say, it is utterly pleasing.

6 large prawns, (uncooked)
1 tsp turmeric powder
1 tbsp cornflour
1 tsp chilli powder
1 tsp salt
6 vanilla pods

Mix turmeric, chilli and salt. Wash prawns and combine with spices. Leave to marinade for 5 minutes. Roll in cornflour and wrap each prawn with one vanilla pod securing firmly with a toothpick.

Deep fry in hot oil for 1 or 2 minutes. Unwrap the pod before eating. You will find that the mixture of spices and vanilla pod combines in a fragrant way that's unique. You can use either chicken or lobster for these delectable little snacks.

Prawn Omelette (illustrated on p. 40)

Cooking time: 4 minutes

4 tbsp oil
2 cloves garlic, crushed
1 carrot
4 eggs, lightly beaten
1 tsp salt
1 tsp pepper
300 g (10 oz) small prawns, shelled

Heat oil and fry crushed garlic until brown. Shred carrot fine, add to pan and fry for 1 minute. Add prawns and fry for 30 seconds. Mix egg with salt and pepper and pour into pan. Spread to form an omelette and cook until egg sets. Add a few more drops of oil if necessary. When egg sets, shred coarsely with ladle and serve with fresh coriander leaves.

Prawns with Walnuts and Celery

Cooking time: 8 minutes

5 tbsp oil
2 cloves garlic, crushed
1 stalk celery
4 tbsp shelled walnuts
400 g (13 oz) prawns
1 tsp sugar
1 tbsp cornflour
200 ml (7 fl oz) water
1 tbsp oyster sauce
1 tsp pepper

Slice celery diagonally into small pieces 3-cm (1¼ in) long. Shell prawns and marinate in sugar for 10 minutes. Heat oil and fry crushed garlic until brown. Add celery, walnuts and prawns and stir for a minute or so.

Add water to cornflour and mix with salt, oyster sauce and pepper. Pour into pan and when gravy thickens dish up to serve.

Aubergine Curry (right, recipe on p. 179),
Deep-fried Spiced Prawns in Vanilla Pods.

Prawns in Yam Basket (illustrated opposite)

Cooking time: 30 minutes

1 large yam (taro) about 500 g (1 lb)
3 tbsp cornflour
1 tsp salt
Oil for deep-frying
2 tbsp sesame oil

FILLING FOR BASKET
3 tbsp oil
2 cloves garlic, crushed
3 slices green ginger, shredded
1 small carrot, cubed
20 button mushrooms
1 stalk celery, sliced 2 cm (¾ in) thick
300 g (10 oz) prawns, shelled with tails left on

TO BE MIXED TOGETHER
1 tbsp sesame oil
1 tsp pepper
1 tbsp ginger juice
1 tbsp Chinese wine or sherry
1 tbsp oyster sauce
1 tbsp cornflour

HOW TO MAKE YAM BASKET

You must have the pair of metal moulds (see picture) which can be specially ordered at hardware stores selling Asian cooking implements. If you can't get these, use the wire mesh ladle for scalding noodles.

Peel yam and cut into thin slices lengthwise. Cut again into strips about the size of matchstick potatoes but longer. The reason for choosing a longish-shaped yam gives you strips long enough to make a deep basket.

Mix yam sticks with cornflour and salt and arrange in mould one at a time to form a basket much like a bird building a nest. Use the short strips for bottom of mould. Yam sticks should be at least 4 cm (1½ in) over rim of mould.

When mould is completely covered, use the other to wedge firmly down on basket of yam sticks. Heat oil until smoking and add sesame oil. This imparts a lovely fragrance to whatever it is you are deep-frying.

Lower basket in to fry for 6 minutes until yam basket is brown and crisp. When it is cooked it will come apart from the mould by itself. Allow to cool and store in an air-tight tin if not using immediately. Take care handling it as it's very brittle.

FILLING

Heat 2 tbsp oil until smoking and fry crushed garlic until brown. Add ginger, carrot, prawns and button mushrooms and fry over high heat for 1 minute. Add celery and stir for a few seconds. Add seasoning mix and bring to fast boil. Gravy should be just thick enough to cover diced food with a sheen. Arrange yam basket on a bed of shredded lettuce or whole lettuce leaves and dish filling into basket.

Indian Spiced Prawns

Cooking time: 10 minutes

4 tbsp oil
500 g (1 lb) prawns, shelled
250 ml (8 fl oz) water
1 tbsp tamarind paste or lemon rind
2 red chillies, chopped
1 tsp salt
1 tsp sugar

SPICES
2 tsp chilli powder
1 tsp cumin powder
1 tsp aniseed powder
1 tsp turmeric powder
3 cloves garlic
2 tbsp coriander powder

Blend spices fine and make into a paste with a few tbsp of water. Marinate prawns with paste for 30 minutes. Mix water with tamarind powder. Heat oil and fry chopped chilli for 1 minute. Add prawns and stir for 1 minute. Add tamarind water, salt, sugar and bring to a boil. Serve heaped on plain boiled rice.

Prawn Tempera

Cooking time: 8 minutes

2 tbsp cooking oil
1 stalk lemon grass or grated lemon rind
3 gloves garlic
2 red chillies
1 green chilli
2 fragrant lime leaves or ½ tsp grated lemon rind
1 tsp turmeric powder
4 French beans
300 g (10 oz) prawns (uncooked)

2 tsp fish sauce
2 tsp malt vinegar
1 tsp shrimp paste powder
2 tsp sugar
1 tsp salt
350 ml (11 fl oz) water

Slice lemon grass, garlic, chillies, fragrant leaves and French beans fine. Combine fish sauce, vinegar, shrimp paste powder, sugar, salt and water. Wash and clean prawns and leave tails on.

Heat oil and fry all sliced ingredients for 2 minutes. Add liquid and bring to the boil. Add prawns and simmer for 3 minutes. Adjust seasoning with more or less sugar or vinegar as your taste dictates.

Sambal Prawns (Very Hot)

Cooking time: 10 minutes

400 g (13 oz) small prawns
1 tsp sugar
2 tbsp tamarind paste
300 ml (½ pint) water
4 tbsp oil
1 large onion, sliced
1 tsp salt
1 tbsp tomato puree

SPICES
3 large onions
15 dry chillies, soaked in hot water until soft
4 fresh red chillies
5 skinned almonds
1 tbsp shrimp paste (powder or paste)

Wash and devein prawns. Sprinkle sugar on them and leave for 10 minutes to marinate. Mix tamarind with water and strain off the pulp if using fresh paste. Fry pounded spices until fragrant. Add sliced onion and fry for one minute. Add tamarind liquid and bring to the boil. Add prawns, salt and tomato puree and simmer for two or three minutes. Serve with bread or rice.

Prawn Fritters

Cooking time: 10 minutes

Oil for deep frying
400 g (13 oz) small prawns
300 g (10 oz) plain flour
2 tbsp cornflour
1 can cold beer
2 egg whites, beaten stiff
1 tsp salt

Wash prawns and leave shells on. Prawns must be no more than 3 cm (1¼ in) long to be prepared this way. Leaving the shells on also makes the fritter crunchy and you eat it shells and all.

Sift flour into a bowl and mix with cornflour. Make a hole in the centre and gradually pour in cold beer to make a thick batter. Add beer a little at a time until you get the batter thick enough to hold a handful of prawns in shape.

Add salt and fold in egg white gently. Using two large spoons, shape small mounds of prawn and batter and lower into smoking oil to fry for 2 minutes until fritters are brown. Serve with chilli and peanut sauce.

POULTRY

Possibly one of the best food buys you can make is a fat chicken. Versatile, tasty and — with battery-reared poultry of every size and grade available at every supermarket — so easy to prepare, a chicken is always good value for money. In Asian cooking, the chicken, and to a lesser extent the duck, lends itself to a limitless range of dishes. Neither boiling, braising, baking or deep-frying and stir-frying can mar the taste and flavour of your chicken if you had a good fowl to being with.

If you are not certain of its age the best guide would be the size. Any chicken over one kilogram is best boiled, curried, stewed or roasted. Smaller chickens or spring chickens are best cooked simply, either deep-fried with a hint of soy sauce and honey or simply grilled.

Ducks are, however, a different fowl altogether. Some people don't like them because they take a long time to cook and tenderise and generally have a strong smell. This is where long, slow cooking with spices can transform this tough bird into a dish fit for your most important guests. Because of its oily richness, duck is best cooked with a strong-flavoured vegetable like salted vegetable or simmered for an hour or two with brandy and sour plums as in the Straits Chinese soup.

But it is the Cantonese and northern Chinese who bring the art of cooking duck to perfection with their delicious roast ducks. These need not be difficult to prepare — who has those enormous clay ovens the Peking and Canton chefs use? — if you have a gas oven and the patience. But once you have mastered the art of stuffing, marinading and roasting duck, you will probably wonder why you didn't like it in the first place.

Long Island ducklings are excellent for roasting and farm-reared ducks are best cut up and stewed in soy sauce, coriander and pepper. On the average a 2 kilogram duck would take an hour and a half to cook.

Steamed Chicken Wings and Mushrooms in Wine

Cooking time: 15 minutes

6 chicken wings
4 Chinese mushrooms
1 thumb-sized knob ginger
1 tbsp Chinese wine or sherry
1 tbsp sesame oil
1 tsp pepper
1 tsp salt
1 stalk spring onions

Cut off small tip of chicken wings and cut each remaining wing into two. Traditionally this dish uses deboned chicken wings but this is a fiddly chore and not really necessary if you are pushed for time.

Soak mushrooms in hot water for 10 minutes. Slice into strips. Pound ginger and squeeze out juice. Mix with wine, sesame oil, salt and pepper and put in steaming plate together with chicken. Steam for 10 minutes and add chopped spring onions. Steam for few minutes more and serve with rice.

Fried Chicken with Salted Vegetable

Cooking time: 15 minutes

3 tbsp oil
2 cloves garlic
3 slices ginger, shredded
200 g (7 oz) salted vegetable
2 chicken breasts
2 red chillies
1 tsp sugar
1 tsp salt
200 ml (7 fl oz) water

Soak salted vegetables in water for 15 minutes and squeeze out all moisture. Shred fine. Cut chicken breasts into shreds about the same size as salted vegetable. Slice chillies into strips.

Heat oil and fry garlic until brown. Add ginger and salted vegetable and fry until almost dry.

Add sugar and salt and stir for 1 minute. Add chicken and stir for 3 minutes until chicken is half-cooked. Add water and simmer for 5 minutes.

Fried Chicken with Ginger

Cooking time: 15 minutes

5 tbsp oil
1 chicken about 1 kg (2 lbs)
2 tsp black pepper
4 tbsp shredded ginger
3 cloves garlic
1 tsp sugar
1 tbsp sesame oil
300 ml (½ pint) water
1 tsp salt

Wash and clean chicken and cut into bite-sized pieces. Heat wok and put chicken pieces in to be dry-fried for 5 minutes. This semi-cooks the chicken for the next stage. When all moisture has evaporated, remove chicken and clean wok.

Heat oil and fry ginger and garlic until brown. Add pepper and chicken and stir-fry vigorously for 4 minutes until all pieces are well coated. Add sugar, sesame oil, salt and water and simmer for 10 minutes until dry.

Chicken Stuffed with Chestnuts and Oysters (illustrated on p. 104)

Cooking time: 1¹/₂ hours

You can use either fresh oysters or dried oysters the latter imparting a delicate smoky flavour to the dish that fresh ones don't. Adding a few spoonfuls of diced liver to the stuffing mix also stretches the dish to feed more persons.

4 tbsp oil
1 large chicken about 1.5 kg (3 lbs) rubbed
   with 1 tbsp black soy sauce
15 dried chestnuts
20 oysters
200 g (7 oz) liver
2 tbsp oyster sauce
2 tbsp black soy sauce
1 tsp pepper
1 tsp sugar
2 tsp five-spice powder
400 ml (13 fl oz) water for stuffing
2 litres (3½ pints) water for braising

Wash and wipe chicken dry. Rub with soy sauce and leave to dry. Heat oil in non-stick wok and brown chicken. Remove chicken. Soak chestnuts in water and remove skins. Soak oysters, if using dry ones, for 10 minutes. Dice liver fine. Heat remaining oil and fry oysters, chestnuts and liver for 2 minutes.

Add oyster sauce, soy sauce, pepper, sugar and five spice powder. Add 400 ml (13 fl oz) water and simmer for 30 minutes until chestnuts and oysters are soft. The liquid should have been reduced considerably by now. Allow to cool.

Put stuffing into chicken cavity and pack loosely. It is not necessary to sew up with thread. There should be plenty of liquid from the stuffing. Mix this with the 2 litres (3½ pints) water and place in a casserole. Put chicken in and stew, covered, for 1 hour or so.

Paper-wrapped Chicken

Cooking time: 8 minutes

This rather odd dish may seem like something out of a news vendor's lunch box but it is very good eating once you get past the paper which acts as a sealant trapping in all the rich juices and seasoning.

1 chicken about 1.5 kg (3 lbs)
1 large knob ginger, pounded for juice
1 tsp light soy sauce
3 tbsp oyster sauce
1 tbsp sesame oil
2 tbsp Chinese wine or sherry
2 tsp sugar
4 tbsp chopped spring onions
15 to 20 sheets rice or ordinary tracing paper,
   cut into 12-cm (4¾ in) square sheets
Oil for deep frying

Wash and cut chicken into bite-sized pieces. Remove as many bones as possible for easier eating. Marinate chicken pieces in seasoning ingredients for 30 minutes.

Place a piece of chicken on one sheet of paper and wrap up firmly tucking in the last triangle to form a small envelope. Deep-fry pieces, a few at a time, for 2 minutes or so and drain on absorbent paper.

If you are using rice paper this wrapping is edible but it is not easy to find rice paper. If you are making a large batch for entertainment using a stapler to fasten parcels is faster but make sure staples are rust-free.

Deep-fried Spiced Chicken

Cooking time: 20 minutes

Oil for deep-frying
1 chicken about 1 kg (2 lbs)
2 tbsp black soy sauce
1 tbsp sugar
1 tsp salt
1 tbsp cornflour
5 tbsp water
1 tbsp lime juice

SPICES
4 red chillies
1 large onion
8 almonds
1 tsp turmeric powder
1 tsp aniseed powder
1 tbsp coriander powder
1 2-cm (¾ in) knob ginger
1 bunch coriander leaves

Pound spices till fine. Cut chicken into bite-sized pieces and marinate in soy sauce, sugar and salt for 5 minutes. Heat oil. Drain chicken pieces and roll in cornflour. Deep-fry for 5 minutes until brown.

Remove from pan and drain. Remove all but 4 tbsp oil and fry pounded spices until fragrant. Add chicken pieces and fry for 1 minute until well coated with spices. Add water mixed with lime juice and simmer for 5 minutes.

Easy Chicken Kurmah

Cooking time: 40 minutes

4 tbsp coconut cream
400 ml (13 fl oz) water
200 ml (7 fl oz) evaporated milk
1 tbsp lime juice
1 chicken about 1 kg (2 lbs)
2 tsp salt
3 tbsp ghee or cooking oil
1 large onion, sliced fine
2 tbsp shredded ginger
1 tsp cinnamon powder
½ tsp clove powder
4 whole cardamoms
1 stalk lemon grass or ¼ tsp grated lemon
  rind

SPICES
4 tbsp ready-made kurmah powder or kurmah
  paste or pound together:
2 cloves garlic
10 almonds
2 tbsp coriander powder
1 tbsp cumin powder
1 tbsp aniseed powder
2 tsp pepper

Mix coconut creme with evaporated milk. Squeeze lime juice into mixture and leave to curdle for 10 minutes. Cut chicken into large joints and rub with 1 tsp salt. Wash and drain.

Heat ghee and fry sliced onion, ginger, cinnamon, cloves, cardamom and lemon grass for 2 minutes. Add kurmah paste or powder and fry until fragrant. Sprinkle a little water in spice mix if it's too dry.

Add chicken joints and fry well for 2 or 3 minutes. Add coconut creme, evaporated milk mixture and salt and simmer for 20 minutes or longer depending on consistency you want. Serve with crusty French bread.

Southern-fried Chicken

Cooking time: 10 minutes

With fast-food type fried chicken enticing at every downtown street corner, I thought I might as well learn how to do it myself and perhaps one day making a million dollars like a certain Colonel has done. Much as I like Kentucky Fried Chicken, I do not wish to be entirely dependent on the fast-food joints but how does one coax the recipe from the fried-chicken people without being involved in a lawsuit? It takes but only a little ingenuity to coax one of the kitchen help to tell me, if not the complete recipe, at least the basic flour mix. And the key to the whole "crisp and brown outside and succulent inside" magic is simple pressure-cooking for about eight minutes.

1 litre (1 ¾ pints) oil for deep frying
1 chicken about 1.5 kg (3 lbs)
10 tbsp plain flour
150 ml (5 fl oz) water
2 tsp salt
1 tsp pepper
1 chicken stock cube
1 egg

Cut chicken into large joints and dry thoroughly. Make depression in centre of flour. Dissolve chicken stock cube in water and mix with salt and pepper. Pour mixture into depression and mix into a fairly thick paste. Add more water if paste is too unyielding. Add egg and stir to incorporate well. Heat oil in pressure cooker until smoking. Coat chicken joints with batter and put in to fry. Cover under 15 pounds pressure and cook for 8 minutes.

Honey Roast Chicken

Cooking time: 45 minutes

1 chicken about 1.5 kg (3 lbs)
4 tbsp honey
2 tbsp black soy sauce
3 bacon rashers (streaky)
2 tsp lime juice

Wash chicken and remove giblets. Rub honey all over and hang to dry for several hours. Pre-heat oven to 150°C (gas mark 2). Rub chicken with soy sauce and lay bacon strips over chicken breast. Place on a rack over a pan of water and roast for 15 minutes.

Turn chicken over and place bacon strips on the back this time. Roast for 15 minutes more and lower heat for last 10 minutes of roasting. Test if chicken is cooked by inserting a metal skewer into thickest part of thigh. If skewer comes out clean, chicken is done. Squeeze lime juice over chicken before serving whole.

Braised Coriander Chicken

Cooking time: 25 minutes

I am never more glad than when cooking this as it is my son's all-time favourite. It is about the only food that will make him take leave of television cartoons willingly and that's something of an achievement for an eight year old hooked on the Pink Panther.

2 tbsp oil
2 large onions, sliced fine
1 clove garlic, crushed
1 chicken about 650 g (1¼ lbs)
3 tbsp black soy sauce
3 tbsp coriander powder
2 tbsp sugar
1 tsp salt
1 tsp pepper
750 ml (1¼ pints) water

Cut chicken and joint into six or eight pieces. Rub all over with black soy sauce, sugar, salt and pepper and marinate for 15 minutes.
An easy way to coat meat or poultry with marinade is to put marinade ingredients in a plastic bag together with meat or poultry and give it a good shake.

Heat oil and fry onions and garlic until soft but not brown. Scrape of marinade ingredients and add to frying pan. Stir for 1 minute and add chicken pieces. Stir until well coated and chicken slightly brown. Add water and simmer for 20 minutes. Adjust seasoning and serve with bread or rice.

Chicken with Cashew Nuts

Cooking time: 25 minutes

2 tbsp oil
2 cloves garlic, crushed
1 chicken breast, cubed
1 carrot, cubed
4 water chestnuts, chopped roughly
3 tbsp cashew nuts
2 tsp light sauce
1 tsp pepper
1 tsp salt
150 ml (5 fl oz) water
2 tsp cornflour
1 tbsp sesame oil
1 bunch coriander leaves

Heat oil and fry onions and garlic until soft but not brown. Scrape off marinade ingredients and add to frying pan. Stir for 1 minute and add chicken pieces. Stir until well coated and chicken slightly brown. Add water and simmer for 20 minutes. Adjust seasoning and serve with bread or rice.

Charcoal-grilled Duck

Cooking time: 45 minutes

1 duck about 2 kg (4 lbs) cut into joints
2 tbsp honey
2 tsp salt
2 tbsp orange juice (freshly squeezed)
2 tsp hoi sin sauce
2 tsp coriander powder
2 tbsp oil

Wash duck joints and dry thoroughly. Combine marinade ingredients and rub all over duck. Refrigerate for an hour. Drain duck and pour marinade into a small container to be used as a basting liquid.

Grill duck over glowing embers for 20 minutes each side turning over frequently and basting with liquid. Heat remaining marinade gently and thicken with a little cornflour mixed with water. Pour over duck and serve.

Roast Duck Cantonese (illustrated opposite)

Cooking time: 1 hour 30 minutes

1 duck about 2 kg (4 lbs)
3 tbsp honey
4 tbsp sherry
Pinch red food colouring
2 tbsp water
2 tsp salt
½ tsp five spice powder

Wash duck and remove any giblets inside body cavity. Prick all over with a sharp fork. This is to release some of the fat when the duck is roasting as duck is extremely fatty. Dry thoroughly.

Combine all other ingredients and rub all over duck. Refrigerate for at least several hours or overnight if possible. Pre-heat oven to 140°C (gas mark 1). Fill a roasting pan with water and place under the centre level rack of your oven. If you have the type of roasting pan that comes with its own rack, make sure the water does not touch the duck.

Place duck breast side upwards and roast for 35 minutes. Baste once or twice while roasting and turn duck over after this time. Roast for 25 minutes or so and turn breast upwards once more.

Serve with sliced cucumber and some of the marinade boiled down a little.

Chicken and Walnuts

Cooking time: 20 minutes

4 tbsp oil
2 chicken breasts, diced
200 g (7 oz) shelled walnuts
1 carrot, diced
2 cloves garlic, crushed
3 slices ginger
2 stalks spring onions, diced
2 tbsp sesame oil
1 tsp salt
1 tbsp light soy sauce
1 tsp pepper
1 tbsp cornflour
4 tbsp water

Heat oil and fry chicken for 2 minutes. Remove and fry walnuts and carrot for minute. Drain and set aside. Reheat oil and fry crushed garlic until brown.

Add ginger and fried ingredients and stir well. Add diced onions, seasoning, sesame oil and water mixed with cornflour. Simmer for 2 minutes until gravy thickens. Serve hot.

Chicken with Honey Lemon

Cooking time: 45 minutes

4 tbsp butter or margarine
2 tbsp lemon juice
2 tsp pepper
3 tbsp honey
1 tsp salt
1 tbsp black soy sauce
2 tbsp brown sugar
1 spring chicken about 650 g (1¼ lbs)

Soften butter and cream with lemon juice, pepper, honey and salt. Clean chicken and rub with soy sauce, sugar and leave aside for 20 minutes.

Pre-heat oven till hot and place chicken on roasting rack with roasting pan underneath. Roast chicken for 10 minutes and spread butter mixture all over. Roast for 20 minutes more and turn chicken over. Scoop dripping from roasting pan and baste chicken with it. Roast 10 minutes more and serve with chilli sauce.

Chicken with Black Beans

Cooking time: 20 minutes

Oil for deep frying
3 chicken breasts, cut into bite-sized pieces
10 shallots, sliced
2 tbsp cornflour
1 tbsp black soy sauce
1 tbsp light soy sauce
2 tbsp Chinese wine or sherry
1 tsp brown sugar
3 stalks spring onions, cut into 5 cm (2 in) lengths
6 cloves garlic, sliced
2 tbsp preserved black beans

Heat oil and deep-fry chicken for 2 minutes. Drain and set aside. Fry shallots until brown and crisp. Drain and set aside. Blend cornflour, soy sauces, sugar and wine.

Remove all but 2 tbsp oil and fry garlic and spring onions for 1 minute. Add preserved beans and fry for 1 minute. Add chicken pieces and fry for 2 minutes. Add liquid and bring to the boil. Simmer until sauce thickens and serve garnished with fried shallots.

Thai-style Chicken and Bamboo Shoots

Cooking time: 10 minutes

3 tbsp oil
2 cloves garlic, sliced
6 shallots, sliced
2 red chillies, sliced
2 chicken breasts, cut into strips
6 slices bamboo shoots cut into strips
1 stalk spring onions, cut into 4 cm (1½ in) lengths
1 tbsp Chinese fish sauce
1 tsp sugar
1 tsp pepper
1 tbsp cornflour
6 tbsp water

Heat oil and fry garlic and shallots until brown. Add chicken and bamboo shoots and fry for 3 minutes. Add spring onions, chillies, fish sauce, sugar, pepper and water mixed with cornflour and bring to the boil. Simmer for 4 minutes and add a little more water if necessary.

Grilled Balinese Chicken (illustrated on p. 114/115)

Cooking time: 30 minutes

1 chicken about 1 kg (2 lbs)
1 tsp salt
2 tsp pepper
4 tbsp butter
2 large onions
2 cloves garlic
3 red chillies
1 thumb-sized knob ginger
2 tbsp tomato puree
1 tbsp sugar
1 tbsp black soy sauce
1 stalk lemon grass, bruised or grated lemon
  rind
2 tbsp lime or lemon juice

Cut chicken into large joints and rub with salt and pepper. Melt butter in heavy-bottomed pan and fry chicken joints until golden brown. Remove and place on a grill rack. Pound together onions, chillies, garlic and ginger. Fry in remaining butter for 2 minutes until fragrant. Mix with tomato puree, sugar and soy sauce and marinate chicken joints in mixture for an hour.

Grill chicken on rack, basting every few minutes with marinade and bruised lemon grass. Grill for 25 minutes turning over once and squeeze lime juice over before serving.

Lemony Chicken Curry

Cooking time: 30 minutes

1 chicken about 1 kg (2 lbs)
4 tbsp oil
2 stalks lemon grass, bruised (or grated peel of
  one lemon)
1 coconut, grated
300 ml (10 fl oz) water
1 tbsp lime juice
1 tsp sugar
1 tsp salt

SPICES
1 large onion
3 cloves garlic
1 tbsp coriander powder
1 tsp cumin powder
½ tsp turmeric powder
2 tbsp chilli powder
8 almonds
1 tbsp shrimp paste or powder

Pound spices till fine. Wash and clean chicken. Grill under hot fire for 10 minutes to singe the skin a little. Heat oil and fry ground spices until fragrant. Add lemon grass and lime leaves and fry for 1 minute. Squeeze coconut milk with water for milk and add to spices. Bring to the boil and add chicken. Simmer for 20 minutes and add salt, sugar and lime juice.

Pigeon Soup

Cooking time: 35 minutes

1 plump pigeon
1.5 litre (3 ½ pints) water
100 g (3 oz) streaky pork
1 tsp salt
1 tbsp light soy sauce
1 tbsp brandy
1 tsp pepper
Fresh coriander leaves

Bring water to the boil and simmer whole pigeon with streaky pork. Simmer for 20 minutes and add salt, soy sauce and pepper. Simmer for 15 minutes more and serve piping hot with brandy spooned into soup just before serving and topped with coriander leaves.

Chicken Soto

Cooking time: 45 minutes

1 chicken about 1 kg (2 lbs)
2 tsp salt
2 tbsp oil
10 shallots, sliced fine
2 cloves garlic, crushed
1 tsp peppercorns
1 tsp shredded turmeric
6 almonds
1 tbsp shredded ginger
2 stalks lemon grass, bruised or grated lemon
 rind
2 tsp salt
3 litres (5¼ pints) water
300 g (10 oz) boiled and diced potatoes
100 g (3 oz) bean sprouts, scalded
Cubed compressed rice (see page 271)
2 bunches Chinese celery
2 stalks spring onions
4 tbsp sliced shallots fried in
3 tbsp oil

SAUCE
10 chilli padi (bird chillies) or red chillies,
 pounded coarsely
4 tbsp black soy sauce
1 tsp sugar
2 tbsp lime juice

Wash chicken and rub with salt. Set aside. Heat oil and fry shallots, garlic, peppercorns, turmeric, almonds, ginger and lemon grass for 1 minute. Add water and salt and bring to the boil. Add whole chicken and simmer for 30 minutes or longer depending on size of chicken.

Remove chicken and allow to cool. Debone chicken and cut meat into shreds. Return bones to stock and simmer for 15 minutes longer. Strain soup and set aside until ready to serve.

Cut Chinese celery and spring onions into 4 cm (1½ in) lengths. Fry sliced shallots in hot oil until brown. Mix pounded chilli with soy sauce, sugar and lime juice.

To serve, place 5 or 6 cubes of compressed rice in individual soup bowls. Top with diced potatoes, scalded bean sprouts and a tsp of chilli mixture. Arrange chicken meat on top, as much as each person wants, and pour hot soup over. Garnish with Chinese celery, spring onions and fried shallots.

Stuffed Duck

Cooking time: 1½ hours

1 duck about 2 kg (4 lbs)
1 tbsp ginger juice
1 tbsp brandy
4 tbsp oil
2 tbsp shredded green ginger
2 cloves garlic, crushed
5 Chinese mushrooms, soaked till soft
200 g (7 oz) streaky pork, minced
4 tbsp diced liver
1 tbsp fish sauce
1 tsp sherry
10 chestnuts, boiled till soft
10 gingko nuts, shelled
10 lotus seeds, boiled and drained
500 ml (16 fl oz) water

Wash duck and wipe dry. Rub with ginger juice and brandy and set aside. Heat wok or non-stick pan with oil and fry garlic and shredded ginger until brown. Slice mushrooms into strips and add to pan together with pork and diced liver.

Stir well and add all other ingredients. Simmer for 20 minutes until almost dry.

Stuff duck with mixture and sew up cavity with strong thread. Place duck in a casserole and steam for an hour or so depending on the tenderness you want. If you use a pressure cooker to steam it will cut the time by half but you have to have a large enough cooker to hold duck. I find that a wide electric wok with a tight lid excellent for this purpose.

Crispy Curried Chicken

Cooking time: 10 minutes

1 chicken about 1 kg (2 lbs)
Oil for deep-frying
1 small head lettuce
2 tomatoes

MARINADE
2 tbsp sugar
1 tbsp curry powder
1 tbsp yoghurt
2 tbsp ginger juice
2 tbsp fish sauce
1 tsp pepper

Wash and cut chicken into bite-sized pieces. Marinate for an hour. Remove chicken pieces after this and drain thoroughly. Heat oil until smoking hot and deep-fry chicken a few pieces at a time. Serve on lettuce leaves and sliced tomatoes. You can deep-fry the chicken whole for better presentation.

Almond Chicken

Cooking time: 15 minutes

3 chicken breasts, sliced
4 tbsp chopped almonds
2 tbsp cornflour
1 egg white
Oil for deep-frying

MARINADE
1 tsp salt
1 tbsp light soy sauce
1 tbsp cornflour
1 tbsp Chinese wine or sherry
4 tbsp water

Marinate chicken for 20 minutes. Mix chopped almonds with cornflour. Beat egg white until stiff peaks form and add chicken pieces to it discarding the marinade. Coat chicken with almond mixture and deep fry until golden brown. Drain on kitchen towels and serve with slices of lemon.

Braised Chicken Wings

Cooking time: 20 minutes

500 g (1 lb) chicken wings
2 tbsp oil
1 clove garlic, crushed
1 tbsp hoi sin sauce
1 square preserved soy bean
1 tsp sugar
600 ml (1 pint) water

Remove small wing tips of chicken wings. Heat oil and fry for a few minutes until half-cooked. Remove chicken wings and add crushed garlic to fry until light brown. Add hoi sin sauce and soy bean, sugar and water and bring to the boil. Simmer chicken wings until cooked. You can also add dried bean curd squares, water convolvulus, spinach, or chicken livers to make a rich stew.

Previous page: Clockwise from top left, Yellow Rice (recipe on p. 205), Balinese Grilled Chicken (recipe on p. 111), Sambal Ikan Bilis (recipe on p. 35), Chilli and Soy Sauce with Lime (recipe on p. 288), Sliced Onions, Chilli Sauce.

Fried Szechuan Chicken

Cooking time: 20 minutes

1 chicken about 1.5 kg (3 lbs)
1 tsp salt
1 tbsp sesame oil
1 tsp five-spice powder
400 ml (13 fl oz) water
1 tbsp cornflour
1 tbsp light soy sauce
1 tbsp Chinese wine or sherry
½ tsp black pepper
5 tbsp oil
10 dried red chillies
3 cloves garlic, crushed
2 tbsp shredded green ginger
1 spring onion, chopped

Cut chicken into bite-sized pieces and mix with salt, sesame oil and five spice powder. Set aside. Mix water, light soy sauce, wine and pepper in a separate bowl. Dissolve cornflour and 2 tbsp water in a small bowl.

Heat oil until very hot and fry chicken pieces until brown. Do a few at a time so chicken browns better. Remove chicken and fry dried chillies, garlic and ginger for 2 minutes. Chillies should have taken on a dark hue by now. Add chopped spring onion and water, wine and soy sauce mixture. Bring to the boil and add chicken. Add cornflour and water mixture and allow to thicken. Serve with boiled rice.

Bird's Nest Soup

Cooking time: 2 hours

50 g (1 ¾ oz) superior bird's nest, cleaned
1 chicken about 1 kg (2 lbs)
3 slices ginger
2 tsp salt
1 tsp fish sauce
1 litre (1 ¾ pints) water

Soak bird's nest overnight and drain. Boil chicken with all other ingredients for 30 minutes and remove chicken to cool. Soak in cold water to cool faster for shredding. Return stock to the boil and add bird's nest to simmer for 45 minutes. Shred chicken and add to soup just before serving. This is a quick way to make this traditional soup. The traditional way is to use a double boiler where you put all the ingredients in and double-boil for three or four hours until chicken melts in your mouth.

Braised Duck with Glutinous Rice

Cooking time: 1 hour

1 duck about 1.5 kg (3 lbs)
200 g (7 oz) glutinous rice, soaked overnight
3 tbsp dried prawns, soaked till soft
2 tsp salt
2 tbsp black soy sauce
2 tbsp sesame oil
2 tbsp Chinese wine or sherry
1 tsp pepper
4 tbsp chopped spring onions
1 litre (1 ¾ pints) meat stock or water
2 tbsp black soy sauce
2 tbsp brown sugar

Steam duck in pressure cooker for 15 minutes. Remove and cool. Mix glutinous rice with dried prawns, salt, soy sauce, sesame oil, Chinese wine, pepper and spring onions. Stuff duck with mixture and sew up with strong thread. Place in deep casserole and simmer with stock or water for 30 minutes.

Remove and reserve liquid. In a clean wok add soy sauce, sherry, brown sugar and 4 or 5 tbsp of the stock and simmer till thick. Add duck and glaze all over. Serve hot.

Deep-fried Spiced Pigeons

Cooking time: 25 minutes

2 plump pigeons
1 tsp salt
2 tsp five-spice powder
1 tbsp black soy sauce
1 tsp sugar
1 tsp pepper
1 tbsp Chinese wine or sherry
Oil for deep frying

Clean pigeons and remove claws and head. Marinate in all other ingredients except oil for 20 minutes turning once. Heat oil until smoking and deep fry pigeons one at a time until dark brown and crisp. Serve with a squeeze of lemon and garlic salt.

Chicken Rendang

Cooking time: 40 minutes

1 chicken about 1.5 kg (3 lbs)
1 coconut, grated
500 ml (16 fl oz) water
1 tbsp tamarind paste or lemon juice
100 ml (3½ fl oz) water
4 tbsp oil
2 large onions, sliced
4 fragrant lime leaves, shredded or 1 tsp grated lemon rind
2 tsp salt
1 tsp sugar

SPICES
2 large onions
2 stalks lemon grass or grated lemon rind
10 almonds
2 cloves garlic
1 tbsp shrimp paste powder
10 dried chillies, soaked till soft
1 tbsp curry powder

Grind spices till fine except curry powder. Add this to paste afterwards. Clean chicken and cut into large joints. Rub a little ground spice paste all over and leave aside. Squeeze coconut with water and mix tamarind with 100 ml (3½ fl oz) water. Remove tamarind pulp. Mix the two liquids. Heat oil and fry sliced onions till light brown. Add spice paste and fry until fragrant. Add lime leaves, salt and sugar and fry for 1 minute more.

Add chicken pieces and fry until well coated. Add liquids and simmer for 20 minutes. You can add potatoes to stretch the dish. Simply peel as many potatoes as required and add to dish in the last 15 minutes of simmering. Serve with bread or rice.

Chicken in Oyster Sauce

Cooking time: 30 minutes

500 ml (16 fl oz) water
500 g (1 lb) chicken breast
4 cloves
14 cm (5½ in) stick cinnamon
3 tbsp honey
2 tsp oyster sauce
1 tsp salt
2 tbsp shredded green ginger
Lettuce leaves

Put chicken in water with cloves and cinnamon and simmer for 10 minutes. Turn off heat and allow chicken to finish cooking in residual heat. Remove chicken and cool before cutting into slices. Mix honey, oyster sauce, salt and ginger and heat over gentle flame. Pour over cooked chicken or add chicken to simmering gravy and serve in lettuce cups as an entree. This dish can also be served chilled as part of a combination cold dish.

Chicken Chop (recipe on p. 120),
Corned Beef and Potato Soup (recipe on p. 279).

Braised Duck with Onions

Cooking time: 1 hour 30 minutes

1 duck about 1.5 kg (3 lbs)
1 tsp salt
1 tbsp black soy sauce
1 tbsp brandy
2 cloves garlic, crushed
4 tbsp oil
4 medium onions, sliced
1 litre (1 ¾ pints) water
1 tbsp cornflour

Rub duck with salt, soy sauce, brandy and garlic and marinate for 20 minutes. Heat oil and fry sliced onions until soft but not brown. Add duck and brown all over. Add water and transfer to a deep casserole. Cover and simmer for an hour or so. Add marinade and simmer for 20 minutes more. When duck is fork tender, dissolve cornflour with a little water and add to gravy. Boil till gravy thickens and serve duck whole with gravy in a sauce boat.

Duck and Black Beans (illustrated on p. 112)

Cooking time: 45 minutes

250 g (½ lb) diced duck meat
1 tsp salt
1 tsp sugar
1 tbsp sesame oil
1 tbsp black soy sauce
1 tbsp cornflour
3 tbsp oil
5 slices green ginger, shredded
2 tbsp preserved black beans
400 ml (13 fl oz) water
1 tbsp Chinese wine or sherry

Steam duck meat for 20 minutes and marinate with salt, sugar, sesame oil, soy sauce and corn flour. Heat oil and fry ginger until light brown and add black beans. Stir fry for 2 minutes and add duck meat. Stir for a few minutes more and add water. Simmer for 20 minutes until sauce thickens and add Chinese wine. Serve hot.

Chicken Chop (illustrated on p. 118)

Cooking time: 20 minutes

2 chicken breasts
4 tbsp plain flour
1 egg, lightly beaten
1 tsp salt
1 tsp pepper
1 tbsp sesame oil
Golden breadcrumbs
Oil for deep-frying

SAUCE
3 tbsp oil
1 large onion
1 small can garden peas
3 tbsp tomato sauce
1 tbsp oyster sauce
4 tbsp water
1 tsp black soy sauce

Flatten chicken breasts with heavy cleaver and cut each into two. Dredge in flour until completely coated. Mix egg, salt, pepper, sesame oil and dip chicken breasts in mixture. Roll in golden breadcrumbs and deep-fry until golden brown. Use low heat as breadcrumbs burn fast.

Slice onion and fry in hot oil for 1 minute. Add all other sauce ingredients and simmer for 2 minutes. Serve chicken breasts either cut up with sauce poured over Chinese style or as individual chops with buttered bread and sauce on the side.

Stir-fried Duck with Ginger (illustrated on p. 112)

Cooking time: 30 minutes

2 duck joints about 400 g (13 oz)
3 tbsp oil
2 tbsp shredded ginger
2 cloves garlic, crushed
1 tbsp black soy sauce
1 tbsp Chinese or ginger wine
1 tsp sugar
1 tsp salt
500 ml (18 fl oz) water

Cut duck into bite-sized pieces and remove skin if it's too fatty. Dry-fry in a wok over moderate heat to semi-cook duck. Sprinkle a few drops of water in to facilitate cooking if duck sticks to wok. Continue to stir for 5 minutes and remove from fire.

Clean wok and heat oil. Fry garlic and ginger for 2 minutes until light brown. Add duck and fry for a few minutes to incorporate flavours. Add soy sauce, wine, sugar and salt and stir for 2 minutes more before adding water. Cover wok and simmer until liquid is reduced by half. Duck should be tender by then. If it isn't, add more water and continue to simmer, adjusting seasoning accordingly.

Salt-baked Chicken

Cooking time: 1 hour

1 chicken about 1 kg (2 lbs)
3 kg (6 lbs) coarse or rock salt
1 tsp salt
½ tsp five-spice powder
1 tbsp Chinese wine or sherry
1 tbsp oil
Coarse tissue paper or napkins

Wash and dry chicken thoroughly. Rub inside of chicken with salt and five-spice powder. Rub chicken skin with salt, wine and oil. Wrap completely with tissue paper or clean napkins making sure every inch is covered.

In a clean, dry wok fry rock salt until very hot. Pour half of the salt into a clay or earthenware pot. Wedge chicken in the centre and top up with remaining salt. Place pot on low heat and cook for an hour or so. If you don't have a fitting lid for your clay pot use any cover that has the same diameter.

Braised Chicken Drumsticks in Ginger Wine

Cooking time: 30 minutes

6 chicken drumsticks
4 tbsp oil
2 tbsp black soy sauce
4 tbsp ginger wine
2 tbsp oyster sauce
1 tbsp sugar
1 piece lard 3 cm (1¼ in) squared
750 ml (1¼ pints) water

Wash and dry chicken drumsticks. Cut into serving pieces. Heat oil and fry until skin shrivels a little and turns brown. Drain and set aside. Combine all other ingredients in a non-stick or heavy-bottomed pot and put chicken in to simmer for 25 minutes. Pot must have a tight-fitting lid to prevent evaporation. When chicken drumsticks are cooked gravy should be thick.

Mock Chicken Drumsticks

Cooking time: 15 minutes

This is an interesting way to use up chicken wings especially if they are rather small. Scraped and shaped into tiny drumsticks, they make very nice finger food during parties and do not cost half as much as the real drumsticks. The important thing is to have a small, sharp knife to work wing meat down towards the bone stump. Only the larger wing joint is used as the wing tip cannot be prepared thus.

20 chicken wings (large joints only)
1 tsp salt
1 tsp pepper
4 tbsp flour
2 tbsp sesame oil
1 tsp sugar
1 tsp light soy sauce
Oil for deep-frying

Using a sharp knife scrape meat from slim end of bone down towards the bone stump. Do not scrape off completely. Force meat and skin downwards until you get a rough lollipop with the little bone exposed. Put mock drumsticks into plastic bag together with all other ingredients except oil and shake well. Marinate for 30 minutes and deep-fry until golden brown. Serve with chilli sauce dip and sliced cucumber.

Red-cooked Chicken (Hung Siew Gai) (illustrated opposite)

Cooking time: 45 minutes

1 large broiler about 1.5 kg (3 lbs)
2 stalks spring onions
2 tbsp shredded ginger
4 tbsp oil
2 tbsp black soy sauce
250 ml (8 fl oz) water
2 tbsp Chinese wine or sherry
2 tbsp brown sugar
2 tsp sherry or any red wine

Wash and dry chicken. Cut spring onions into 5 cm (2 in) lengths and stuff chicken cavity together with shredded ginger. Sew up cavity with strong thread. Heat oil and fry chicken all over until evenly browned.

Blend all other ingredients and bring to the boil. Add chicken and simmer, covered, for 20 minutes. Turn chicken over once and simmer for a further 15 minutes until liquid is reduced considerably. Remove chicken and allow to cool. Carve into serving slices and serve in a flat plate with gravy poured over. Tinned asparagus makes a nice accompaniment.

Stir-fried Chicken and Spring Onions

Cooking time: 25 minutes

3 tbsp oil
2 cloves garlic, sliced thinly
2 chicken breasts, diced
4 stalks fat spring onions
2 tbsp sesame oil
1 tbsp black soy sauce
1 tsp salt
5 tbsp water

Heat oil and fry garlic until light brown. Remove and fry chicken in remaining oil. Cut spring onions into 5 cm (2 in) lengths and add to chicken together with sesame oil, black soy sauce, salt and water. Simmer for 2 or 3 minutes or until chicken is cooked. Serve with plain boiled rice.

Chicken in Tomato Gravy

Cooking time: 30 minutes

1 chicken, cut into large joints
4 tbsp oil
2 tbsp curry paste
3 tbsp tomato sauce
4 red tomatoes, quartered
3 green chillies, slit lengthwise
2 tsp salt
1 tsp sugar
1 tbsp lime juice
½ coconut, grated
600 ml (1 pint) water

SPICES
1 large onion
6 macadamias or almonds
1 tbsp shredded ginger
3 red chillies
1 tsp pepper

Blend spices till fine. Squeeze coconut with water for milk. Heat oil and fry chicken until light brown. Remove chicken and fry curry paste and blended spices for 3 minutes. Add tomato sauce, quartered tomatoes, chillies, salt, sugar and lime juice and stir for 3 minutes.

Add chicken joints and fry for 2 minutes until well coated. Add coconut milk and simmer for 20 minutes until liquid is reduced by one-third. This is a dry, mild curry that should appeal to those not used to hot curries.

Garlic Chicken

Cooking time: 30 minutes

This is a pungent dish only for those who have a passion for garlic. One word of caution. After eating the chicken and whole cloves of garlic, do not, on any account, breathe near another human being unless he or she has eaten of the same dish.

5 tbsp oil
15 cloves garlic, skinned and left whole
2 chicken breasts, cut into chunks
1 tbsp oyster sauce
1 tbsp Chinese wine or sherry
1 tbsp black soy sauce
1 tsp salt
1 tbsp sesame oil
150 ml (¼ pint) water

Heat oil and fry garlic cloves until light brown. Remove and drain. In remaining oil fry chicken pieces until cooked. Add oyster sauce, wine, soy sauce, salt and simmer for 10 minutes. Add garlic cloves and simmer for five minutes more.

Add water and sesame oil last and simmer for 2 or 3 minutes. Serve in a small clay pot or pre-heated dish as this dish has to be hot to be enjoyed.

Sweet-sour Chicken with Pineapple

Cooking time: 35 minutes

2 chicken breasts, cubed
1 tbsp cornflour
1 tsp salt
4 tbsp oil
1 large onion, quartered
1 tbsp shredded ginger
1 can pineapple cubes, reserve juice

SAUCE
2 tbsp water
4 tbsp tomato sauce
1 tbsp oyster sauce
4 tbsp pineapple juice
1 tsp vinegar

Mix chicken with salt and cornflour. Heat oil and fry chicken until half-cooked. Drain and set aside. In remaining oil fry onion and ginger for 1 minute. Add pineapple and combine all sauce ingredients to be added afterwards. Simmer for 1 minute and add chicken to cook for 5 minutes.

White Chicken Curry

Cooking time: 20 minutes

This is a very mild curry with only the barest hint of chilli. You can, in fact, leave out the chilli altogether and it will still be a spicy curry.

1 whole chicken about 1.5 kg (3 lbs)
1 coconut, grated
900 ml (1½ pints) water
4 tbsp oil
1 tsp salt
**1 stalk lemon grass, bruised or grated lemon
   rind**
1 tbsp light soya sauce
1 tsp sugar

SPICES
8 shallots
2 cloves garlic
½ tsp chilli powder
1 tbsp cumin powder
1 tbsp aniseed powder
2 tbsp coriander powder

Pound or blend spices fine. Wash chicken and remove giblets if using supermarket fowl. Squeeze coconut with water for milk. Heat oil and fry spices until fragrant and put in whole chicken to coat for a few minutes. Add coconut milk and all other ingredients and simmer for 20 minutes.

This chicken dish is delicious if you take the trouble to grill it for a few minutes after it has been boiled in the coconut milk. Serve with chunks of crusty French bread.

MEAT

For various reasons, religion and tradition being the two chief ones, many older Chinese people do not eat beef. My own mother refused to touch it and it wasn't because of religious taboo. Her mother had told her never to eat beef and it provoked me to think it must have something to do with the cow as an indispensible beast of burden in China.

Actually religion has little to do with it but the reasons probably got mixed up over the decades and with so many Chinese migrating to Singapore, the exhortations must have worn a little thin and confused.

My mother-in-law till today feels she should not eat beef though she does not know why. So we turn to the next most easily available meat,

pork, which is less expensive and easier to cook. But pork is rarely, if ever, eaten in the way beef is eaten as steaks and chops by westerners.

If used, it is invariably cut up and stir-fried or simmered in soup. Mutton and lamb rarely figure in Singaporean meals though, with plenty of it being imported from New Zealand and Australia, more and more people are trying them out in Asian recipes.

Being rather "strong" meats they are cooked mostly in curries with the occasional stir-fried or stewed lamb or mutton dish that came by way of northern China. The modern Singaporean eats beef with as much gusto as the westerner though in smaller quantities.

Beef with Lotus Root

Cooking time: 10 minutes

300 g (10 oz) fillet steak
1 tbsp black soy sauce
1 tbsp oyster sauce
2 cloves garlic, crushed
1 tsp five-spice powder
3 tbsp oil
400 ml (13 fl oz) water
1 tbsp cornflour
1 can lotus root

Cut meat into thin slices and pound with flat edge of cleaver to tenderise further. Marinate in soy sauce, oyster sauce, garlic and five spice powder for 20 minutes.

Heat oil and fry beef slices for 1 or 2 minutes and add water. Bring to the boil and add cornflour mixed with a little cold water. Add lotus root slices and simmer for 5 minutes.

Braised Pork and Chestnuts (illustrated opposite)

Cooking time: 45 minutes

500 g (1 lb) belly pork, without skin
3 cloves garlic, crushed
1 tbsp light soy sauce
1 tbsp Chinese wine or sherry
1 tbsp ginger juice
20 dried chestnuts
3 tbsp oil
2 litres (3½ pints) water or more
2 tbsp black soy sauce

If pork is too large for braising pot cut into two. Otherwise leave the piece whole. Marinate in garlic, soy sauce, wine and ginger juice for 2 hours. Turn every half an hour or so.

Soak chestnuts in water for 15 minutes and remove brown skin. Boil a large pot with water and simmer chestnuts for 15 minutes until half-cooked. Heat oil and fry drained pork for 3 or 4 minutes until well singed. Add marinade, boiled chestnuts, water and black soy sauce and simmer for 30 minutes until pork melts in your mouth.

Savoury Mince Sambal

Cooking time: 15 minutes

4 dried chillies (soaked till soft)
16 shallots, sliced
4 cloves garlic
1 tbsp shrimp paste, toasted
1 tsp salt
3 tbsp oil
400 g (13 oz) minced beef
1 tbsp tomato puree
3 tbsp tamarind juice or
2 tbsp lime juice
1 tbsp sugar

Pound chillies, shallots, garlic and shrimp paste till fine. Add salt. Heat oil and fry paste till fragrant and add mince. Stir for 1 minute and add tomato puree, tamarind juice or lime juice, sugar and stir for 2 minutes more. Add a few drops of water if mixture is too thick. Serve as a dip or a sandwich spread.

Braised Pork with Chestnuts (right,),
Fried Pork Strips with Salted Vegetable (recipe on p. 141)

Pork Chops Hainanese Style

Cooking time: 20 minutes

This dish has an interesting history though a few may disagree with my explanation. In the absence of another version I shall stick with this one and any dispute herein can only make it that much more memorable. Back when the British colonials lived and entertained in their spacious bungalows — you still see these houses around — they often had in their employ Hainanese cooks.

These newly-arrived migrants from South China, or at least descendants of earlier migrants, anxious to please their tuans and mems called upon all their culinary skills and ingenuity to prepare meals that went beyond simple enjoyment. Mem, most probably longing for a good chop, must have told cook to make some for dinner to be eaten with buttered toast. And don't forget the peas and chips. Thus was born Hainanese pork chops with gravy, peas and potatoes.

Oil for deep-frying
4 pork chops
1 egg, lightly beaten
Golden bread crumbs
1 can garden peas
2 large potatoes
2 large onions, sliced

Gravy
1 tbsp HP or Lea and Perrin Sauce
2 tbsp black soy sauce
½ tsp salt
2 tsp cornflour
½ stock cube
400 ml (13 fl oz) water

Cut pork chops into bite-sized pieces and pound a little with a mallet or the blunt edge of a cleaver. Dip in beaten egg and roll in bread crumbs. Deep fry for 3 minutes each and drain on absorbent paper. Set aside. Peel and slice potatoes into 1-cm (½ in) thick rounds.

Slice onions. Fry potatoes in oil until brown. Pour off all but 3 tbsp of oil and fry onions until soft but not brown.

Mix gravy ingredients and add to pan. Bring to the boil and simmer for 2 minutes. Add potatoes and peas and simmer for 1 minute. To serve, pour gravy over fried pork chops.

Fried Liver with Ginger

Cooking time: 8 minutes

3 tbsp oil
2 cloves garlic, crushed
4 slices stem ginger shredded
300 g (10 oz) liver
1 tbsp black soy sauce
1 tsp salt
2 red chillies, sliced
5 tbsp water

Slice liver thin and marinate in soy sauce and salt. Chill liver for a while for easier slicing. Heat oil and fry garlic and ginger until light brown. Add liver and fry for 1 minute. Add chillies and water and marinade and simmer for 1 minute.

Fried Minced Pork in Pig's Caul

Cooking time: 15 minutes

350g (¾ lb) minced pork
150 g (5 oz) minced prawns
2 stalks spring onions, chopped
6 water chestnuts
1 tsp salt
1 tsp fish sauce
1 tbsp cornflour
1 egg
1 sheet pig's caul, cleaned
8 pieces cream crackers, crushed fine
2 eggs lightly beaten
Oil for deep frying
4 tbsp Chinese sweet sauce

Peel water chestnut and chop fine. Mix with pork, prawns, spring onions, salt, fish sauce, cornflour and egg and knead until well mixed. Using a tablespoon, scoop up one amount and lay it on caul lining. Fold over and pat down firmly.

Make up all rolls and place in a steamer. Steam for 5 minutes until fat veins in caul are creamy white. Dip rolls in egg and then in crumbs. Deep fry until light brown. Serve with sweet sauce and pickled carrots.

PICKLED CARROTS
1 large carrot, scraped and sliced very thin. Sprinkle 1 tsp salt all over and set aside for 10 minutes. Squeeze out all moisture and add 1 tsp sugar and 1 tsp malt vinegar.

Skewered Beef Satay

Cooking time: 20 minutes

Probably one of the nicest ways of eating meat and one which lends itself beautifully to outdoor entertaining; satay, either in skewers or simply fried, can be anything from beef to seafood. The important thing is the marinade which, if well-done, even obviates the need for a spicy sauce. However if you simply must have the sauce, making it is simplicity itself if you use crunchy peanut butter. (see page 206)

500 g (1 lb) rump steak
1 tbsp cumin powder
2 cloves garlic, crushed
1 tsp salt
1 tbsp sugar
1 tsp chilli powder
300 ml (½ pint) coconut cream
30 satay skewers
1 cucumber
1 or 2 large onions

Cut meat into thin slices and pound with blunt edge of cleaver until twice as thin again. Mix with cumin, garlic, salt, sugar, chilli and coconut cream and leave in fridge for an hour. Thread about five or six slices of beef onto one skewer until all done. Grill over hot charcoal or under electric griller until meat sizzles and chars a little. Eat with satay sauce and slices of cucumber and onions.

Beef Ribs in Black Bean Sauce

Cooking time: 15 minutes

2 stalks spring onions, chopped
3 tbsp shredded ginger
2 cloves garlic, crushed
1 tsp black pepper
2 tbsp fermented black beans
½ tsp salt
2 tsp sugar
1 tbsp Chinese wine or sherry
1 tbsp black soy sauce
1 tbsp oyster sauce
250 ml (8 fl oz) oil
400 g (13 oz) spare ribs
2 tbsp cornflour

Combine all ingredients except oil, spare ribs and cornflour. Coat the ribs with cornflour and dust off. Heat oil and fry ribs a few at a time until brown. Pour off all but 3 tbsp of oil and heat until smoking. Pour in seasoning mixture to boil. Add spare ribs and simmer for 10 minutes until liquid is reduced slightly. Serve hot.

Dry Meat Curry (Pork, Lamb or Beef)

Cooking time: 30 minutes

400 g (13 oz) meat
1 tbsp sugar
3 potatoes
2 carrots
½ coconut squeeze with 400 ml (13 fl oz) water
2 tbsp sliced shallots
3 cm (1¼ in) piece green ginger
5 tbsp oil
3 tbsp curry powder
1 tsp salt

Cut meat into small cubes about 2 cm (¾ in) square and sprinkle sugar all over. Leave aside. Cut potatoes and carrots into equal sized chunks. Chop shallots and ginger roughly.

Heat oil and fry ginger and shallots until brown. Add curry powder moistened with 2 tbsp of the coconut milk. Fry until fragrant or until oil seeps out again.

Add coconut milk and boil. Add all other ingredients and simmer until gravy is dry. Stir occasionally to prevent sticking.

Pork in Soy Sauce

Cooking time: 35 minutes

2 tbsp oil
4 cloves garlic, lightly bashed
500 g (1 lb) lean pork with a little fat and skin
4 tbsp thick black soy sauce
1 tsp salt
600 ml (1 pint) water
1 tsp sugar (optional)

Cut pork into large chunks, wash and drain. Heat oil and fry garlic for 30 seconds. Add pork and singe in oil thoroughly. Add next ingredient, soy sauce, only when pork pieces shrink a little and change colour. Stir well after adding soy sauce until pork absorbs sauce and glistens. This is an important step to a perfect dish and cannot be compromised.

When pork is well stirred, add water and seasoning and simmer for 35 minutes. Top up with more water if necessary and a tbsp or 2 of soy sauce.

Cantonese Roast Pork (illustrated on p. 132)

Cooking time: 1 hour

1 kg (2 lbs) pork fillet or "koo loo yok". This is
   the strip from the spine that is excellent for
   this or sweet and sour pork.
2 tbsp honey
3 tbsp Chinese wine or ordinary rice wine
3 cloves garlic, finely minced
1 tsp five-spice powder
1 tsp salt
1 tsp sugar
1 tbsp ginger juice
1 tsp red food colouring mixed with a little
   water

Pork should ideally be about 18 cm (7 in) strips for roasting. If you do not have an oven large enough to accommodate hanging meat, cut into shorter pieces and roast on a rack.

Combine all ingredients and marinate pork for at least 3 hours or overnight. Pre-heat oven and place pork either hanging on metal hooks from roof of oven or placed flat down on a roasting rack. Catch drippings with a roasting tin. Roast for an hour or so basting every 20 minutes until bits of pork are charred and the rest succulent and red. The food colouring is optional but without it your roast pork will be pale looking.

Pork Rolls

Cooking time: 20 minutes

1 kg (2 lbs) boned pork chops
1 tbsp honey
1 tsp salt
1 tsp pepper
1 tsp cornflour
1 egg, lightly beaten
1 packet golden breadcrumbs
Oil for deep frying

Cut pork chops into thin slices and pound a little to soften. Season with honey, salt, pepper and cornflour and roll up each slice to form sausage-shapes. Dip in beaten egg and dredge with breadcrumbs. Fry in hot oil for 3 minutes each and serve with HP or Lea and Perrins sauce.

Sweet Pork Satay

Cooking time: 15 minutes

500 g (1 lb) pork fillet
1 tsp garlic powder
1 tsp salt
2 tbsp black soy sauce
1 tbsp cumin powder
1 tbsp aniseed powder
2 tbsp coriander powder
2 tbsp melted palm sugar or golden syrup
2 tbsp oil
20 satay skewers
1 stalk lemon grass, bruised or grated lemon
   rind
2 tbsp oil mixed with 4 tbsp water

Cut pork into thin slices and marinade in the rest of ingredients for an hour. Stir once in a while to make sure all meat gets well coated with marinade. Thread each skewer three-quarters of the way and grill over hot charcoal or under electric grill. Turn once or twice during 10 minutes of grilling. Brush with oil and water mixture with bruised lemon grass. This imparts a lovely aroma to the meat.

Curried Meatballs

Cooking time: 30 minutes

This originates from Kashmir where Brahmins who do not eat beef, use lamb instead. A basic kofta curry, it became adapted by ingenious Singapore cooks in the last century or so with minced pork being used fairly often. The choice is yours.

1 kg (2 lbs) mince
3 tbsp curry powder
1 large onion, finely chopped
1 tbsp shredded green ginger
1 tsp salt
1 tbsp cornflour
1 tsp pepper
1 can coconut cream about 500 ml (16 fl oz)
1 tsp sugar
4 tbsp oil
2 tbsp curry paste

Mix meat with curry powder, onions, shredded ginger, salt, cornflour and pepper. Form into balls the size of walnuts. If mixture is too dry and crumbly, add a little water or half and half water and coconut cream. Heat oil and fry curry paste until fragrant. Add coconut cream and bring to the boil. Add meatballs and simmer for 25 minutes . Serve on a bed of boiled rice.

Pork Vindaloo

Cooking time: 30 minutes

1 kg (2 lbs) lean pork
2 tbsp tamarind paste
1 litre (1¾ pints) water
20 whole peppercorns
4 fragant lime leaves or bay leaves
4 tbsp oil

MARINADE
1 tbsp garlic powder
1 tbsp shredded green ginger
2 tsp chilli powder
1 tbsp cumin powder
2 tbsp coriander powder
1 tsp turmeric powder
1 tbsp aniseed powder
1 tsp powdered cloves
1 tsp powdered cinnamon
1 tsp salt
500 ml (16 fl oz) malt or wine vinegar

Cut pork into chunks and combine with marinade to leave for a few hours or overnight. Mix tamarind with water and squeeze out juice. Discard pulp. Heat oil and add meat, marinade, peppercorns and bay leaves or fragrant lime leaves. Fry for 2 minutes until well mixed. Add tamarind liquid and simmer for 30 minutes or longer depending on consistency you want.

Simple Mutton Curry (illustrated opposite)

Cooking time: 1 hour

This is one of the simplest and spiciest curries to make if you use a commercial curry powder mix.

1 kg (2 lbs) mutton or lamb, boned
3 tbsp ghee or half butter and oil
2 large onions, chopped fine
2 tsp shredded green ginger
3 cloves garlic, crushed
2 tbsp curry powder
2 tsp salt
3 limes
2 tbsp tomato puree
4 tbsp water
3 green chillies left whole

Cut mutton or lamb into large cubes. Heat oil and fry garlic, onion and ginger until light brown. Moisten curry powder with a little water and add to pan. Fry for 1 minute and add lime juice and salt. Add meat and stir well until chunks are coated with spice mixture. Add tomato puree and water and cover to cook over gentle heat for an hour or so. Top with liquid if necessary but adjust with salt. Add chillies in the last 15 minutes of simmering.

Steamed Pork Ribs with Black Beans

Cooking time: 30 minutes

500 g (1 lb) pork ribs
1 tsp salt
1 tbsp cornflour
4 tbsp water
2 tbsp black beans
1 tsp pepper

Wash pork ribs and cut each into two if too large. Place in a flat metal tray to fit into steamer. Mix cornflour with water and pour over ribs. Sprinkle black beans evenly over ribs and do likewise with pepper. Steam covered for 30 minutes and serve hot.

Spiced Fried Pork

Cooking time: 20 minutes

1 kg (2 lbs) belly pork
4 tbsp oil
2 large onions
3 cloves garlic
5 macadamia nuts or almonds
1 tsp shrimp paste powder
1 tsp chilli powder
2 stalks lemon grass or grated lemon rind
1 tbsp sugar
1 tsp salt

Boil a little water and simmer whole piece of belly pork until partly cooked and firm enough to slice into small strips. Drain pork until dry. Blend onions, garlic and macadamia nuts and mix with powdered ingredients. Heat oil and fry spice blend for 2 minutes or until oil seeps out again. Add sliced pork and fry over slow heat for 15 minutes. Add sugar and salt and keep in enamel or glass container. This dish can be refrigerated for up to a month.

Minced Pork with Szechuan Vegetable

Cooking time: 10 minutes

2 tbsp oil
1 clove garlic, crushed
200 g Szechuan vegetable, sliced
200 g minced pork
1 tsp salt
1 tbsp sesame oil
4 tbsp water

Soak Szechaun vegetable in water to remove some of the spiciness. Remove and drain well. Heat oil and fry garlic for 1 minute. Add vegetable and fry for 1 minute more. Add minced pork and stir well so it doesn't become lumpy. Fry for 2 minutes and add salt and sesame oil. When pork is completely cooked add water and bring to brisk boil to finish cooking. Serve garnished with celery or parsley.

Beef with Bamboo Shoots

Cooking time: 10 minutes

2 tbsp oil
500 g fillet beef
10 slices canned bamboo shoot
1 tbsp shredded green ginger
4 tbsp water
1 tbsp Chinese wine or sherry
1 tbsp sesame oil
1 tsp salt
1 tsp pepper
1 tsp cornflour mixed with
2 tbsp water

Cut beef into strips and pound with the blunt edge of a cleaver or heavy knife. Heat oil and fry beef over high heat for 30 seconds. Add bamboo shoot and ginger and fry for 30 seconds more. Add water, wine, sesame oil and seasoning and bring to a brisk boil. Add cornflour mixture and serve when gravy thickens.

Beef in Black Bean Sauce

Cooking time: 15 minutes

3 tbsp oil
500 g rump or fillet steak
1 tbsp cornflour
1 tsp salt
2 tbsp Chinese wine
2 cloves garlic, crushed
1 tbsp black beans
1 tbsp shredded green ginger
2 tbsp black soy sauce
1 tsp sugar
200 ml water

Cut steak into thin strips and marinate with cornflour, salt and wine. Heat oil and fry garlic until light brown. Add ginger and black beans and fry for one minute more. Add beef strips and fry for 2 minutes. Add marinade and water and bring to brisk boil. When gravy thickens add soy sauce and sugar and simmer for one minute. Serve hot.

Sweet Pork Slices

Cooking time: 8 minutes

500 g (1 lb) boned pork chops
2 tbsp black soy sauce
2 tbsp sugar
1 tbsp pepper
5 tbsp oil

Slice pork into thin rounds and hammer with blunt edge of cleaver. Marinate in soy sauce, sugar and pepper for 30 minutes. Heat oil and fry a few slices at a time until crisp and cooked. Serve with toasted French bread or as an appetiser.

Braised Beef Brisket

Cooking time: 45 minutes

1 kg (2 lbs) beef brisket
3 tbsp oil
1 stalk celery
2 large onions
2 carrots
2 tbsp black soy sauce
1 beef stock cube
1 litre (1¾ pints) water
1 tsp salt
4 cloves
1 5 cm (2 in) piece cinnamon or
1 tsp cinnamon powder

Cut beef into chunks. Quarter onions, dice carrots into wedges and cut celery into 3 cm (1¼ in) pieces. Heat oil and fry beef until surfaces are well sealed. Add vegetables and stir for one minute. Add soy sauce, water and stock cube and simmer for 30 minutes. Add all other seasoning and simmer for 15 minutes more or until beef is of the tenderness required.

Fried Beef with Herbs

Cooking time: 15 minutes

500 g (1 lb) fillet steak
2 tbsp oil
2 cloves garlic, crushed
1 stalk parsley, chopped
1 tsp chopped oregano
1 tsp chopped chives
1 stalk lemon grass, sliced fine or grated lemon
   rind
2 red chillies, sliced fine
1 tsp salt
1 tsp pepper
2 tbsp Chinese wine or sherry

Slice steak into strips and dry thoroughly. Heat oil and fry crushed garlic until brown. Add beef strips and fry for one minute. Add herbs and fry for one minute. Add salt and pepper and wine and simmer for 1 minute. Serve on a bed of rice.

Fried Pork Strips with Salted Vegetable (illustrated on p. 129)

Cooking time: 10 minutes

I remember this dish fondly. There used to be a hawker stall manned by a kindly Hainanese man who sold rice, cooked food and a beancurd soup which he gave away free. This Hainanese "curry png" (curry rice) man cooked the same dishes every day but what wonderful dishes.

Fried pork with salted vegetables, pork chops with green peas, chicken curry, steamed pork in bean curd, fried fish in turmeric and chilli, stewed pork with bean curd squares and prawns fried with cucumbers in chilli gravy. There are still similar hawker stalls in Housing Board estates today but the dishes are rather more watered-down versions. And the beancurd soup, far from being gratis, can cost a few dollars.

3 tbsp oil
2 cloves garlic, crushed
300 g (10 oz) fillet of lean pork, cut into strips
250 g (½ lb) salted vegetable, sliced fine and
   soaked for 10 minutes
1 tsp sugar
1 tbsp cornflour
400 ml (13 fl oz) water
2 red chillies, sliced

Heat oil and fry garlic until brown. Squeeze salted vegetable dry and add to pan. Fry for 1 minute and add fillet pork. Fry for 2 minutes more and add sugar, cornflour mixed with water and chillies. Simmer for 5 minutes.

Sweet Sour Pork (illustrated opposite)

Cooking time: 20 minutes

Of all the pork dishes that tourists eat this deserves to be elevated to the hall of fame. It is an invariable together with fried rice and a star item at all Chinese restaurants. When cooking it at home remember to use pork that has some fat on it else you will end up with dry chunks instead of succulent cubes.

Oil for deep-frying
400 g (13 oz) pork
4 tbsp cornflour
1 tsp salt
½ tsp pepper

SAUCE
2 tbsp plum sauce
2 tbsp tomato sauce
200 ml (7 fl oz) water
2 tomatoes
1 large onion
1 red chilli
2 tbsp pineapple chunks

Wash pork and cut into bite-sized cubes. Mix cornflour with salt and pepper. Roll pork cubes in mixture until well coated. You may use an egg to bind but this tends to toughen the fried pork. Dust off excess and deep-fry until golden brown. Drain off oil and set aside.

Mix plum sauce and tomato sauce and dilute with water. Quarter tomatoes and onion and slice chilli into strips. Put all ingredients in a small pot and bring to the boil. To serve either pour sauce over pork or simmer pork gently in sauce for 30 seconds to let flavour blend well.

Fragrant Beef Slices

Cooking time: 10 minutes

Oil for deep-frying
400 g (13 oz) fillet beef
2 tbsp sesame oil
1 tbsp oyster sauce
1 tsp pepper
1 tbsp cornflour
4 tbsp water
Spring onions for garnish

Cut beef into bite-sized slices. Mix sesame oil, oyster sauce, pepper, cornflour and water and marinate beef for 1 hour. Heat oil and fry drained beef for 1 minute for rare or 3 minutes for well done. Drain on absorbent paper. Garnish with spring onion blossoms.

To make spring onion blossoms.

Cut 2 stalks spring onions into 5 cm (2 in) lengths. With a sharp knife, shred 1 cm (½ in) at both ends and soak in ice water. In a few minutes the spring onions will curl nicely into little blossoms.

Stewed Beef in Soy Sauce

Cooking time: 35 minutes

2 tbsp oil
4 cloves
1 4 cm (1½ in) piece cinnamon
3 star anise
3 cloves garlic, crushed
4 tbsp black soy sauce
650 ml (1¼ pints) water
2 tsp salt
1 beef stock cube
1 kg (2 lbs) rump steak

Cut beef into 4 cm (1½ in) cubes. Heat oil and fry cinnamon, cloves and star anise for 1 minute. Add crushed garlic and fry till fragrant. Add beef cubes and fry till beef is well sealed by hot oil. Add black soy sauce and continue frying till beef cubes are well coated. This is an important step as beef will take on a pallid look if improperly fried with sauce. Add all other ingredients and simmer for 30 minutes or longer if necessary. For this dish, beef should melt in the mouth. Serve with plain boiled rice and steamed mustard greens.

Spiced Shredded Beef

Cooking time: 30 minutes

5 tbsp oil
1 kg (2 lbs) rump steak or sirloin
2 tbsp lime juice
½ cococnut
400 ml (13 fl oz) water
1 tsp salt

SPICES
1 large onion
3 cloves garlic
1 tbsp shrimp paste
2 tbsp coriander powder
1 tsp cumin powder
1 tsp fennel powder
3 fragrant lime leaves or bay leaves

Blend all spices till fine. Cut steak into large chunks. Squeeze coconut with water for milk and add lime juice to it. Add blended spices and steak and bring to the boil. Simmer for 40 minutes until liquid is almost completely absorbed. Remove meat and allow to cool.

Pound meat in a pestle and mortar or use fingers to shred meat. Heat oil and fry till meat turns dark brown. Pour whatever residue there is from the pot onto beef shreds and serve hot or cold.

Beef Rendang Padang Style (illustrated on p. 144)

Cooking time: 40 minutes

1½ coconuts
2.5 litres (4½ pints) water
2 screwpine leaves or vanilla pods
1 kg (2 lbs) topside beef
2 tsp salt

SPICES
2 slices green ginger
2 large onions
15 dried chillies, soaked in water till soft
4 tbsp brown sugar
2 tbsp salt

Squeeze coconut with water for milk. Wash screwpine leaves and tie each into a firm knot. Cut topside in large chunks and rub with a little salt. Pound spices till fine and add to coconut milk. Bring to the boil in a heavy-bottomed pot or non-stick pot. Add beef and simmer for 15 minutes stirring occasionally to prevent sticking. Add screwpine leaves.

Add remaining salt and continue simmering for another 30 minutes or so until beef is tender and comes apart when pricked with a fork. Discard screwpine leaves and serve with crusty French bread. When rendang is cooked for more than 30 minutes, there should be a layer of rich, red oil on top.

Rich Spiced Leg of Lamb

Cooking time: 40 minutes

Oil for deep-frying
1 small leg of lamb about 1 kg (2 lbs)
3 tbsp coriander powder
1 tbsp cumin powder
1 tbsp aniseed powder
1 tsp chilli powder
3 tbsp black soy sauce
2 tbsp sugar
1 tsp pepper
4 large onions
1 5 cm (2 in) stick cinnamon
750 ml (1¼ pints) water

Score deep cuts along leg of lamb at 4 cm (1½ in) intervals to the bone. Mix spices, soy sauce, sugar and pepper and rub all over lamb making sure deep vents are well seasoned. Refrigerate for 30 minutes.

Heat oil and deep fry lamb for 3 minutes on each side until surface is brown and well-sealed. Slice onions fine. Remove all but 2 tbsp of oil and fry onions until soft. Transfer onions, lamb and water to pressure cooker. Add cinnamon stick and cook under 15 pounds pressure for 20 minutes.

Remove pressure cooker lid and lift out lamb. If there is still liquid left, transfer to casserole and simmer over gas ring until liquid is reduced further. By now your lamb should be very tender and come away in shreds. Serve hot with bread or rice.

Quick Pork and Watercress Salad

Cooking time: 8 minutes

200 g (7 oz) lean pork
150 g (5 oz) watercress
2 tbsp French or Thousand Island dressing

Boil pork for 5 minutes and slice across the grain. Wash and drain cress and mix with pork. Pour in dressing and mix well.

Szechuan Spiced Beef

Cooking time: 45 minutes

2 tbsp oil
500 g (1 lb) beef sirloin
2 star anise
1 tbsp Chinese wine or sherry
1 tsp sugar
1 litre (1 ¾ pints) water

SAUCE
2 tbsp black soy sauce
500 ml (16 fl oz) water
3 cloves garlic, sliced
1 tbsp Chinese wine or sherry
6 dried chillies, soaked till soft
4 tbsp oil

Heat oil and brown sirloin in one whole piece till brown on all sides. Add star anise, wine, sugar and water and braise in a pot with a tight-fitting lid for 30 minutes. Check to see if there is enough liquid. Top up with half and half water and soy sauce if necessary and simmer for 15 minutes more until beef is tender. Remove to a plate to cool.

Heat oil and fry dried chilli until oil turns red. Discard chilli pods. Add garlic and fry till brown. Add all other ingredients and bring to the boil. Simmer for 10 minutes until sauce thickens a little. Slice beef and pour sauce over.

Liver Satay

Cooking time: 15 minutes

500 g (1 lb) calf's liver, boiled and diced

MARINADE
6 cloves garlic, crushed
1 tsp pepper
1 tsp chilli powder
10 almonds, ground
2 stalks lemon grass, sliced fine or grated
   lemon rind
1 large onion, grated

SPICES
1 tsp chilli powder
2 tbsp coriander powder
1 large onion
1 tsp turmeric powder
1 coconut, grated and dry-fried
750 ml (1 ¼ pints) stock

Dice boiled liver into pieces large enough to be threaded through satay skewers. Mix with marinade and let steep for several hours. Pound or blend spices till fine. Bring stock to boil and add ground spices. Simmer for 10 minutes until slightly thick. Cool and reserve. Grill skewered liver for 5 or 6 minutes and serve with compressed rice(p, 271).

Beef Rendang Padang Style (recipe on p. 143).

MOSTLY MUSHROOMS

Would anybody eat fungus? If it's a mushroom, most certainly yes. And there are mushrooms and mushrooms that make Asian cuisine the splendid thing it is. Dried black mushroom caps from China with woodsy flavour and spongy texture unlike anything else in this world, soft, delicate fresh mushroom caps that can be added to just about anything, cute little button mushrooms for amusing eating, straw mushrooms in cans, and something called "hairy" mushrooms, the strange transliteration not diminishing its flavour one whit.

Whatever, mushrooms are known for their versatility if not low price but like cheese, there are inexpensive ones and pricey ones. Boil them, bake them, braise them or eat them raw — mushrooms are fat in nutrition and very thin in calories. Dried ones keep for years and nothing, not even the most pungent spice mixture, can rob it of its distinctive flavour.

This perhaps is the mushroom's most endearing quality. Whatever you add it to it remains a mushroom giving a nudge to other ingredients without stealing too much of their thunder. One can easily wax endlessly lyrical about this humble fungus.

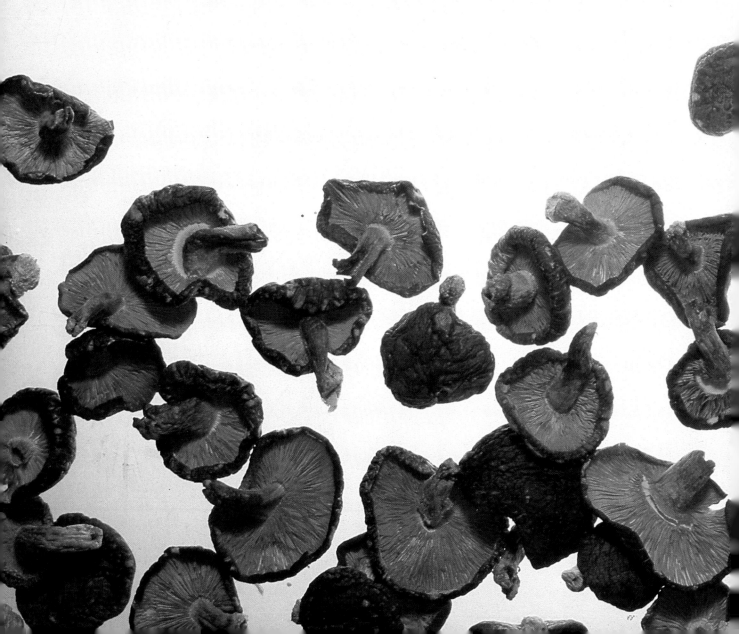

Braised Mushrooms in Oyster Sauce

Cooking time 40 minutes

10 large dried Chinese mushrooms
1 piece of pork fat
4 tbsp oyster sauce
2 cloves garlic, crushed
400 ml (13 fl oz) water

Soak mushrooms in hot water until soft. Remove stalks. Heat oil and fry crushed garlic until brown. Add mushrooms and oyster sauce and bring to the boil. Add pork fat and water and simmer, covered for 35 minutes. The pork fat is important to give the mushrooms a smooth velvety texture.

Button Mushrooms with Prawns in Milk Sauce

Cooking time: 8 minutes

3 tbsp oil
2 cloves garlic, crushed
1 small can button mushrooms
1 can prepared crab meat
300 ml (½ pint) milk
1 tsp cornflour
2 egg whites
1 tsp salt
Pinch of monosodium glutamate
2 large lettuce leaves

Drain mushrooms and slice each into two. Beat egg whites until stiff peaks form. Heat oil and fry garlic until brown. Add mushrooms and crab and fry for 1 minute.

Mix cornflour with milk and egg white and add to pan. Add seasoning and stir over low heat until lumps begin to form. Milk burns very easily so your flame must be low.

Do not stop stirring until mixture becomes soft, cheesy-like lumps. Serve on washed and dried lettuce leaves. This is a modified dish, the basis of several "yam basket" dishes (see page 98.)

Mushroom Compote

Cooking time: 5 minutes

This is a good way to use up left over mushrooms, whatever type they may be. It is also by no means a "left-over" dish as vegetarians will attest to the fame of some Lohan (Buddhist) vegetarian dishes with their basis in mushrooms. This one uses three types and a few vegetables for colour but you could use more if you wish.

4 tbsp oil
2 cloves, garlic
1 carrot, sliced
10 mange tout
10 button mushrooms
4 Chinese mushrooms
6 straw mushrooms
1 tbsp fish sauce
300 ml (½ pint) water
1 tsp cornflour

Drain button and straw mushrooms of liquid. Soak Chinese mushrooms in hot water and cut each into two. Heat oil and fry garlic until brown. Add mange tout and carrot and stir-fry for 1 minute. Add mushrooms and stir for another minute or so. Add water mixed with cornflour and fish sauce and simmer for 3 minutes.

Button Mushrooms with Cashew Nuts and Chicken

Cooking time: 10 minutes

3 tbsp oil
2 cloves garlic, crushed
1 chicken breast
3 tbsp cashew nuts
1 small can button mushrooms
1 tsp salt
Pinch monosodium glutamate
3 tbsp water
1 tbsp cornflour
1 tbsp sesame oil
1 tsp pepper

Cube chicken breast. You could also par-boil chicken breast to save time. Heat oil and fry garlic until brown. Add chicken and and stir-fry for 2 minutes. Add mushrooms and cashews and stir for 2 minutes more.

Mix water with cornflour and add together with all other ingredients. When gravy thickens, dish up and serve garnished with fresh coriander leaves.

Mushrooms with Bamboo Shoots and Prawns

Cooking time: 6 minutes

3 tbsp oil
2 cloves garlic, crushed
6 Chinese mushrooms
1 wedge bamboo shoot, sliced
150 g (5 oz) prawns, shelled
3 slices green ginger
2 tbsp Chinese wine or sherry
1 tbsp sesame oil
1 tbsp oyster sauce
1 tbsp cornflour
300 ml (½ pint) water

Soak Chinese mushrooms in hot water for 5 minutes and remove stalks. Bamboo shoots should be sliced about 1/2 cm thick. Most bamboo shoots come in cans of three of four wedges but if you can find ready sliced ones, it'll save some time.

Reserve extra shoots for another meal by immersing in water and keeping them refrigerated. Cut mushrooms into two or leave whole as you wish. Heat oil and fry crushed garlic and ginger until light brown. Add bamboo shoots and mushrooms and stir-fry for 2 minutes. Add prawns, wine, sesame oil, oyster sauce and stir for another minute. Dissolve cornflour in water and add to pan. Simmer for 3 minutes and serve hot.

Steamed Mushrooms with Chicken Wings

Cooking time: 6 minutes

6 Chinese mushrooms
6 chicken wings
4 slices green ginger
2 tbsp Chinese wine or sherry
1 tbsp sesame oil
1 tbsp dark soy sauce
1 tsp salt
1 tsp sugar

Soak Chinese mushrooms in hot water for 5 minutes and remove stalks. Bamboo shoots should be sliced about 1/2 cm (½/¾ in) thick. Most bamboo shoots come in cans of three of four wedges but if you can find ready sliced ones, it'll save some time.

Braised Mushrooms and Lettuce (illustrated opposite)

Cooking time: 30 minutes

8 Chinese mushrooms
1 head lettuce
4 tbsp oyster sauce
1 piece lard about 4 cm (1½ in) squared
500 ml (16 fl oz) water

Wash mushrooms and remove stalks. Soak in hot water for 5 minutes. This is not absolutely necessary as the braising process will soften the mushrooms. But soaking the mushrooms beforehand will shorten cooking time. Remove lettuce stalk and separate individual leaves. Do not cut leaves. Wash and drain thoroughly in colander.

Mix oyster sauce and water and bring to the boil in a deep pot. Arrange mushrooms along the bottom and top with lettuce leaves. Add piece of lard and braise covered for 30 minutes. As oyster sauce is a rich seasoning in itself it is not necessary to add more seasoning.

Stuffed Mushroom Curry

Cooking time: 30 minutes

8 Chinese mushrooms
200 g (7 oz) minced pork
1 tbsp cornflour
1 tsp salt
300 g (10 oz) coconut
300 ml (½ pint) water
1 tsp salt
1 tsp sugar
4 tbsp oil

SPICES
1 tbsp shredded ginger
4 shallots, pounded
2 tbsp curry powder

Wash mushrooms and soak in hot water for 10 minutes. Remove stalks. Mix minced pork with cornflour and salt and stuff each mushroom cap. Squeeze coconut with water. Heat oil and fry pounded shallots and ginger for 2 minutes. Add curry powder and fry for 4 minutes. Add coconut milk and bring to the boil.

Add mushroom caps, seasoning and simmer for 10 minutes. Serve with plain rice.

Button Mushroom Omelette

Cooking time: 5 minutes

4 tbsp oil
3 eggs
1 tsp salt
1 can button mushrooms
1 stalk spring onions
1 bunch fresh coriander leaves

Slice button mushrooms. Lightly beat egg and add salt. Heat oil until smoking and pour in egg to fry over low heat. When surface is still mushy, add sliced mushrooms and cook until set. Flip over to form a half-moon shape and serve garnished with spring onions and coriander leaves.

Mushrooms in Wine Sauce

Cooking time: 15 minutes

15 Chinese mushrooms
3 tbsp oil
4 slices green ginger
2 cloves garlic, crushed
2 tbsp Chinese wine
1 tbsp sesame oil
1 tbsp black soy sauce
1 tsp salt
300 ml (½ pint) water

Soak mushrooms in hot water for 5 minutes. Remove stalks and squeeze out excess moisture. Slice each mushroom into strips. Heat oil and fry crushed garlic and ginger until light brown.

Add mushrooms and stir-fry for 2 minutes. Add wine, salt and soy sauce for 1 minute. Add water and sesame oil and simmer for 10 minutes. Serve with plain rice.

Stuffed Mushroom Caps in Coconut Gravy

Cooking time: 15 minutes

10 large Chinese mushrooms
200 g (7 oz) minced pork
100 g (3 oz) minced prawns
1 tsp cornflour
2 tbsp chopped spring onions
1 tsp oil
1 tsp salt
1 tsp pepper
4 tbsp oil

FOR THE GRAVY
½ coconut, shredded
400 ml (13 fl oz) water
1 tsp salt

SPICES
1 tsp chilli powder
1 tsp lemon grass powder or 1 stalk fresh
   lemon grass or 1 tsp grated lemon rind
6 shallots
8 almonds
1 tsp turmeric powder
2 tsp shrimp paste powder (belacan)
1 tbsp coriander powder

Blend spices till fine. Soak mushrooms in hot water for 5 minutes and remove stalk. Mix pork, prawns, cornflour, spring onions, oil, salt and pepper and stuff each mushroom cap with mixture pressing down firmly.

Steam for 4 minutes and remove from steamer. Squeeze coconut with water. Heat 4 tbsp oil and fry pounded spices till fragrant.

Add coconut milk and bring to the boil. Add steamed mushroom caps and simmer for 2 minutes. Add 1 tsp salt and serve garnished with fresh coriander leaves.

Steamed Mushrooms with Mustard Greens

Cooking time: 8 minutes

250 g (½ lb) young mustard greens
8 Chinese mushrooms
1 tsp salt
1/2 tsp monosodium glutamate
1 tsp cornflour
200 ml (7 fl oz) water
1 tsp oil

Wash mustard greens and leave whole. Soak mushrooms in hot water for 5 minutes. Remove stalks. Lightly oil a deep pyrex dish and lay mushrooms cap-side down to fill up whole dish. Steam mushrooms for 5 minutes. Coil mustard greens over mushrooms and steam for 3 minutes more.

You do not steam both at the same time as greens will be over-cooked. For attractive presentation, upturn mushrooms and greens onto another plate so you get a nice mound of black mushroom caps on top and just-done mustard greens at the bottom. Pour out gravy before doing this and put it back afterwards.

Mushroom, Pork and Prawn Soup

Cooking time: 15 minutes

4 tbsp oil
10 shallots, sliced
2 cloves garlic, crushed
1 small bunch coriander leaves
750 ml (1¼ pints) water
1/2 chicken stock cubes
200 g (7 oz) prawns, shelled
150 g (5 oz) pork fillet, sliced
6 Chinese mushrooms, soaked and stalks
  removed
1 tsp pepper

Heat oil and fry sliced onions until brown. Dish up and set aside. In the remaining oil fry crushed garlic until brown. Add pork and mushrooms either sliced or whole and fry for 2 minutes.

Add prawns, water, coriander leaves and bring to the boil. Crumble stock cube in and simmer for 5 minutes. Garnish with fried onions and pepper.

VEGETABLES

Ancient ingenuity — scarcity being the supreme mother of inventiveness — of the old country Chinese resulted in a culinary method that is second to none. Stir-frying, which is not at all the same as sauteeing, does the best justice to vegetables and it is a method of cooking that has been extended to all types of Asian dishes.

But it is vegetables that come into their own when cooked very quickly in a wok (nothing else will do). In my three decades of cooking I have learnt to appreciate the tender sweetness of zucchinis or courgettes, the crunch of Australian lettuce, the nut-like flavour of chicory and fragrant celery the size and likes of which were not seen 10 years ago.

Then again, modern farming methods in Malaysia have resulted in better, sweeter and cheaper vegetables indigenous to this part of

the world. Fat round cabbages like cannonballs, crinkly Chinese celery cabbage that can be cooked to velvet smoothness, dark green mustard greens that need no more than a minute to cook, sweet vegetable melons, smooth, ridged, bitter or brown gourds, several types of spinach all delicious and nutritious, snow peas eaten pod and all, string beans, radishes, carrots, eggplants, yams, sweet potatoes and the indispensible bamboo shoot are all available all year round.

Chinese broccoli or Kai Lan is very similar to the western broccoli but has far less crinkly leaves. But stir-frying is by no means the only way to cook vegetables to perfection. Fried lettuce might seem a horrendous murder but if you've eaten it cooked thus and smothered in oyster sauce, you are likely to became an afficionado.

Spiced Leeks

This is somewhat of an acquired taste especially for those who don't like garlicky flavours of which the leek has plenty of as it belongs to the same family. There is no cooking involved but the combination of leeks, vinegar and sliced herbs is mouth-watering especially when you're feeling surfeit of too much meat.

2 whole leeks
3 shallots
2 red chillies
2 cloves garlic
1 tsp salt
1 tbsp vinegar
1 tsp sugar
1 tsp light soy or fish sauce
1 lime

Slice leeks, shallots, chillies and garlic as thin as possible. Wash and drain thoroughly. They must be completely dry or the finished dish will become watery instead of crunchy. Sprinkle salt over and let stand for 10 minutes. Squeeze out all moisture and mix with vinegar, soy sauce, sugar and juice of one lime. Serve as a side dish with seafood.

Leeks with Beancurd

Cooking time: 10 minutes

2 whole leeks
1 large square beancurd or tofu
200 g (7 oz) prawns, shelled
4 tbsp oil
1 clove garlic, crushed
300 ml (½ pint) water
1 tsp salt
1 tbsp oyster sauce
1 tsp pepper

Slice leeks into diagonal pieces. Cut beancurd into quarters. Heat oil and fry beancurd until light brown. Remove and cool. Cut beancurd into thin slices. In remaining oil fry crushed garlic until brown. Add leeks and fried beancurd and fry for 1 minute. Add water, salt and oyster sauce and simmer for 3 minutes. Serve garnished with pepper.

Leeks with Cod Slices

Cooking time: 8 minutes

2 whole leeks
200 g (7 oz) cod fillet, sliced
1 tbsp sesame oil
1 tsp salt
3 tbsp oil
4 shallots, sliced
200 ml (7 fl oz) water
1 tbsp fish sauce
1 tbsp pepper
1 tbsp sesame seeds, dry-fried

Cut leeks into diagonal slices. Marinate cod slices in sesame oil and salt for 10 minutes. This helps prevent the fish slices from breaking up when they are put in to fry. Heat oil and fry shallots until light brown. Add leeks and fry for 2 minutes. Add fish slices and stir gently for 1 minute. Add water, fish sauce and pepper and simmer for 2 minutes until fish is cooked. Serve and garnish with sesame seeds.

Leeks with Pineapple

Cooking time: 10 minutes

This may seem an unlikely combination but the two flavours are perfectly compatible as you'll discover. You may add prawns, chicken livers, diced cooked pork or whatever you fancy but start with fresh, firm leeks and pineapple.

2 leeks
1 small pineapple
2 tbsp oil
2 cloves garlic, crushed
300 ml (½ pint) water
1 tbsp cornflour
1 tbsp fish sauce

Wash and slice leeks into diagonal pieces. Slice pineapple into fan-shaped wedges about 1 cm (½ in) thick each. Heat oil and fry garlic until brown. Add leeks and pineapple and fry for 2 minutes or so. Add water mixed with cornflour and simmer for 3 minutes. Add fish sauce last and serve hot.

Leeks with Prawns

Cooking time: 8 minutes

2 leeks
2 tbsp oil
2 cloves garlic, crushed
200 g (7 oz) prawns, shelled
1 tbsp fish sauce
1 tsp cornflour
200 ml (7 fl oz) water
1 tsp pepper

Slice leeks into diagonal pieces about 2 cm (¾ in) long. Use only the white part and perhaps a few centimetres into the pale green part. Wash and remove sand and grit that tend to gather between the leek folds. Heat oil and fry garlic until brown. Add leeks and fry over high heat for 2 minutes. Add prawns, fish sauce and fry for 1 minute more. Dissolve cornflour in water and add to pan. Simmer for 5 minutes and add pepper.

Boiled Okra (Lady's Fingers)

Cooking time: 5 minutes

This is one of the simplest and tastiest ways of eating okra. The accent is really on the special sauce but the okra must not be overboiled. Choose okra that is pale green and firm. Old okra tend to be dry and the tip rigid. If tip is pliant and bends without snapping off, the okra is okay for plain boiling. Use older okra for fried dishes.

3 litres (5¼ pints) water
12 okra
1 tsp salt

SAUCE
2 tbsp black prawn paste (hae ko) or fish sauce
1 tbsp sambal belacan (see page 288)
2 limes
2 tsp sugar
2 tbsp hot water
2 tbsp pounded peanut brittle

Boil whole okra after removing stalks. Water must be furiously boiling. Boil for 1 or 2 minutes and remove from water. Run okra under cold running tap and drain throughly. This will help retain the green colouring and refresh okra so they don't look squashed and limpid. They can be chilled until you need them. Mix prawn paste with sambal belacan, juice of 2 limes, hot water and peanut brittle. Add sugar at the last minute and serve as a dip for boiled okra.

Okra Tempura

Cooking time: 5 minutes

The Japanese have the nicest way to deep-fry vegetables in a thin batter. The secret lies in a special tempura flour sold at supermarkets that feature Japanese foodstuffs. The oil you use must be clean and hot and, if you like, augmented for fragrance with a little sesame oil. Just about every type of firm vegetable can be sliced thin and deep-fried this way.

Oil for deep-frying
2 tbsp sesame oil
10 okra

BATTER
3 tbsp tempura flour
Cold water or beer
2 egg whites
1 tsp salt
1 tsp pepper

Mix tempura flour with cold water or beer for a batter that just flows, about the consistency of honey. Beat egg whites until stiff peaks form. Fold in batter together with salt and pepper and allow to chill for an hour. Remove okra stalk and cut into two. Dip in batter and allow excess to run off. Fry in hot oil for 1 or 2 minutes until batter is light brown. Drain on absorbent paper and serve with tempura sauce.

Spicy Fried Okra

Cooking time: 8 minutes

3 tbsp oil
8 okra
200 g (7 oz) prawns, shelled
1 tsp salt
1 tsp sugar
500 ml (16 fl oz) water

SPICES
2 red chillies
1 tsp dried shrimp paste
4 shallots
1 tsp turmeric powder
2 cloves garlic
6 almonds

Pound spices fine. Remove stalk from okra and cut each into three or four diagonal pieces. Heat oil and fry spices until fragrant and oil seeps out again. Add okra pieces and continue frying until well-coated. Add prawns, salt and sugar and fry for 2 minutes more. Add water and simmer for 5 minutes. If you like your okra with crunch in them, simmer for a shorter time. Okra also tends to soak up liquid so top with more water if necessary and adjust seasoning. This dish should have a thickish gravy.

Beansprouts with Cod

Cooking time: 10 minutes

4 tbsp oil
100 g (3 oz) cod
2 cloves garlic, crushed
300 g (10 oz) beansprouts

Heat oil and fry cod until brown and fragrant. Remove to cool. When cool enough to handle, cut into small cubes or flakes.

Reheat oil and fry crushed garlic for 1 minute. Toss in washed and drained beansprouts and fry for 30 seconds. Add salt with fish and stir well before serving.

Plain Fried Beansprouts

Cooking time: 1 minute

This ubiquitous vegetable has fired the imagination of cooks from London to Jakarta, New York and Singapore elevating it to an international reputation. There was a time when it was merely synonymous with Chinese cuisine abroad, its easy availability and cheapness being legend. And until the primary production people have successfully farmed rootless beansprouts — they are trying I believe — people will continue to remove the fine roots before cooking. Personally I like 'em roots and all and there is nothing quite like unadorned stir-fried beansprouts.

2 tbsp oil
2 cloves garlic crushed
300 g (10 oz) beansprouts
1 tsp salt

Heat oil until smoking. Toss in garlic and fry till brown. Add beansprouts and stir-fry over high heat for 30 seconds and no more. In fact I like my sprouts just tossed in the hot oil for barely 10 seconds. It's more crunchy this way. Add salt and serve.

Beansprouts with Prawns

Cooking time: 3 minutes

3 tbsp oil
2 cloves garlic, crushed
200 g (7 oz) prawns, shelled
300 g (10 oz) beansprouts
2 stalks spring onions
1 red chilli, sliced
1 tsp salt

Heat oil and fry crushed garlic until brown. Add prawns and fry until they turn pink. Make sure the prawns are completely dry before you add to the oil or the moisture will make your finished dish rather limp.

Beansprouts are high in water content and should never be fried with water. When prawns turn pink add beansprouts and spring onions and stir well. Add salt and serve with sliced chilli garnished on top.

Beansprouts Omelette

Cooking them: 4 minutes

4 tbsp oil
2 cloves garlic, crushed
2 eggs
1 tsp salt
250 g (½ lb) beansprouts
3 tbsp chopped shrimps
1 tsp pepper
1 red chilli, sliced
1 bunch fresh coriander leaves or parsley

Heat oil and fry garlic until brown. Wash bean sprouts and toss in hot oil for 20 seconds. Lightly beat egg in a deep dish. Scoop up bean sprouts and stir into egg mixture.

Add salt, pepper, shrimps and red chilli and pour mixture back into pan to finish cooking. Serve with coriander leaves or parsley.

You can also first fry the egg and just before it sets, toss in beansprouts and shrimps but you won't get crunchy sprouts this way.

Fried Rice with Corned Beef and Cabbage (top, recipe on p. 267),
Steamed Cabbage Parcels (recipe on p. 163).

Cabbage and Chicken

Cooking time: 40 minutes

750 ml (1¼ pints) water
½ coconut, grated
2 chicken drumsticks
1 tsp salt
1 tsp fish sauce
½ cabbage

SPICES
1 tbsp coriander powder
1 tsp chilli powder
1 tsp pepper
½ tsp turmeric powder

Squeeze coconut with water for milk and set aside. Chop chicken drumsticks into bite-sized pieces. Cut cabbage into rough shreds. Blend spices with coconut milk and bring to the boil. Add chicken and simmer for 30 minutes. Add seasoning and cabbage and simmer for 10 minutes more.

Raw Cabbage Sambal

Cooking time: 5 minutes

I recall this unusual appetiser — I have often made a complete meal of it — from my childhood when cabbage was a few cents each and the "fish were jumpin." It was a classical composition of deep-fried mackerel mixed with sambal belacan and a squeeze of lime and nothing else on the table was taken any notice of.

My uncle used to buy several heads of the fattest cabbage he could find, toss them into the family well (tap water was a decade away) to crisp for a whole morning before he shredded the leaves coarsely. Then he would exhort my aunt to fry a whole mackerel to the exact degree of browness and crispness.

Anything less would provoke a mild storm of anger for this was my uncle's almost-ritualistic meal which made a lamb out of his demon. Afterwards he would go off to sleep on the raised platform which no Singapore Straitsborn family could do without then. Peace would reign amid the torpor from a surfeit of raw cabbage.

1 head cabbage, soaked till crisp
2 mackerel steaks
1 tsp salt
5 tbsp oil

SAMBAL BELACAN (see page 288)

Rub salt over fish after washing and fry in hot oil until brown and cooked through. Leave to cool. Drain cabbage and shred coarsely or leave whole in a large basin of water for diners to help themselves to however large or small a piece.

The way to eat is to mix a little fried fish with the belacan and wrap up each cabbage leaf with mixture to form little morsels. It is an acquired taste but once you acquire it life won't be the same.

Cabbage Rice

Cooking time: 10 minutes

I must admit this was born of teenage ingenuity at a time when the free spirit of camping days gnawed at the vitals every half an hour. So faced with not much more than cabbages (they're the easiest, most durable vegetables for travelling) and rice, my inventiveness knew no bounds. Actually it turned out to be a remarkably tasty dish with a fine balance of textures that I had occasion to cook many times over the past 20 years.

4 tbsp oil
2 eggs
Cold, cooked rice for four, about 350 g (¾ lb)
½ head cabbage
2 tsp chilli powder
2 tsp salt
4 tbsp small prawns, shelled
2 red chillies, sliced

Wash cabbage and slice very fine. If you have an electric food processor it'll do the job just fine within seconds. Lightly beat eggs and fry in hot oil to make an omelette. Remove from pan.

In the remaining oil, add sliced cabbage and fry for 1 minute. Add rice, chilli powder, salt and prawns and fry for 4 minutes. Add omelette, roughly cut up and sliced chillies and stir well. Serve with sliced cucumber and chopped pineapple.

Cabbage and Pork Soup

Cooking time: 10 minutes

3 tbsp oil
6 shallots, sliced
1.5 litres (2¼ pints) water
½ cabbage
200 g (7 oz) pork fillet
1 tsp salt
1 tbsp fish sauce
1 tsp monosodium glutamate or
½ chicken stock cube
1 tsp pepper

Heat oil and fry sliced shallots until brown and crisp. Set aside. Bring water to the boil and add fillet pork. Simmer for 10 minutes and remove pork. Slice into thin pieces and put back into soup. Wash cabbage and cut into small squares. Add to soup and simmer for 5 minutes. Add salt, chicken stock and fish sauce and serve garnished with pepper.

Steamed Cabbage Parcels (illustrated on p. 161)

Cooking time 10 minutes

6 large cabbage leaves
2 litres (3½ pints) hot water for scalding
300 g (10 oz) minced pork
100 g (3 oz) minced prawns
1 tbsp oil
2 tbsp salt
1 tsp pepper
1 tbsp sesame oil
1 stalk spring onions, chopped
1 tbsp cornflour

Boil water and immerse cabbage leaves to simmer making sure you don't tear them. Simmer for about 3 minutes then drain and set aside. Mix minced pork with all other ingredients and knead well.

Divide mixture into six amounts and roll up each with cabbage leaf. Fold under neatly into parcels or secure with toothpicks. Place in a deep dish and steam for 5 minutes. Serve hot.

Pickled Cabbage

This is a pungent dish usually eaten as an appetiser before a rich Chinese meal. It's easy to make and keeps indefinitely. Because of its sharp, sweet taste you can eat only a little at a time.

1 head cabbage
1 tbsp salt
500 ml (16 fl oz) malt vinegar
3 red chillies
2 tbsp sugar

Do not wash cabbage. Peel off leaves one by one and wipe with kitchen paper thoroughly. Slice cabbage into 1 cm (½ in) wide strips and put in large enamel basin. Do not use aluminium as the vinegar will turn the metal black and render the pickle an unpleasant taste.

Sprinkle salt all over cabbage and cover to set aside for 30 minutes. Boil the vinegar, sugar and chillies and allow to cool completely. Squeeze cabbage, a handful at a time, to remove as much moisture as possible. Place in a glass jar or enamel container and mix in vinegar mixture. Allow at least one day of steeping before eating.

To serve, scoop up as much cabbage as you want and drain off liquid. Add more sugar if you like it sweet.

Cabbage in Coconut Milk

Cooking time: 15 minutes

3 tbsp oil
2 tbsp dried shrimps
½ coconut
600 ml (1 pint) water
½ cabbage, shredded
1 tsp salt

SPICES
1 large onion
2 cloves garlic
3 red chillies
½ tsp turmeric powder
6 almonds
1 tbsp shrimp paste powder

Pound spices fine. Squeeze coconut with water for milk. Soak dried shrimps in hot water for 5 minutes and pound till fine. Heat oil and fry pounded spices for 4 minutes until oil seeps out again. Add shrimps and stir fry for 1 minute more.

Add coconut milk and salt and bring to the boil. Add cabbage and simmer for 10 to 15 minutes. To this basic dish can be added a plethora of things like fish balls, fresh prawns, beancurd squares, sliced French beans, turnips and even meat.

Cabbage in Cream Sauce

Cooking time 15 minutes

5 tbsp oil
2 tbsp sesame oil
2 cloves garlic, crushed
1 head cabbage, shredded
1 tsp salt
1 tsp pepper
150 ml (¼ pint) single cream or light cream
2 tsp light soy sauce

Heat both types of oil and fry crushed garlic until brown. Add shredded cabbage and fry for 2 minutes more. Add salt and pepper and fry cabbage until half-cooked but still crisp. Add cream and soy sauce and simmer over gentle heat for 5 minutes. Serve hot.

Cabbage and Beancurd in Spicy Gravy (top, recipe on p. 166), Compressed Rice (recipe on p. 271).

Cabbage and Beancurd in Spicy Gravy (illustrated on p. 164)

Cooking time: 15 minutes

5 tbsp oil
½ head cabbage
3 squares beancurd (tofu)
2 tsp salt
1 tsp fish sauce
2 tbsp dried prawns, soaked till soft
1 coconut, shredded and squeeze with
2 litres (3½ pints) water

SPICES
5 dried chillies, soaked till soft
1 stalk lemon grass or grated lemon rind
1 large onion, sliced
1 tsp turmeric powder
8 almonds
1 tbsp coriander powder
1 tsp shrimp paste powder (belacan)

Pound dried prawns until fine. Pound or blend spices till fine. Heat oil and fry beancurd for a few minutes to seal the surface so the pieces won't break up when they are simmered later.

Remove and fry spices in same oil until fragrant. Add pounded dried prawns and fry for 2 minutes more. Add coconut milk and bring to the boil. Add shredded cabbage and beancurd and simmer for 10 minutes. Add seasoning and serve.

Fried Cabbage with Dried Prawns

Cooking time: 15 minutes

4 tbsp oil
2 cloves garlic
2 tbsp dried prawns
½ cabbage
2 tsp salt
1 stock cube
500 ml (16 fl oz) water

Soak dried prawns in hot water and pound slightly. Cut cabbage into shreds about 1 cm (½ in) wide. Heat oil and fry crushed garlic for 1 minute. Add dried prawns and stir for 1 minute more.

Add shredded cabbage and stir throughly until well coated in oil and prawns mixture. Add water and simmer for 12 minutes. Add stock cube in the last 5 minutes of simmering.

Cauliflower with Beef

Cooking time: 8 minutes

1 cauliflower about 300 g (10 oz)
4 tbsp oil
1 clove garlic, crushed
3 slices ginger, cut into strips
200 g (7 oz) fillet beef
1 tbsp oyster sauce
1 tbsp Chinese wine or sherry
1 tsp pepper
1 bunch fresh coriander leaves
5 tbsp water
2 tsp cornflour

Cut cauliflower into florets and scald for 1 minute in boiling water. Refresh under cold running tap and set aside. Cut beef into thin slices and marinate in oyster sauce, wine and pepper. Heat oil and fry garlic and ginger strips until light brown.

Drain beef from marinade and reserve liquid. Add beef and cauliflower to pan and stir for 1 minute. Dissolve cornflour with water and add to beef and cauliflower. Bring to boil and serve immediately.

Cauliflower Compote (illustrated on p. 158)

Cooking time: 8 minutes

4 tbsp oil
2 cloves garlic, crushed
200 g (7 oz) prawns, shelled
1 cauliflower about 350 g (¾ lb)
1 carrot
1 green pepper
2 tbsp cashew nuts
1 tsp salt
1 tsp pepper
250 ml (8 fl oz) water
1 tbsp sesame oil

Wash and cut cauliflower into florets. Dice green pepper and slice or cube carrot. Boil a small pot of water and scald all three vegetables for 1 minute. This par-cooks them so they retain their colour and crunchiness when you stir-fry them quickly afterwards.

After scalding refresh under cold running tap immediately and drain. Heat oil and fry crushed garlic for 1 minute. Add prawns and vegetables and give the lot a quick a stir. Add seasoning, and cashew nuts, water and sesame oil and bring to a brisk boil. Serve immediately. Water may not be necessary if vegetables are already moist.

Stir-fried Broccoli with Mushrooms

Cooking time: 5 minutes

This is a more luxuriant version of Chinese kale or kai lan but with basically similar texture. It has fatter stalks and heads that look more like tight clumps of tiny buds than leaves. Broccoli has almost the same taste as kai lan and, because of its firmer texture, holds its shape better during cooking. Use as you would kai lan.

1 litre (1¾ pints) water
400 g (13 oz) broccoli
6 Chinese mushroom caps
1 tsp salt
1 knob ginger, pounded for juice
2 cloves garlic, crushed
4 tbsp oil

Wash and cut broccoli into bite-sized pieces. Heat water till boiling and scald broccoli for 1 minute. Refresh under cold tap immediately to retain the greenness. Set aside. In the same hot water soak the mushrooms for 5 minutes.

Remove stalks and slice each cap into strips. Squeeze out liquid. Heat oil and fry crushed garlic until brown. Add mushrooms and fry for 1 minute. Add broccoli, ginger juice and salt and stir for 30 seconds. Serve hot.

Steamed Broccoli with Ham

Cooking time: 8 minutes

400 g (13 oz) broccoli
4 slices cooked ham
3 tbsp oyster sauce
1 tsp cornflour
4 tbsp water
1 tsp pepper
1 tsp lard or oil

Wash broccoli and leave whole. Cut each slice of ham into two. Lay broccoli in a deep dish and lay ham slices across. Steam for 2 minutes and add gravy consisting of oyster sauce, cornflour mixed with water and pepper.

Steam for 2 more minutes and add 1 tsp of oil just before serving. This dish must be served piping hot.

Broccoli and Prawns

Cooking time: 5 minutes

4 tbsp oil
2 cloves garlic, crushed
300 g (10 oz) broccoli
150 g (5 oz) prawns, shelled
1 tsp salt
1 tsp monosodium glutamate (optional)
150 ml (¼ pint) water
2 tsp cornflour

Wash prawns and sprinkle with sugar. Set aside for 10 minutes. Wash broccoli and cut into bite-sized pieces. Heat oil and fry garlic until brown. Add broccoli and stir-fry for 1 minute over high heat. Add prawns, salt, monosodium glutamate and cornflour dissolved in water. When gravy boils and thickens serve immediately.

Kai Lan (Kale) with Ginger Wine

Cooking time: 5 minutes

This is a favourite vegetable of the Cantonese and very versatile, lending itself to a wide range of fried, braised and soupy dishes. This one is absolutely simple but fit for a king if you use a top-quality Chinese wine. Sherry will do as well if you can't get Chinese wine.

3 tbsp oil
2 cloves garlic, crushed
1 large knob ginger
3 tbsp Chinese wine or sherry
1 tbsp oyster sauce
250 g (½ lb) kai lan or curly kale
5 tbsp water mixed with
2 tsp cornflour

Pound ginger roughly and extract every drop of juice. Mix with wine and set aside. Wash kai lan and cut into 6 cm (2¼ in) lengths. Skin the stalks if they look a little old and tough.

If you use tender kai lan with thin stalks, use them unskinned. Heat oil and fry garlic until brown. Do not lower heat at this point as a high heat is important when you toss in vegetables to stir-fry. Add kai lan and fry for 1 minute. Add wine or sherry and water and stir well. The minute gravy bubbles, dish up. Overfried kai-lan not only looks insipid but tastes like shoe leather.

Kai Lan (Kale) with Fish

Cooking time: 5 minutes

4 tbsp oil
2 cloves garlic, crushed
300 g (10 oz) kai lan or curly kale
1 tsp salt
1 tbsp Chinese wine or sherry
200 g (7 oz) cod
1 tbsp sesame oil
1 tsp pepper
1 tsp oil
4 tbsp water

Wash kai lan and cut into 6 cm (2¼ in) lengths. Cut fish into bite-sized pieces and marinate in sesame oil, oil and pepper. Heat 4 tbsp oil and fry crushed garlic until brown.

Add kai lan and stir for 1 minute over high heat. Drain fish and add to kai lan. Add marinade, salt and water and bring to a quick boil. Dish up immediately after giving it a good stir.

Kai Lan (Kale) with Beef (illustrated on p. 172)

Cooking time: 5 minutes

Oil for deep frying
400 g (13 oz) kai lan or curly kale
2 cloves garlic, crushed
200 g (7 oz) fillet beef
1 tbsp cornflour dissolved in 2 tbsp water
2 tbsp oyster sauce
1 tbsp wine or sherry
1 tsp pepper

Wash and drain kai lan. Heat oil till smoking and deep fry kai lan very quickly. Kai lan must be dry and oil very hot. About 20 seconds should do it. Drain immediately and aside.
Cut beef into thin slices and marinate in corn flour, oyster sauce, wine and pepper. Remove all but 3 tbsp of oil from wok and fry crushed garlic until brown.

Drain beef slices and toss in wok for 1 minute. Add fried kai lan and toss quickly. Add marinade and bring to boil over high heat. Serve immediately. The reason for deep-frying the kai lan first is to preserve its crunchy texture and cook it through without resulting in soggy vegetables.

French Beans in Tamarind Soup (illustrated on p. 178)

Cooking time: 10 minutes

I had this dish at a friend's restaurant once and he told me it originated from Banjarmasin in Indonesia. My father's people were from this town which explained why he had a passion for this rather unlikely dish. Unlikely, because French beans are rarely, if ever, used in soup. It is, I assure you, delicious especially served with a dip of sambal belacan, (see page 288).

4 French beans
650 ml (1 pint) water
2 tbsp fresh tamarind paste
1 tsp salt
1 tsp fish sauce
3 tbsp small prawns, shelled
2 red chillies, slit lengthwise and deseeded
1 tsp pepper

Cut French beans into 8 cm (3 in) lengths. Blend tamarind paste with 100 ml (3 ½ fl oz) water and squeeze out juice. Discard pulp. Add to the rest of the water and bring to the boil. Add all other ingredients and bring to the boil again. Simmer for 3 minutes and serve with a side dip of sambal belacan.

French Beans with Preserved Soy Beans

Cooking time: 10 minutes

10 French beans
3 tbsp oil
2 cloves garlic, crushed
2 tbsp preserved soy beans, washed and
    drained
2 red chillies
150 g (5 oz) prawns, shelled
1 tsp salt
5 tbsp water

Wash and cut French beans into 3 cm (1 ¼ in) pieces. Slice red chillies. Heat oil and fry crushed garlic for 1 minute. Add preserved beans and fry for 1 minute more. Add chillies, French beans and fry for 3 minutes. Add salt and water and simmer for 3 minutes.

French Bean Omelette (illustrated on p. 168)

Cooking time: 5 minutes

This simple but delicious egg dish is a great standby. The crunchy texture of chopped French beans in the egg mixture provides a tasty contrast of flavours. It also makes an unusual sandwich filling. You may omit the chillies if you don't like a hot omelette.

4 tbsp oil
2 large eggs, lightly beaten
1 tsp salt
4 French beans
2 red chillies

Wash and chop French beans into ½ cm (¼ in) nuggets. An easy way to do this fast is to line all the beans in a straight row and slice across with a sharp knife. Cut chillies fine. Heat 2 tbsp of the oil and fry chopped beans for 2 minutes until slightly shrivelled.

Add chillies and give pan a quick stir. Scoop up and add to beaten egg. Put in remaining oil to heat and pour egg mixture back to fry for 2 minutes. When egg is set, chop up roughly with ladle and serve. To save time, after frying the beans simply pour beaten egg into pan and finish cooking.

French Beans with Sambal

Cooking time: 10 minutes

10 French beans
4 tbsp oil
1 tbsp shrimp paste (fresh or powder)
3 red chillies
2 cloves garlic
200 g (7 oz) prawns, shelled
5 tbsp water
1 tsp sugar
½ tsp salt

Cut French beans into 6 cm (2¼ in) lengths. Wash and drain. Toast shrimp paste over naked flame or under a grill for 3 minutes. If using powder, add to chilli after it has been pounded. Pound with chillies and garlic until fine.

Heat oil and fry pounded mixture for 1 minute. Add beans and fry for another 2 minutes. Add shelled prawn and stir for 1 minute. Add water, salt and sugar and simmer for 3 minutes until beans are just soft.

Pickled Cucumber

Preparation time: 10 minutes

Any cook worth his salt knows this cool character of the vegetable family is worth a lot more than being an ignominious filling between sandwiches. For novice cooks, cucumbers are an excellent introduction to culinary mysteries, and basically bland flavour notwithstanding, lend themselves to fast cooking. The following are extensions of the cool theme, some simple and some a little less so but all interesting to try out.

1 cucumber
1 tsp salt
3 tbsp malt vinegar
2 tbsp sugar

Skin cucumber and slice into four lengthwise. Remove pulp and cut into diamond-shaped pieces. Sprinkle salt all over, cover and set aside. After 4 minutes squeeze out all moisture making sure not to bruise cucumbers.

Mix with vinegar and sugar and let steep for a few minutes. Cucumbers remain crisp only when most of their moisture is removed. The easiest way to do this is to "sweat" out the moisture. I remember when my mother used to make me stand guard over trays of cucumber slices drying in the sun for her fabulous acar.

Cucumber and Prawn Salad

Cooking time: 5 minutes

2 tbsp oil
1 large onion, finely sliced
3 cloves garlic, sliced
150 ml (¼ pint) water
1 tsp salt
400 g (13 oz) prawns, shelled
2 cucumbers

SAUCE
3 red chillies or 6 birds eye chillies (chilli padi)
1 tbsp sugar
1 tbsp fish sauce
2 tbsp lime or lemon juice

Heat oil and fry sliced garlic and onion until brown and crisp. Dish up and set aside. Boil water and cook prawns until just done. Add salt and set aside.

Skin cucumbers and remove pulp after cutting into four lengthwise. Cut each into diamond-shaped pieces. Drain prawns and mix with cucumbers. Roughly crush chillies and mix with sugar, fish sauce and lime juice. Add a little of the prawn liquid and pour over salad. Sprinkle with fried garlic and onions and serve.

Cucumber and Onion in Coconut Milk

Preparation time: 10 minutes

1 cucumber
1 large onion
1 tsp salt
½ coconut, shredded
100 ml (3½ fl oz) water
1 red chilli
1 lime

Skin cucumber and slice very thin. Slice onion into thin rings. Sprinkle salt over both and cover for 5 minutes. Squeeze coconut with water for milk. Squeeze lime juice over and allow to curdle slightly.

Squeeze moisture from cucumbers and onion rings and add to coconut milk. Add sliced red chilli for extra zest. This is a good side dish for a curry meal.

Cucumber Boats

Cooking time: 5 minutes

2 cucumbers of even size
2 tbsp oil
1 large onion, finely sliced
200 g (7 oz) minced beef (topside)
2 red chillies, sliced fine
2 limes
1 tsp sugar
1 tsp pepper
2 sprigs coriander leaves

Choose cucumbers that are not curved or mis-shapen. Holding firmly slice away 3 cm (1¼ in) from each and 1 cm (½ in) deep to form a "dugout". Using a sharp knife or spoon, gently scoop out pith so cucumber becomes a boat.

Cut away the pith on the part you sliced away and soak in cold water. Heat oil and fry sliced onion until soft but not brown. Add beef, chillies, salt, pepper and sugar and stir fry for 1 minute. Squeeze juice of 2 limes into beef mixture and stir for one minute more. Scoop out and fill cucumber boats. Garnish with coriander leaves and lay each sliced "cover" across slightly askew for attractive presentation.

Kai Lan (Kale) with Beef (recipe on p. 170).

Cucumber and Chicken Livers

Cooking time: 6 times

3 tbsp oil
1 clove garlic, crushed
1 cucumber
4 chicken livers
5 tbsp water
1 tsp salt
1 tsp cornflour
Pinch monosodium glutamate

Cut off cucumber ends 2 cm (¾ in) from the dark green and 1 cm (½ in) from light green ends and cut into four lengthwise. Remove pith and cut into diamond-shaped pieces.

Wash chicken livers and cut each into 2 or 3 pieces depending on size. Heat oil and fry garlic until fragrant. Add cucumbers and livers and fry for 2 minutes over high heat.

Mix cornflour and water and add to pan. Stir until gravy thickens and seasoning. Serve hot.

Stir-fried Bitter Gourd and Beef

Cooking time: 15 minutes

The bitter gourd is not everybody's favourite vegetable on account of its bitterness. But this can be tamed to a certain degree. All it needs is a little salt to "sweat" out the moisture and with further squeezing, you have rather unbitter gourd that goes particularly well with prawns and beef. Some people eat it because it's bitter.

4 tbsp oil
2 cloves garlic, crushed
1 large bitter gourd (dried) about 300 g (10 oz)
1 tsp salt
250 g (½ lb) fillet beef
2 tsp light soy sauce
1 tsp pepper
250 ml (8 fl oz) water
1 tbsp cornflour

Cut bitter gourd into half lengthwise. Scoop out pith and pink seeds. Make sure all the pith is removed as this is the bitter part of the gourd. Cut diagonal slices from each half about 1 cm (½ in) thick. Sprinkle 1 tsp salt all over and set aside.

Slice fillet beef into bite-sized pieces and mix with cornflour. Heat oil and fry garlic for 1 minute until brown. Squeeze all moisture from bitter gourd.

The salt would have coaxed most of it out by now. Add to pan and stir-fry for 1 minute over high heat. Add beef and fry for another minute or so and add soy sauce and pepper. Add water and bring to a quick boil. The gravy should be just thick and barely cover the food.

Bitter Gourd with Fish Meat (illustrated on p. 176)

Cooking time: 10 minutes

4 tbsp oil
1 large onion, sliced
1 tbsp preserved soy beans, washed and
   drained
1 red chilli, sliced
1 stalk spring onion
3 slices ginger, sliced fine
1 large bitter gourd (dried) about 300 g (10 oz)
250 g (½ lb) fish meat
200 ml (7 fl oz) water
1 tsp sugar
1 tsp salt

Cut bitter gourd into rings each 2 cm (¾ in) thick. Scoop out pith and seeds. Stuff each ring with fish meat patting it in firmly. Heat oil and shallow fry until light brown.

Bitter gourd takes on a wrinkled appearance when fried without first being parboiled but this is alright and saves you the bother of an additional cooking step. Dish up and set aside.

In remaining oil, fry sliced onions, ginger and spring onions for 1 minute. Add preserved soy beans and water and bring to the boil. Add bitter gourd rings, sugar and salt and simmer for 1 minute. Add sliced chilli and serve.

Bitter Gourd Lemak

Cooking time: 20 minutes

3 tbsp oil
3 tbsp dried prawns, soaked in hot water
1 large bitter gourd (dried) about 300 g (10 oz)
200 g (7 oz) fish meat
1 tsp salt
½ coconut
500 ml (16 fl oz) water

SPICES
3 red chillies
1 large onion
1 tbsp prawn paste powder
6 almonds
2 cloves garlic

Pound dried prawns until fine. Squeeze coconut with water. Cut bitter gourd into 2 cm (¾ in) thick rings and remove pith. Stuff with fish meat.

Heat oil and fry pounded spices until fragrant. Add pounded prawns and continue frying for 2 minutes. Add coconut milk and salt and bring to the boil. Add bitter gourd and simmer for 5 minutes.

Stuffed, Deep-fried Bitter Gourd

Cooking time: 5 minutes

Oil for deep frying
2 large (dried) bitter gourds about 300 g (10 oz) each
300 g (10 oz) minced pork
4 medium-sized prawns, shelled
2 tsp fish sauce
1 tbsp cornflour
1 tsp pepper
1 egg

Cut bitter gourd into half lengthwise and scoop out pith and seeds. Make sure not to puncture the soft green flesh. Scald in plenty of boiling water for 3 minutes, drain and set aside.

This semi-cooks it so when you deep-fry, the bitter gourd will not shrink and look shrivelled. Chop prawns fine and mix with minced pork. Add cornflour, fish sauce, pepper and the egg lightly beaten. Stuff bitter gourd halves and deep-fry for 2 minutes. This makes a tasty lunch in itself if you don't feel like eating rice.

Stir-fried Bitter Gourd with Prawns

Cooking time: 10 minutes

4 tbsp oil
2 cloves garlic, crushed
1 large bitter gourd (dried) about 300 g (10 oz)
1 tsp salt
300 g (10 oz) prawns, shelled
2 tsp light soy sauce
300 ml (½ pint) water
1 bunch coriander leaves

Cut bitter gourd into half lengthwise and remove pith and seeds. Cut diagonal slices about 2 cm (¾ in) thick and sprinkle with salt.

Set aside. Squeeze out moisture after 10 minutes. Heat oil and fry garlic until brown. Add bitter gourd and fry for 1 minute.

Add prawns and fry for 1 minute more or until prawns turn pink. Add seasoning and water and bring to the boil. Simmer for 5 minutes or until bitter gourd is soft. Serve garnished with coriander leaves.

Bitter Gourd in Coconut Milk

Cooking time: 10 minutes

4 tbsp oil
1 large bitter gourd (dried)
1 tsp salt
250 g (½ lb) prawns, shelled
10 fish balls, (available from Chinese grocers)
½ coconut, shredded
300 ml (½ pint) water
1 tsp salt

SPICES
6 dried chillies, soaked in hot water for 5
    minutes
5 shallots
2 cloves garlic
6 skinned almonds

Squeeze coconut with water for milk. Set aside. Boil fish balls for 5 minutes until they float. Cut bitter gourd into half and remove pith and seeds. Cut into 4 cm (1½ in) wedges and sprinkle salt over.

Squeeze out moisture after 10 minutes. Heat oil and fry pounded spices until fragrant. Add bitter gourd and prawns and fry for 1 minute. Add coconut milk, fish balls and salt and simmer for 5 minutes.

Bitter Gourd with Turmeric and Chilli

Cooking time: 5 minutes

4 tbsp oil
1 large bitter gourd (dried) about 250 g (½ lb)
150 g (5 oz) small prawns, shelled
2 cloves garlic, crushed
1 tsp turmeric
1 tsp chilli powder
1 tsp salt
150 ml (¼ pint) water

Prepare bitter gourd as you would for other dishes. Heat oil and fry crushed garlic for 1 minute. Add bitter gourd, turmeric and chilli and fry for 1 minute more.

Add prawns and water and simmer for 3 or 4 minutes. Add salt and give it a quick stir. Serve with plain boiled rice.

Mange Tout and Prawns (illustrated on p. 158)

Cooking time: 8 minutes

4 tbsp oil
2 cloves garlic, crushed
20 mange tout
300 g (10 oz) prawns, shelled
1 tsp sugar
1 tsp salt
1 tsp pepper
4 tbsp water
1 tsp cornflour
1 tbsp sesame oil

Marinate prawns in sugar for 10 minutes. This makes them crunchy when stir-fried. Heat oil and fry garlic until brown. Add mange tout and fry over high heat for 1 minute. Add prawns and fry for 2 minutes.

Add seasoning and continue stirring for 1 minute more. Mix water with cornflour and add to pan. Bring to the boil and when gravy thickens add sesame oil. Serve hot.

Bitter Gourd with Fish Meat (recipe on p. 174).

Spinach with Shrimp Paste

Cooking time: 10 minutes

4 tbsp oil
2 cloves garlic
4 red chillies
1 5 cm (2 in) square pieve shrimp paste,
   toasted
300 g (10 oz) spinach
200 ml (7 fl oz) water
2 tsp salt
1 tsp sugar

Pound chillies, garlic and shrimp paste until fine. Wash spinach thoroughly. Slice thick stalks and leave thin stalks whole in 6 cm (2¼ in) lengths.

Heat oil and fry pounded ingredients until fragrant. Add spinach and stir fry for 2 minutes until vegetable absorbs spices and is thoroughly mixed. Add water and seasoning and simmer for 30 seconds. Serve hot.

Aubergine Curry (illustrated on p. 94)

Cooking time: 25 minutes

3 aubergines cut into three each
3 tbsp oil
1 thumb-sized piece ginger, shredded
2 cloves garlic, pounded
½ coconut, grated
300 ml (½ pint) water
2 tbsp tamarind paste
200 ml (7 fl oz) water
2 tsp salt
2 green chillies, deseeded and sliced
1 tbsp sugar

SPICES
1 tbsp coriander powder
2 tsp cummin powder
2 tsp aniseed powder
2 tsp chilli powder

Blend spices and moisten with water or coconut milk from allowance. Slit each aubergine piece halfway down. Heat oil and fry ginger and garlic until light brown. Add spices and fry until fragrant. Squeeze coconut with water for milk. Mix tamarind with water and drain off pulp. Add to spices and bring to the boil. Add salt, sugar, aubergines and green chillies and simmer for 10 minutes or until aubergines are soft.

Aubergines with Dried Prawns and Sambal

Cooking time: 10 minutes

2 tbsp dried prawns, soaked in hot water
3 red chillies
2 cloves garlic
4 shallots
6 almonds
2 slices ginger
3 tbsp oil
2 aubergines, (diced)
1 tsp sugar
2 tbsp lime juice
6 tbsp water

Pound dried prawns separately and remove. Pound together chillies, garlic, shallots, ginger and almonds until fine. Heat oil and fry prawns until oil seeps out again. Add pounded spices and fry for 3 minutes until fragrant. Add aubergines, sugar, salt, lime juice and water and simmer gently for 2 minutes. Serve hot.

French Beans on Tamarind Soup (top, recipe on p. 170),
Grilled Aubergines (recipe on p. 180).

Grilled Aubergines (illustrated on p. 178)

Cooking time: 20 minutes

2 aubergines
1 tsp pepper
1 tbsp black soy sauce
2 tbsp oil

Cut aubergines into two lengthwise and split each half three quarter way down. Soak in water to prevent them turning black. Roughly score surface with a knife and marinate with soy sauce, pepper and oil. Grill for 15 minutes on each side and serve with sambal belacan.

Aubergines with Preserved Soy Beans and Chilli

Cooking time: 10 minutes

2 aubergines
1 tbsp lime juice
3 tbsp oil
2 cloves garlic, crushed
2 red chillies, sliced
1 tbsp preserved soy beans, washed and
  drained
1 tsp sugar
4 tbsp water

Cut aubergines into two lengthwise and slice into bite-sized pieces. Mix with lime juice and set aside. Heat oil and fry garlic and chillies for 1 minute. Add preserved soy beans and fry for 1 minute. Add aubergines and fry for 2 minutes. Add water and simmer for 3 minutes until aubergines are soft and change colour. Add sugar and serve.

Runner Beans with Beef

Cooking time: 8 minutes

3 tbsp oil
2 cloves garlic, crushed
300 g (10 oz) Runner beans, sliced
  diagonally into thin strips
200 g (7 oz) fillet beef, sliced very thin
1 tsp salt
2 limes
½ coconut
300 ml (½ pint) water

SPICES
1 stalk lemon grass or 1 tsp grated lemon
  rind
4 slices ginger
4 cloves garlic
4 red chillies
1 tbsp coriander powder
1 tsp chilli powder
½ tsp turmeric powder
1 tsp sugar

Pound spices till fine. Season beef slices with salt and lime juice. Squeeze coconut with water for milk. Heat oil and fry garlic till brown. Add spices and fry till oil seeps out again. Add beans and beef and fry for 1 minute. Add coconut milk and simmer for 5 minutes. Serve with plain rice or bread. This dish can be adapted to any other meat, seafood or a mixture of both.

Stuffed Beancurd

Cooking time: 15 minutes

I really do miss that hawker who used to ply the streets in the area I grew up with his delicious stuffed beancurd and duck stewed in soy sauce. He would ride his bicycle — yes, bicycle — and balance an enormous round cane basket at the rear.

When hailed, he would get off his bicycle, open the basket cover and reveal his goodies. There would be a few ducks, dozens of beancurd squares, fresh coriander leaves, bottles of sauces, sugar, syrup, vinegar and gizzards, livers and fish balls all waiting to be diced and stuffed. His chilli sauce was something else again. Today if I want to eat this I have to prepare it myself.

6 tbsp oil
6 cakes beancurd or tofu
200 g (7 oz) beansprouts
1 cucumber
6 fishballs (available from Chinese grocers),
    deep fried
1 stalk fresh coriander leaves
A few leftover pieces duck or chicken
Livers (cooked)

SAUCE
12 red chillies
3 cloves garlic
2 tbsp vinegar
1 tbsp sugar
2 tbsp black soy sauce or duck stew gravy
200 ml (7 fl oz) water
6 pieces peanut brittle or 6 tbsp crunchy
    peanut butter

Heat oil and fry bean curd squares until brown on both sides. If you can find the type of bean curd squares that are practically hollow inside they are ideal. If not, use ordinary yellow or white bean curd squares. When cooled after being fried cut each into two triangles and hollow out at widest part.

Boil a little water and scald beansprouts for 20 seconds. Drain and cool. Peel cucumber and shred roughly using a vegetable shredder. Dice fried fishballs and duck or chicken pieces; chop coriander leaves and dice cooked livers if using them. Stuff each beancurd piece with a tbsp of filling. Use up all filling and fry extra beancurd if there is excess.

Pound chillies and garlic and mix with vinegar, sugar and sauce. Pound peanut brittle if using them and mix with sauce and water. Adjust consistency of sauce by adding water a little at a time. To serve pour a little sauce into each beancurd triangle or let diners help themselves to however much they want.

FESTIVE FARE

Singaporeans need but the simplest reason to lay a festive table. Be it a birthday, wedding, a child's first haircut or even — excuse the morbidity — a funeral, there are always special dishes to commemorate the occasion. The special dishes served at the Long Table (Tok Panjang) meals of yesteryear's Straitsborn wedding parties were an experience of exquisite taste.

Recent attempts by restaurants to resuscitate this delicious tradition has reawakened interest in the cuisine and more Singaporean tastebuds, somewhat dulled by fast foods, have been quivering overtime. Today, it is rare for any Straits Chinese to serve food at a similar long table — where does one have the place for a rectory-like medieval table? — because most of the rambling pre-war houses are gone.

But my experience of festive dining was by no means restricted to our heritage. We had Malay, Indian and Eurasian neighbours and if it was not an invitation to a Hari Raya (Malay New Year and Ramadan Feast), an Indian wedding or Eurasian birthday party, it was to some other occasion where tables creaked with food.

I remember too the delightful tradition of Malay families who sent their young ones, old enough to bear a large tray laden with curries, sambals, yellow rice and sweetmeats, to their non-Malay neighbours so they too could enjoy whatever it was they cooked for a wedding or new year.

This practice, unfortunately, has waned somewhat because working couples today have little time to prepare huge feasts to distribute to six, seven or eight families living in the same village. The "villages" today are government housing estates and people make do by inviting neighbours over for special occasions.

The open-house tradition, thank goodness, is still practiced during all the festive seasons and every Hari Raya, Chinese New Year or Deepavali lunch at the humblest two-room flat or the poshest bungalow is likely to be a multi-racial mix of Chinese, Malays, Indians, Europeans and — if they should be lucky — tourists.

The special dishes here are all I have eaten at friends' homes over the past 25 years and which I have had occasion to cook at home.

As has been said, Singaporean meals at home are a fascinating mixture of Chinese, Malay, Indian, Indonesian, Thai and European types. My family still eat this way and I wouldn't change it for anything in the world.

Combination Cold Dish (Chinese)

Cooking time: 30 minutes

This is now firmly entrenched as the supreme entree for Chinese festive meals and takes many forms depending on the taste and pocket. It can be a gloriously imperial cold lobster borne on silver plate or a humble dish of sliced meats. Whatever, it lends a challenge to the innovative host who likes using up cold cuts without turning them into sorry sandwiches. The selection below is merely a basis and you can go to town with any and every type of food that can be served cold and sliced thinly. Serve several dips like mustard, chilli sauce and oyster sauce.

6 slices cooked ham
6 slices cold roast beef
1 can abalone, thinly sliced
1 cooked chicken breast
6 slices cold roast duck
1 cucumber, thinly sliced
300 g (10 oz) boiled, sliced king prawns
4 tbsp shredded lettuce
2 tbsp salad cream or mayonnaise

Arrange sliced foods all around platter overlapping one another. Put shredded lettuce in centre and pile boiled prawns on top. Top with salad cream and chill whole plate for half an hour or so. Serve as an appetiser for eight or 10 people at a sit-down Chinese meal.

Yam Cake (Chinese)

Cooking time: 1 hour

Though this is not strictly a festive dish, it has been so in my family with my mother-in-law being an expert at making trays of it for special occasions. It's delicious eaten steamed or cut up into slices and fried.

6 tbsp oil
15 shallots, sliced
4 tbsp dried prawns, soaked
300 g (10 oz) diced roast pork
3 tbsp light soy sauce
3 tbsp sugar
1 tsp salt
5 Chinese sausages, (available from Chinese supermarkets) diced fine
400 g (13 oz) rice flour
100 g (3 oz) tapioca flour
100 g (3 oz) plain flour
750 ml (1¼ pints) water
2 tsp salt
1 kg (2 lbs) yam
2 stalks spring onions, chopped

Heat oil and fry shallots until crisp and brown. Remove shallots and drain. In remaining oil fry dried prawns until fragrant and add roast pork, seasoning and diced Chinese sausages. Remove and set aside.

Blend all flours, water and salt till smooth. Add cooked mixture and stir well.

Peel yam and cut into chunks for steaming. Steam for about 10 minutes and allow to cool a little. Mash roughly with fork and add flour and cooked mixture. Mix well to incorporate ingredients.

Continue steaming for 10 minutes more. When completely cool, cut into diamond shapes and sprinkle with spring onions or fry in oil till crisp and brown. Serve with chilli sauce as a hearty breakfast dish.

Penang Laksa (illustrated on p. 186)

Cooking time: 30 minutes

This is one of Penang's most beautiful culinary exports though some Singapore laksa lovers have proclaimed otherwise. They shouldn't even be compared to begin with as the two dishes are totally different though they are both laksas. I love both versions but Penang laksa is a lot more amusing to eat as it comes with lots of different accompaniments.

A good friend's mother, Mrs K. K. Lim, cooks it to perfection and I coaxed her to part with her recipe. But not before I tasted at least two bowls of her Penang Laksa. It was superb and Mrs. Lim's reputation for Penang Laksa, among her other culinary gems, is known on both sides of the causeway.

MAIN INGREDIENTS
1½ kg (3 lbs) mackerel
350 ml (11 fl oz) water
1½ kg (3 lbs) laksa noodles

SOUP
2 litres (3½ pints) water
2 tbsp dried prawns, pounded fine
350 g (¾ lb) tamarind paste
2 tsp salt
1 tbsp sugar

SPICES
3 tbsp chilli powder
2 tbsp shredded fresh turmeric
600 g (1 lb 2 oz) shallots
7 stalks lemon grass or 1 tsp grated lemon rind
150 g (5 oz) shrimp paste

GARNISHES
1 pineapple, shredded
2 cucumbers, peeled and shredded fine
200 g (7 oz) mint leaves
300 g (10 oz) Chinese lettuce, shredded
3 stalks bunga siantan, (ginger flowers),
   sliced fine (available from Chinese
   grocers)
4 Red chillies (optional), sliced fine or
   chopped
250 ml (8 fl oz) prawn paste (hae ko) diluted
   with
200 ml (7 fl oz) water
15 shallots, sliced fine

Bring 350 ml (11 fl oz) water to the boil and simmer fish in it for 10 minutes. When cooked, remove to flake flesh. Reserve fish stock. Pound spices fine. Bring 2 litres (3½ pints) water to the boil. Add dried prawns, tamarind paste, salt, sugar, fish stock and pounded spices. Simmer for 10 minutes and adjust seasoning to taste. Add flaked fish and simmer for a few minutes more.

To serve Penang Laksa, place enough noodles in serving bowl and top up with gravy. Garnish with pineapple, cucumber, lettuce, ginger flowers, pickles, chillies, shallots and diluted prawn paste as much or as little as each person wants.

Spicy Cauliflower (Indian)

Cooking time: 15 minutes

I am privileged to have, as a neighbour, a Punjabi family whose matriarch cooks the most delicious Indian dishes. She will always say, with a smile, that their food is not Punjabi, Tamil or whatever that is representative of a particular region on the Indian sub-continent. Rather, she experiments with different Indian recipes and concocts her own. It is on this premise that I do not indicate whether a dish is from a particular regional school. Suffice that it is either Indian, Chinese, Malay, Indonesian, Eurasian or European.

4 tbsp vegetable oil
1 tsp mustard seeds
2 tbsp shredded ginger
1 onion, sliced fine
1 tsp turmeric powder
1 red chilli, chopped
1 large cauliflower
1 tsp salt
1 tbsp lemon juice

Heat oil and fry mustard seeds until they pop. Add ginger, onion, turmeric and chilli and fry for 2 minutes more. Cut cauliflower into florets and add to pan.

Add salt and lemon juice and stir well. Cover the pan and simmer cauliflower for 15 minutes until tender.

There is no need to add water as the cauliflower has high moisture content but if it seems too dry, sprinkle a few drops of water in. Serve hot.

Dry Beef Curry (Malay)

Cooking time: 40 minutes

1.5 kg (3 lbs) rump or sirloin beef
2 tsp salt
5 tbsp oil
2 stalks lemon grass, (bruised), or grated
   lemon rind
2 large onions, sliced
3 fragrant lime leaves or ¾ tsp grated
   lemon rind
2 coconuts, grated
1 litre (1¾ pints) water
3 tbsp lime juice

SPICES
1 tbsp coriander powder
2 tsp cumin powder
1 tsp pepper
1 tsp turmeric powder
1 tbsp chilli powder
10 almonds
3 tsp shredded ginger
4 green chillies
1 tsp salt
6 cloves garlic
2 large onions

Pound or blend spices till fine. Cut beef into large chunks and season with salt. Set aside. Heat oil and fry spices until fragrant. Add meat and bruised lemon grass and fry for 1 minutes. Add sliced onions and fry for 3 minutes. Add lime leaves and fry for 1 minute.

Squeeze coconut with water for milk and squeeze lime juice into it to curdle a bit. Add to beef and simmer, covered, for 20 minutes stirring occasionally until gravy is reduced by half. Cook on low heat until almost dry and very oily. Serve with crusty French bread.

Chicken Biryani (Indian)

Cooking time: 40 minutes

More than any other Indian dish I have enjoyed, this is a perennial favourite and one that I cook often when entertaining. It has also been adopted by most Singaporeans as one of their old standbys for Sunday lunches.

RICE
3 or 4 saffron strands
5 tbsp water
500 g (1 lb) Basmati or long-grain rice
2 tbsp ghee or cooking oil
6 shallots, sliced
100 ml (3½ fl oz) evaporated milk
1 litre (1¾ pints) water
1 tsp salt
1 packet raisins

BIRYANI CHICKEN
½ coconut, grated
500 ml (16 fl oz) water
100 ml (3½ fl oz) evaporated milk
4 tbsp ground almonds
juice of 1 lime
3 tbsp ghee or cooking oil
2 tbsp ground ginger
5 cm (2 in) stick cinnamon
6 cardamoms
3 green chillies, split lengthwise
1 bunch coriander leaves, chopped
1 chicken about 1.5 kg (3 lbs) cut into 6 joints

SPICES
5 cloves garlic
1 tbsp coriander powder
1 tsp turmeric powder
1 tsp cumin powder
1 tsp aniseed powder
1 tsp chilli powder
1 tsp pepper

Soak saffron strands in 5 tbsp water until liquid is golden yellow. If you cannot get saffron, which is very expensive, use turmeric powder (about 1 tsp) with the same amount of water. You won't get the same fragrance but the dish won't suffer too badly.

Wash rice and drain. Heat pan with ghee and fry shallots until brown. Add rice and fry quickly, making sure rice does not stick to pan. Add milk mixed with water and salt and transfer contents to a pot or rice cooker to finish cooking. When rice is almost dry, sprinkle saffron water on top and stir gently to get a combination of white and yellow grains.

This is strictly for presentation and does nothing to the taste. Cover and cook until rice is dry. Add raisins in the last few minutes and leave to plump up in hot rice.

Squeeze coconut with water for milk. Mix coconut milk and evaporated milk and add ground almonds. Squeeze lime juice over mixture and leave to curdle for a few minutes. Heat ghee and fry ground ginger for 1 minute.

Add pounded spices, cinnamon, cardamoms, green chillies and coriander leaves and fry for a further 2 minutes. Add chicken joints and fry until all the pieces are well coated with spices.

Add prepared liquid and salt and simmer for 25 minutes. Gravy should be reduced by half after this time. Pile chicken joints onto rice and let steep for awhile before serving.

Fried Tamarind Prawns (Straits Chinese)

Cooking time: 5 minutes

3 tbsp tamarind paste
300 ml (½ pint) water
1 tsp salt
10 king prawns
Oil for deep frying

Mix tamarind with water for a thick paste. Wash prawns and cut off feelers but leave unshelled. Marinate in tamarind with salt for 10 minutes. Drain off tamarind but do not wash. Heat oil till smoking and deep fry five at a time until crisp and brown.

Chinese New Year Raw Fish

Preparation time: 1 hour

Traditionally eaten from the seventh until the fifteenth day of the Lunar New Year, raw fish makes a timely appearance after a week's surfeit of meat and rich festive food. The Chinese are, unlike the Japanese, wary of anything raw but will drink endless toasts to this special dish once a year.

By far the most popular is the Cantonese version using a plethora of greens and spices but the Teochews have a slightly different version. Eating raw fish during Chinese New Year is supposed to bring good luck and prosperity.

1 whole mackerel about 500 g (1 lb)
4 carrots
2 whole white radishes
4 fragrant lime leaves or grated lemon rind
1 4 cm (1½ in) knob ginger
10 slices preserved red ginger
2 tbsp candied lemon peel
3 tbsp mixed pickled vegetables

SAUCE
5 tbsp fragrant oil or corn oil
2 tbsp sugar
2 tsp fivespice powder
2 tsp salt
Juice of 6 limes
4 tbsp crushed peanuts or peanut brittle
2 tbsp toasted sesame seeds

Wash fish and hang to dry for a few hours. When completely dry, cut along side and remove one fillet from centre bone.

Slide knife under end tip of centre bone and cutaway whole bone. Slice away head and flesh near the gill reserving only clean, boneless fillets for use. Slice very thin and arrange in a circular pattern on one large round plate. Use a food processor and grate peeled and washed carrots, radish and cabbage as fine as possible. Cut lime leaves, gingers, lemon peel and mixed vegetables into fine shreds.

Now comes the fun and ritualistic part. The Cantonese have a chant when preparing raw fish at the table and diners are supposed to join in to "Lo Hei" or stir well for good luck and prosperity.

Combine the sauce ingredients except peanuts and sesame seeds and pour all over shredded vegetables in a large plate. Add peanuts and sesame seeds and fish and stir the lot well. Raw fish is traditionally served with two types of porridge, one plain and the other simmered with dried scallops and fish, the recipe for which follows.

Porridge with Dried Scallops and Fish

Cooking time: 2 hours

6 litres (10½ pints) water
750 g (1½ lbs) broken rice
10 dried scallops
3 tbsp sesame oil
400 g (13 oz) sliced raw mackerel
2 tsp salt
2 tbsp fish sauce
4 tbsp chopped spring onions
2 tsp pepper

Wash rice until clean. Put to boil with water and dried scallops. Simmer for 1½ hours and add salt and fish sauce. If scallops are all shredded and soft reduce heat and simmer for 10 minutes more.

Add sliced fish and simmer for 2 minutes. Add sesame oil and fish sauce and serve in individual bowls with chopped spring onions, pepper and more sauce if necessary.

Grilled Chicken (Malay)

Cooking time: 30 minutes

This is an invariable dish during the Malay end of Ramadan celebration and is quite different from the western-style grilled chicken. It takes a little effort but the result is well worth it.

2 chickens each about 1 kg (2 lbs)
1 tsp salt
1 coconut, grated
400 ml (13 fl oz) water
2 bay leaves
2 tsp salt
1 tsp sugar

SPICES
1 tbsp shredded ginger
4 cloves garlic
1 large onion
5 dried chillies, soaked till soft
1 tsp turmeric powder

Pound spices till fine and set aside. Wash chickens and cut each into four joints. Rub with salt. Squeeze coconut with water for milk.
Mix with pounded spices and bay leaves and bring to the boil. Put chicken joints in and simmer for 5 minutes.

Remove chicken joints and place on a grilling rack. Grill for 5 minutes on each side basting with extra liquid. Serve grilled chickens with extra gravy poured on top.

Rich Sharksfins Stew (Chinese)

Cooking time: 30 minutes

The quality of sharksfins is directly proportional to the pocket and this has to be the guideline as there is sharksfin and there is sharksfin. On the whole, prepared sharksfin sold dried and packed in cellophane paper or plastic boxes is of good quality depending on whether you are using it for a simple dish or a festive one. There is not much point in buying sharksfin that you have to boil and clean as this takes hours. Prepared sharksfin can be cooked after being soaked a while in water.

2 litres (3½ pints) chicken stock
300 g (10 oz) prepared sharksfin (dried)
2 tsp salt
1 tbsp light soy sauce
1 tbsp lard
250 g (½ lb) crab meat
4 tbsp cornflour
5 tbsp water or stock
3 egg yolks
3 tbsp sesame oil
Good shake of pepper
2 bunches coriander leaves
4 tbsp black vinegar
2 tbsp pickled green chillies

Soak sharksfin for 20 minutes and, drain well. Put stock to boil and add sharksfin salt and soy sauce. Simmer for 15 minutes and add 1 tbsp lard. Add crab meat, cornflour dissolved in 5 tbsp water, beaten egg yolks and sesame oil.

Stir well until it thickens. Serve with individual dips of soy sauce, pickled green chillies, coriander leaves and black vinegar. This last condiment is as vital to sharksfin as the fin was to the shark in the first place.

Pumpkin cake (recipe on p. 192)

Gado Gado (Indonesian) (illustrated opposite)

Cooking time: 15 minutes

This bears some similarity to rojak but for the addition of boiled potatoes and compressed rice cubes. There seems to be several versions of this for I have been served it without the rice or potatoes and sometimes with potatoes and fish cutlets. Whatever, the basis of gado gado lies in the spicy peanut sauce.

3 large potatoes, boiled and cut into chunks
12 compressed rice cubes (see pg 271)
½ cabbage, boiled till soft
6 French beans, boiled and cut into
    4 cm (1 ½ in) pieces
4 squares hard beancurd (tofu), fried and
    sliced
1 cucumber, sliced into wedges
2 hard-boiled eggs, quartered
Handful of fried prawn crackers

SAUCE
3 tbsp oil
4 dried chillies, soaked till soft
4 red chillies
2 tsp shrimp paste, toasted
10 shallots
3 cloves garlic
8 tbsp crunchy peanut butter
2 tsp brown sugar
¼ coconut
200 ml (7 fl oz) water
2 tbsp tamarind paste
200 ml (7 fl oz) water
1 tsp salt

Arrange cooked ingredients on individual plates or a large central plate. Don't add prawn crackers until just before serving or they will go soft. Crumble them a little.

Pound chillies, shrimp paste, shallots and garlic until fine. Heat oil and fry for 3 minutes until fragrant. Mix coconut with water and squeeze for milk.

Mix tamarind with water and squeeze for milk. Combine the two liquids and add to spices. Bring to the boil and add peanut butter, sugar and salt. Pour over gado gado and serve topped with crumbled prawn crackers.

Whitebait in Sambal

Cooking time: 10 minutes

10 dried chillies
1 large onion
8 almonds
1 tbsp shrimp paste
1 tbsp tamarind paste
200 ml (7 fl oz) water
6 tbsp oil
200 g (7 oz) whitebait
1 tsp salt
1 tsp sugar

Soak dried chillies in hot water until soft. Remove stalks. pound together with onions, almonds and shrimp paste till fine.

Squeeze tamarind with water to get juice. Wash and dry whitebait thoroughly or they won't brown properly. Heat oil and fry whitebait until crisp. Set aside. In the remaining oil fry the pounded spices until fragrant. Add tamarind juice, salt and sugar and simmer until gravy thickens. Add fried whitebait and remove from fire immediately. Serve with coconut rice.

Indonesian Chicken (Ayam Percel)

Cooking time: 30 minutes

1 chicken about 1.5 kg (3 lbs)
1 coconut
500 ml (16 fl oz) water
3 fragrant lime leaves or ¾ tsp grated lemon
   rind
1 tbsp lime juice
1 tsp salt

SPICES
4 cloves garlic
6 red chillies
1 thumb-sized piece ginger
14 almonds
1 tsp pepper
1 tbsp shrimp paste powder

Wash and cut chicken into four joints. Grill for 10 minutes until golden brown. Pound or blend spices until fine. Squeeze coconut with water for milk. Mix with pounded spices and bring to the boil.

Simmer over low heat for 5 minutes stirring to prevent liquid from sticking to pot bottom. Add lime juice and salt and remove pan from heat. Put chicken joints under grill and pour gravy over.

Baste with gravy while chicken is being grilled. There should be charred bits here and there. Serve with extra gravy poured over chicken.

Pumpkin Cake (Chinese) (illustrated on p. 190)

Cooking time: 1 hour

This is not, as the name might suggest, a dessert dish but rather a savoury that also makes a tasty snack. It was not part of our family cuisine until my sister married into a typical Fukien family. They had a retinue of cooks, one of whom was a robust peasant from Amoy who made an excellent version of this cake.

Of course, sister who did not want to disgrace my mother's good Straistborn name and reputation as a cook, dug in and learnt it in next to no time and every weekend for months thereafter whenever she came visiting, we would have pumpkin cake coming out of our ears.

It's much nicer fried a little after it has been steamed. It's also a good way to cook pumpkin which does not figure very much in Chinese cooking.

1 small pumpkin to yield 2 kg (4 lbs) mashed
   pumpkin
300 g (10 oz) rice flour
30 shallots, sliced fine
10 tbsp dried shrimps, soaked and pounded a
   little
2 tsp salt
4 tbsp oil

Skin pumpkin and cut into wedges. Boil or steam until flesh is soft and cooked through. Allow to cool. Sieve rice flour and add to pumpkin mash. If its texture is too dry add a few tbsp of liquid from boiling liquid until mixture is like mashed potatoes in consistency. Heat oil and fry sliced shallots until light brown.

Add pounded dried shrimps and fry for 2 minutes before adding salt. Drain off half the oil and stir mixture into pumpkin mash. Taste for seasoning and adjust with more salt. Add a good shake of pepper if you like a spicy taste. Grease a round baking tin and fill with pumpkin mixture.

Steam for 45 minutes to 1 hour depending on how small and how low or high your tin is. When cool pumpkin cake can be cut into squares and eaten as is with chilli sauce dip or fried in oil until crisp. It's quite an unusual taste and different from the hawker version of radish cake.

Spiced Liver (Rendang Hati — Malay)

Cooking time: 10 minutes

I would have been turned off liver had I not been introduced to the Malay style of cooking this offal. As a child, whenever I showed any signs of fatigue, my mother would immediately mince a hunk of the bloody stuff — and I do mean bloody in the literal sense — pour boiling water over the mess, add a few slices of ginger and a pinch of salt and watched me down the lot in 3 seconds.

As a remedy for anaemia it supposedly knew no rival and I was expected to be gung-ho within minutes. I do not now recall if I was or not but I grew up to hate liver. It's a different story now and I have the utmost respect for this time-honoured offal.

But it's a delicate meat and deserves tender loving care in its preparation else it turns into boot leather. I fell in love with this dish that a Malay neighbour was fond of cooking during Hari Raya.

4 tbsp oil
2 large onions, sliced
3 stalks lemon grass, bruised or grated lemon rind
2 bay leaves
500 g (1 lb) calf's liver, cubed
300 g (10 oz) potatoes, cubed
1 carrot, cubed
1 tsp salt
1 tsp sugar
1 coconut, grated
400 ml (13 fl oz) water

SPICES
1 tsp turmeric powder
6 red chillies
5 cloves garlic
2 tsp cumin powder
1 tsp aniseed powder
1 tbsp coriander powder
1 tsp salt

Pound spices till fine and sets aside. Squeeze coconut with water for milk and moisten pounded spices with 2 tbsp of coconut milk. Whenever you pound spices that do not include onions, it is better to do this to aid frying.

Heat oil and fry sliced onions until soft. Add spices and fry for 2 minutes until fragrant. Add bruised lemon grass and bay leaves and fry for 1 minute more.

Add potatoes and carrots and stir for 30 seconds. Add coconut milk and simmer for 5 minutes than add cubed liver. Simmer until gravy thickens and add salt and sugar. Serve with crusty French bread.

Hainanese Chicken Rice (Chinese) (illustrated opposite)

Cooking time: 40 minutes

Although this is not strictly a festive dish, its fame having come by way of the hundreds of chicken rice stalls in Singapore, I like to cook it for special occasions. Simplicity in itself, Hainanese Chicken Rice should be elevated to the hall of fame among culinary greats.

It is, if you like, to the Chinese what Coq au Vin is to the French. Its popularity whipped around Singapore with such gusto that even posh hotel coffee houses jumped on the band wagon and began serving (some decent some not quite) versions of it.

There is no difference between what the chicken rice hawker and what the coffee house sell except for the price. You might jump on the band wagon too and attempt it at home.

CHICKEN
1 plump chicken about 2 kg (4 lbs) (it must be plump)
2.5 litres (4½ pints) water
1 large knob of ginger about the size of a walnut
2 tsp salt
2 tbsp sesame oil
3 tbsp corn or vegetable oil

RICE
5 tbsp lard or half and half lard and chicken fat
5 cloves garlic, crushed
1 stalk celery, chopped
Enough chicken stock (see above) to cover rice up to 3 cm (1¼ in) above level of rice.
1 tsp salt

SAUCES
6 red chillies
2 cloves garlic
1 tsp salt
2 tbsp vinegar

1 large knob ginger about 100 g (3 oz)
½ tsp salt
1 tbsp oil

Clean chicken and rub all over with a little salt. Cut ginger into two and bruise one piece. Put into chicken cavity. Bring water to the boil and put chicken together with the rest of the ginger and salt and cover.

Boil over medium heat for 6 minutes and turn off heat. Allow to cool completely and turn on flame again. Simmer for another 20 minutes and remove chicken immediately. Plunge chicken into cold water and hang up with a deep plate underneath to catch liquid. Mix two oils and rub chicken all over with mixture. When cool enough, cut up and serve with chicken rice.

Wash rice and drain. Heat oil and fry garlic and chopped celery for 2 minutes. Add rice and stir for a few minutes making sure rice does not stick to pan. Transfer to rice cooker or deep pot and add stock.

Cook over moderate heat until almost dry. Stir rice once to separate grains and cover to finish cooking. Turn off heat after 5 minutes and serve with chicken and sliced cucumber, spring onions and sliced tomatoes.

Traditionally chicken rice is served with the trio of chilli sauce, ginger sauce and thick black soy sauce.

Pound chillies and garlic till fine. Add vinegar and salt.

Pound ginger until fine and mix with salt and oil.

Deep-fried Spiced Spring Chicken (Chinese)

Cooking time: 15 minutes

More and more, Singaporeans are opting for fast-to-cook dishes for entertaining and fried chicken, in one form or another, remains a firm favourite. This one is ideal for small parties and very tender inside and crisp outside if properly cooked. Use a chicken no more than 650 g (1¼ lbs) in weight. Any heavier or older and it might as well be boiling fowl.

1 spring chicken, trussed but with head intact
3 tbsp Chinese wine
2 tbsp black soy sauce
1 tsp pepper
2 tsp salt
1 tsp sugar
3 tbsp ginger juice
Oil for deep frying
Cucumber slices for garnish

Clean chicken inside and out and dry thoroughly. Mix wine with soy sauce, pepper, salt, sugar and ginger juice and marinate chicken for 1 hour. Turn every 15 minutes so every part of chicken is steeped in marinade.

Drain after an hour or longer. Heat oil until smoking and deep fry for 10 minutes or so. To test if chicken is done, poke a metal skewer through thickest part of thigh. If no blood oozes out chicken is done. Serve cut up and garnished with cucumber slices.

Fried Tientsin Cabbage (Gai Choy) in Crab Sauce

Cooking time: 30 minutes

Fresh Tientsin cabbage or Gai Choy as it is called in Cantonese is a large, cabbage-like vegetable with pale green colouring throughout. It is from this that the salted vegetable so famous in Chinese cooking is made. It has a rather nut-like bitter taste eaten fresh and must be first scalded before being fried or steamed.

400 g (13 oz) Tienstsin Cabbage (tinned)
3 tbsp lard
3 cloves garlic, crushed
250 g (½ lb) crab meat
250 g (½ lb) prawns, shelled
500 ml (16 fl oz) water
2 tbsp cornflour
2 tsp salt
1 tsp sugar
1 tbsp light soy sauce
2 tbsp sesame oil
1 tsp pepper
2 eggs

Boil plenty of water and blanch cabbage cut into large pieces. Blanch for 3 minutes and run under cold tap immediately. This helps to refresh the colour and texture. Drain and set aside. Heat lard and fry crushed garlic until brown. Add prawns and crab meat and fry for 1 minute. Mix cornflour with water and add to pan. Bring to the boil and add all other seasoning. Crack two eggs in and stir well to diffuse. Add scalded vegetables and simmer for 30 seconds. Serve hot.

Mee Siam (Thai)

Cooking time: 30 minutes

As the name indicates, this dish came to Singapore by way of Siam, the old name for Thailand and is now firmly entrenched in Singapore cooking. There are as many versions of Mee Siam as there are nationalities here and each is delicious in its own way.

There's mild Mee Siam as the Malays cook it. The Indians have a version which uses few ingredients and the Straitsborn Chinese go to town with coconut milk, tamarind and a spicy prawn sambal.

The version here is of course Straitsborn and my firm favourite because it makes an excellent dish for entertaining. Once prepared you can sit back and enjoy it with your guests without to-ing and fro-ing, fetching and carrying.

1 packet coarse vermicelli
200 g (½ lb) beansprouts
150 g (5 oz) chives
500 g (1 lb) small prawns
4 tbsp oil
4 firm soy bean cakes or tofu
5 tbsp oil
2 large onions, sliced
300 ml (½ pint) water
2 tbsp tamarind paste
5 hard-boiled eggs

SPICES
4 large onions
4 cloves garlic
10 almonds
15 dried chillies, soaked till soft
2 tbsp shrimp paste or powder
2 tsp sugar
1 tsp salt

GRAVY
3 litres (5½ pints) water
5 tbsp tamarind paste
4 tbsp of fried spices (see method)
3 tbsp preserved soy beans, washed and
  drained
3 tsp sugar
¼ coconut, grated
200 ml (7 fl oz) water

Boil large amount of water and scald vermicelli until soft and strands are pliable. If you cannot get coarse vermicelli the fine type will do as well.

Treat as you would the coarse type. Wash beansprouts and cut chives into 5 cm (2 in) lengths. Wash and peel prawns. Heat 4 tbsp oil and fry soy bean cakes until brown. Cut into fine pieces.

SPICES
Pound or blend all spices except sugar and salt until fine. Reheat oil and fry the 2 sliced onions until soft. Add pounded spices and fry for 3 minutes until fragrant. Add sugar and salt and fry for 1 minute more. Scoop up about half the mixture and set aside.

To the remaining spices add prawns and first amount of tamarind and water (300 ml (½ pint) and 2 tbsp). Simmer for 3 minutes and scoop up to reserve as garnish. Take half of the remaining lot of fried spices and put back in the pan. Fry scalded vermicelli and bean sprouts, stirring all the while, for about 10 minutes.

Sprinkle with tamarind liquid from the gravy allowance if vermicelli gets too dry. Add soy beancurd and half the chives and stir well. Adjust with little more salt if necessary. Dish up and arrange on a large plate. Garnish with sliced hard-boiled eggs and chives.

GRAVY
Mix tamarind paste with water and strain off pulp. Bring to the boil and add fried spices, soy beans, sugar and coconut milk from squeezing grated coconut with water. Add sugar or salt to adjust taste and serve Mee Siam with prawn sambal.

Buddhist Vegetarian Stew (illustrated opposite)

Cooking time: 45 minutes or more

This is a favourite Chinese New Year dish because it tempers the surfeit of meat and fowl meals beautifully. I learnt it first from one of our family retainers, a lady from the Fukien province of South China. Many years later, after I married my Cantonese wife, her mother rekindled the vegetarian ilk in me by unfailingly producing the same dish on Chinese New Year's Eve.

And the beautiful thing is that it tastes better the day or even two days after. Such is the mystery of certain Chinese dishes that really know no regional boundaries cooked as they are by Cantonese, Fukien and Swatow peoples. Festive dishes, in fact, transcend all barriers in modern Singapore because non-Chinese are just as likely to cook them during their festivals having learnt from friends.

1 litre (1¾ pints) oil for deep frying
3 tbsp sesame oil
20 fresh dates
20 gingko nuts (tinned variety)
10 dried Chinese mushrooms
1 can straw mushrooms
30 g (1 oz) "hair vegetable" (In Cantonese this
    is pronounced Fatt Choy which is the same
    meaning as prosperity, thus its appearance
    during Chinese New Year)
20 mange tout
4 tbsp tree fungus
½ Chinese cabbage
2 bunches transparent vermicelli
2 squares preserved red beancurd
1 large knob ginger about 70 g (2¼ oz)
4 cloves garlic, crushed
2 tbsp sugar
1 litre water (1¾ pints) or more if necessary

Soak dried mushrooms, tree fungus and hair vegetable in hot water for 5 minutes. Drain and dry thoroughly.

Cut Chinese cabbage into 5 cm (2 in) lengths, wash and dry. Soak vermicelli in water until soft and drain. All ingredients must be clean and absolutely dry for the next step.

Heat oil until smoking and add sesame oil. Using a wire mesh ladle lower each ingredient separately and deep-fry for 30 seconds. This seals in all the natural juices and keeps them crisp even after being stewed.

Drain all deep-fried ingredients and remove all but 4 tbsp oil. Bruise knob of ginger and fry in hot oil. Mash preserved red bean curd and add to pan. Fry for 1 or 2 minutes and add all ingredients including sugar and water. Stew for 40 minutes or so over low heat.

When you reheat the next day or the next, add a little more water and 2 tbsp of oyster sauce for seasoning. I have left oyster sauce out in the recipe because it's not strictly necessary as the rich compote of ingredients have their own natural flavours.

Teochew Spiced Duck (Chinese)

Cooking time: 45 minutes

This may seem a very simple dish, calling as it does, for not much more than a good, fat duck and soy sauce. But like the famous Hainanese Chicken Rice it is magnificent eating when well-done.

The secret lies in the balance of flavours in the sauce in which the duck is left to simmer for as long as it takes to tenderise. Then comes the chilli and garlic sauce which is an integral part of the whole. Here again, there is no mystique but good vinegar and fresh chillies.

1 duck about 1.5 kg (3 lbs)
250 ml (8 fl oz) good, black soy sauce
3 tbsp sugar
2 tsp salt
2 litres (3½ pints) water or more if needed

CHILLI SAUCE
6 red chillies
3 cloves garlic
5 tbsp malt or rice vinegar
1 tsp salt

Buy a duck with the head still on. This is important, whatever your feelings about fowl ends in general and duck's heads in particular, because you need to manipulate the duck around in the simmering gravy and the curve of the neck is where you grip the duck with chopsticks or tongs.

Heat a large wok or non-stick pan till smoking. Add sugar in dry pan and stir vigorously to caramelise.

Add the whole duck and make sure every inch is coated with this glaze. Dribble in a few drops of soy sauce if caramel threatens to burn. When duck is well coated, add soy sauce and continue turning the duck well around till it turns a rich, red brown.

Add water and salt and simmer for 45 minutes, turning every now and then to make sure duck is cooked through.

Do not leave duck to soak in gravy once it's cooked. Remove and boil gravy down to about half its amount. Dissolve 3 tbsp cornflour in water and add to simmering gravy. Remove from heat when it thickens. Serve this in a gravy boat with duck.

Pound chillies and garlic till fine. Mix with vinegar and salt and serve with duck.

Top Hats (Kuih Pie Tee — Chinese)

Cooking time: 45 minutes

These crispy little cups, shaped like top hats, when filled with a compote of bamboo shoots, prawns and pork make tasty tidbits for entertaining. I'm not sure how the name was derived but one version has it that it was originally filled with a sweetmeat mixture and served as kuih party or party cakes. Today, kuih pie tee is very much an item in the Singapore cuisine and once you have mastered how to make the batter cups the rest is relatively easy.

BATTER FOR PIE TEE
300 g (10 oz) plain flour, sifted
5 eggs, lightly beaten
1 tsp salt
600 ml (1 pint) water
Oil for deep frying

5 tbsp oil
2 cakes hard beancurd or tofu
4 cloves garlic, crushed and
** mashed**
400 g (13 oz) bamboo shoots, shredded
300 g (10 oz) runner beans, shredded
300 g (10 oz) prawns, shelled
300 ml (½ pint) water
1 cucumber, peeled and shredded fine
3 bunches coriander leaves
4 tbsp chilli sauce

Put flour in a deep bowl and make a well in the centre. Add water a little at a time and mix into a thickish batter. Stir eggs in slowly and incorporate until batter has the consistency of condensed milk. Add salt and strain through fine wire sieve or muslin cloth. Allow to stand for 30 minutes.

Heat oil in a deep container (not a wok). Heat the pie tee mould in oil and dip into batter up to rim of mould. Return to hot oil quickly and fry for 1 or 2 minutes until batter cup separates and floats away. Lift out with slotted spoon and drain on kitchen paper. When cool, store in airtight tins.

Heat oil and fry beancurd until brown. Remove to cool and shred fine. Reheat oil and fry crushed garlic until brown. Add preserved soy beans and fry for 1 minute. Add prawns, bamboo, runner beans and water and simmer for 25 minutes. Add more water if mixture is too dry and adjust seasoning with a little more salt.

Keep warm and serve in a deep bowl with another small bowl upturned in it. This allows each person to scoop up filling without too much liquid to fill pie tee cups. Top with shredded cucumber, coriander leaves and chilli sauce.

Double-boiled Spring Chicken and Mushroom Soup (Chinese)

Cooking time: 1 hour

600 ml (1 pint) water
1 spring chicken about 650 g (1¼ lbs)
8 Chinese mushrooms
2 tsp salt
1 tsp pepper
2 tbsp chopped spring onions

Wash chicken and remove head, neck and claws. Put in soup container of double boiler with water. Fill lower container with water up to halfway mark and bring to boil. Soak mushrooms and remove stalks. Add to soup with salt. Double boil for an hour and serve with pepper and spring onions.

Steamboat (Chinese)

Probably one of the most impressive and heart-warming ways to dine; the steamboat has chugged, bubbled and simmered its way into the hearts of not only Singaporeans, but visitors too. Utterly charmed by its hearty goodness, many a foreign tourist has lugged back home steamboats with charcoal burners and a few electric models.

The latter, while not having as much character, is perfect for entertaining in a flat where you do not have an open patio to dispel the plumes of steam from the steamboat funnel. What's best about having steamboat is you don't have to know how to cook.

You don't even have to have stock if the list of ingredients used is extensive, as by the end of half an hour you will have a rich stock anyway.

5 or 6 litres (9 pints) meat stock or water
250 g (½ lb) chicken breast, diced
250 g (½ lb) fillet beef, sliced thin
250 g (½ lb) fillet pork, sliced thin
200 g (7 oz) liver, sliced
400 g (13 oz) prawns, shelled
250 g (½ lb) squid, sliced
250 g (½ lb) firm white fish (monkfish or huss)
** sliced and marinated in oil**
40 fishballs (available from Chinese grocers)
** boiled for 5 minutes**
500 g (1 lb) Chinese cabbage, sliced
1 whole head lettuce any variety
10 eggs
250 g (8 oz) lard
300 ml (½ pint) light soy sauce
Salt and pepper for each diner

The food list is a typical one but there is no reason why you cannot improvise and toss in things that you can find in your supermarkets. The whole range of seafood from lobsters to mussels and cockles can be cooked in the steamboat.

Likewise, you may opt for a meat-only steamboat or a strictly vegetarian meal. If you are using stock, pre-heat to boiling point and pour around the funnel. If using charcoal, heat charcoal until glowing and place in funnel making sure embers do not drop onto your table. Place a thick chopping board or any protective plate on your table before serving steamboat. This is not necessary with an electric model.

Place all ingredients in individual plates or bowls. Provide chopsticks, spoons and little brass wire ladles for scalding food. Let each diner take as much or as little as pleases and make his own combination. Individual soup bowls and dips of light soy sauce should also be provided so seasoning can be done to taste rather than season the whole steamboat.

Remember that most of the sliced ingredients take only a few seconds to cook — pork must be completely cooked — and the soup drunk only after some cooking has been done so you get a rich taste.

Yellow Rice (Nasi Kuning — Malay) (illustrated on p. 114/115)

Cooking time: 20 minutes

This is traditionally served with grilled chicken or deep fried tamarind prawns.

1 kg (2 lbs) glutinous rice
3 cm (1¼ in) piece fresh turmeric
4 screwpine leaves (or vanilla pods)
2 tbsp lime juice
1 coconut, grated
750 ml (1¼ pints) water
2 tsp salt

Ideally, glutinous rice should be soaked in enough water to cover it and mixed with pounded turmeric and lime juice overnight.

Drain glutinous rice and spread in a deep tray for steaming. Wash screwpine leaves and tie into a knot. Push it deep among the rice grains. Squeeze coconut with water for milk.

Pour half of coconut milk into rice, add salt and steam for 5 minutes. Check if rice is well moistened and sprinkle more coconut milk all over if necessary. Continue steaming for 5 more minutes until grains are cooked.

Satay (recipe on p. 206).

Satay (Beef, Pork or Chicken — Malay) (illustrated on p. 204)

Cooking time: 10 minutes

1 kg (2 lbs) beef, chicken or pork
2 tbsp coriander powder
1 tbsp cumin powder
1 tsp aniseed powder
1 large onion
3 cloves garlic
2 stalks lemon grass or grated lemon rind
3 slices ginger
2 tsp salt
1 tsp turmeric powder
2 tsp sugar
3 tbsp oil
40 satay skewers

SATAY SAUCE

If you can find a specialist food store that sells ready-made satay sauce, it's a boon. Otherwise, you simply have to knuckle down to make your own and while you're at it you might as well make more to refrigerate for another day. I have taken the liberty of using commercial peanut peanut butter (crunchy) and the sky did not fall when I served it to friends. They, believe me, did not know the difference.

3 tbsp oil
10 dried chillies, soaked till soft
2 medium onions
10 ground almonds
2 cloves garlic
1 stalk lemon grass or grated lemon rind
750 g (1 ½ lbs) crunchy peanut butter
2 tbsp tamarind paste
500 ml (16 fl oz) water
2 tbsp sugar
1 tsp salt

Cut meat into small pieces that can be threaded through skewers. Pound a little with blunt edge of cleaver. Combine all other ingredients in a blender until fine and marinate meat in mixture for at least 2 hours. Thread skewers up to slightly more than half the length to leave a short end for handling during boiling. Brush each skewer with a little oil and cook on hot charcoal for five to 10 minutes. Serve with chunks of raw onion, cucumber and compressed rice cakes and satay gravy.

The skill in making the coconut frond compressed rice baskets (ketupat) is within the grasp of mainly the Malays and my attempts at learning how to weave them are best not talked about. The compressed rice cakes (page 271) serve just as well.

Pound or blend chillies, onions, almonds, garlic, lemon grass until fine. Heat oil and fry until fragrant and red oil seeps out again. Mix tamarind with water and add to spices. Bring to the boil and add peanut butter, sugar and salt and simmer over slow fire until oil rises to the top. Adjust thickness of gravy with more or less peanut butter and tamarind liquid to the consistency desired.

Singapore Salad (Rojak — Indonesian)

Preparation time: 30 minutes

This delectable spicy salad is believed to hail from Java originally and the enterprising Singaporean in the heyday of itinerant hawkers adopted and adapted it to what we know it as today. Just about every hawker complex in Singapore sells one version or another and slummers will have their favourite rojak stall north, south, east and west of here. As a special occasion dish, I like to serve it direct from the glazed earthenware bowl in which it is made.

200 g (7 oz) beansprouts, washed and tailed
200 g (7 oz) water convolvulus or spinach
300 g (10 oz) runner beans
1 small pineapple
1 cucumber
4 squares dried beancurd
2 small green mangoes
1 small sweet potato
3 limes

SAUCE
200 g (7 oz) fried, skinned peanuts
5 dried chillies, soaked till soft
1 tbsp shrimp paste, toasted
3 tbsp prawn paste
2 tbsp brown sugar
2 tbsp tamarind paste
150 ml (5 fl oz) water
1 tsp salt

Boil plenty of water and scald beansprouts for 20 seconds. Scald water convolvulus for 1 minute until limp. Cut into 4 cm (1 ½ in) lengths and drain well. Peel pineapple and cucumber and cut into fine slices. Cut beancurd square into strips or whichever way you want.

Wash mangoes and runner beans well and cut into small pieces. Peel sweet potatoes and slice into fine pieces.

Take a handful of each prepared ingredient and mix well for one portion serving. When well mixed, squeeze a little lime juice over, add 1 or 2 tbsp pounded peanuts. Never make rojak in bulk to wait for guests or you'll end up with a watery mess. Use only the best quality prawn paste and if too thick, may be mixed with a little boiled water.

Pound peanuts beforehand and put in small bowl. Clean basin and put in soaked and drained chillies. Use the wooden mallet that comes with the earthen basin to grind chillies in a circular motion. Add shrimp paste and salt and grind for a few seconds. Add sugar, prawn paste, tamarind paste mixed with water and stir well.

Take a handful of each prepared ingredient and mix well for one portion serving. When well mixed, squeeze a little lime juice over, add 1 or 2 tbsp pounded peanuts. Never make rojak in bulk to wait for guests or you'll end up with a watery mess. Use only the best quality prawn paste and if too thick, may be mixed with a little boiled water.

Eurasian Mixed Meat Curry (Feng)

Cooking time: 45 minutes

The impoverished moments of my early life were given a great boost by my Eurasian neighbours. And there were many to the left, right and front of our home. I never knew what Christmas meant — our family was strictly Taoist — until invited to a few of parties held by the Wilson family. I still remember fondly Auntie Minnie and Uncle Alfred, both of whom could cook up a storm. It was during their Christmas parties that I was introduced to Feng, a compote of different meats in a spicy gravy.

4 tbsp oil
200 g (7 oz) pork (belly or leg with some fat)
200 g (7 oz) sirloin beef
200 g (7 oz) pig's liver
1 pair pig's kidneys
200 g (7 oz) tripe
2 tsp cinnamon powder
2 tsp salt
½ star anise
2 large onions, quartered
4 potatoes quartered
400 ml (13 fl oz) sherry or ordinary red wine
100 ml (3½ fl oz) malt vinegar

MARINADE
3 tbsp coriander powder
1 tbsp cumin powder
1 tbsp aniseed powder
1 tsp pepper
½ tsp turmeric powder
2 large onions
4 slices ginger
6 cloves garlic
3 tbsp brown sugar
1 tsp vinegar

Cut pork, beef and tripe into bite-sized pieces. Buy pre-cooked tripe to save time as raw tripe takes several hours to tenderise. Wash kidney's and remove white membrane to reduce ammonia smell.

Boil kidney and liver whole for 3 minutes and allow to cool. Dice as with meats. Blend all marinade ingredients well and pour over meats in a casserole. Refrigerate for 2-3 hours.

Heat oil and fry whole spices for 1 minute. Add marinated meats, salt and onions and fry for 3 minutes until almost dry and meats well sealed. Add wine and vinegar and bring to the boil. Simmer for 30 minutes.

Add potatoes and simmer for 25 minutes more or until potatoes are soft but do not fall apart. Adjust seasoning and serve hot.

Coconut Rice (Nasi Lemak — Malay)

Cooking time: 15 minutes

300 g (10 oz) rice
300 ml (1½ pint) water
1 coconut, grated
500 ml (16 fl oz) water
1 tsp salt
2 screwpine leaves (or vanilla pods)

Wash rice in several changes of water and drain. Put rice and 300 ml (½ pint) of water in a steaming tray. Squeeze coconut with 500 ml (16 fl oz) water for milk. Mix coconut milk with salt and stir into rice.

Push screwpine leaves into rice and steam for 10 minutes.

Coconut rice is traditional served with sambal ikan bilis (p 35), fried tamarind prawns (p 188) chicken curry (p 209), plain omelette and sliced cucumber.

Chicken Curry (Straits Chinese)

Cooking time: 20 minutes

5 tbsp oil
3 tbsp shredded ginger
10 shallots, pounded roughly
1 chicken about 1 kg (2 lbs)
500 g (1 lb) potatoes
1 coconut, grated
1 litre (1 ¾ pints) water
2 tsp salt

SPICES
4 tbsp curry powder
4 tbsp water

Squeeze coconut with water for milk. Cut chicken into bite-sized joints. Mix curry paste and rub 1 tbsp all over chicken pieces. Leave aside.

Heat oil and fry garlic and onions until light brown but not crisp. Add curry paste and stir-fry until fragrant. Add chicken pieces and stir well until coated.

Add coconut milk and bring to the boil. Skin potatoes and cut into two. Add potatoes after five minutes of simmering. Simmer for 15 minutes more.

Spicy Beancurd Soup (Straits Chinese)

Cooking time: 10 minutes

4 tbsp oil
100 g (3 oz) cod with bones
200 g (7 oz) small prawns, shelled
750 ml (1 ¼ pints) water
1 tsp fish sauce
½ tsp pepper
1 large piece beancurd (soft) silken tofu
Pepper
1 bunch coriander leaves

SPICES
8 almonds
2 large onions
2 red chillies
1 tbsp belacan (shrimp paste)

Pound spices till fine. Soak cod in water for 5 minutes and cut beancurd into large chunks. Heat oil and fry spices till fragrant. Drain cod and add to spices. Fry for 2 minutes and add prawns, water, fish sauce and ½ tsp pepper. Bring to the boil and add beancurd to simmer for 3 minutes. Serve with extra dash of pepper and chopped coriander leaves.

SIMPLY STRAITSBORN

This truly ethnic Singaporean cooking comes closest to my heart and stomach. It is the result of marriage between Malay and Chinese culinary styles with a sprinkling of Indian, Indonesian and Thai influences that make it a unique hybrid not found anywhere else in the world. The recipes in this section do not do total justice to the beautiful heritage that is Straitsborn cuisine but have been included in this book as a sort of appetiser.

I have chosen the classics of Straitsborn cooking with some modification to make them easier and within reach of more people. I believe a beginner is not going to be very inspired if faced with complicated recipes that really have short cuts that rob nothing from the finished product.

Fish in Thick Tamarind Gravy (Ikan Masak Asam Pekat)

Cooking time: 15 minutes

4 mackerel steaks cut into bite-sized cubes
1 tsp salt
4 tbsp tamarind paste
400 ml (13 fl oz) water
3 tbsp sugar
1 tsp salt
4 green chillies
4 red chillies
1 tsp lard or oil

SPICES
½ tsp powdered turmeric
2 tbsp shrimp paste
10 shallots

Pound or blend spices to a fine paste. Slit both types of chillies lengthwise almost to the stalk and deseed for milder flavour. Remove stalk, wash and drain. Wash fish and rub with salt.

Mix tamarind paste with water to a thick paste and discard pith. Use a wire strainer with large holes to do this or use your fingers. Blend tamarind liquid, pounded spices, sugar and salt and simmer over low heat for 10 minutes. Add fish after washing off salt and simmer for 5 to 6 minutes more. Add chillies last and simmer for 1 minute. Put in lard or oil last and serve with compressed rice.

Singapore Salad (Jaganan)

Cooking time: 15 minutes

This is a favourite Straits Chinese salad that is a meal in itself and excellent for entertaining. Once you have prepared the vegetables and sauce it leaves you free to be the perfect host or hostess because guests simply help themselves and create their own salads with more or less of this or that.

200 g (7 oz) water convolvulus (use spinach as a substitute)
½ cabbage
10 French beans
200 g (7 oz) beansprouts
2 soy bean cakes (taukwa) or tofu
2 tbsp oil
3 hard-boiled eggs
1 cucumber
Prawn crackers (substitute with potato crisps)

GRAVY
10 dried chillies
1 tbsp shrimp paste powder
10 shallots
10 pieces peanut brittle or
10 tbsp crunchy peanut butter
600 ml (1 pint) water
3 tbsp tamarind paste
1 tsp salt

Scald water convolvulus or spinach for 1 minute in hot water. Make little bundles with each stalk. Cut cabbage and long beans into serving sizes and scald for 1 minute. Scald bean sprouts for 20 seconds.

Fry soy bean cakes in oil until light brown then quarter and cut into 1 cm (½ in) thick slices. Slice hard-boiled eggs into quarters. Cut cucumber into wedge-shape pieces. Arrange all ingredients on a large platter.

GRAVY
Soak dried chillies in hot water for 2 minutes and pound with shrimp paste and shallots. Pound peanut brittle separately until fine.

Mix tamarind with water and bring to the boil. Add all pounded ingredients and salt and simmer for 5 minutes.

If gravy is too thin simply add more pounded peanut brittle or peanut butter. Pour over vegetables and garnish with prawn crackers or crisps.

Alternatively, let each diner make his own combination and pour a few tablespoons of gravy over his concoction.

Duck and Salted Vegetable Soup

Cooking time: 1 hour

There is no reason why you cannot use chicken instead for this Straitsborn classic though the characteristic richness will be missing.

1 whole duck, cut into 6 pieces
1 tbsp brandy
500 g (1 lb) salted vegetable
3 litres (5½ pints) water (2 if you are using a pressure cooker)
200 g (7 oz) foreleg of pork or a small hind trotter
2 tomatoes
1 piece tamarind skin
3 green chillies
1 tbsp brandy or sherry

Rub duck pieces all over with brandy and set aside for 10 minutes. Soak salted vegetable in several changes of water for 10 minutes to reduce their salt content.

Bring water to the boil and put duck and trotters, cut into pieces, to simmer for a good hour. Pressure cooking will take less than half the time and does not alter the taste one bit.

Add the rest of the ingredients in the last ten minutes of simmering on the range. Do not pressure-cook vegetables or they will disintegrate. To serve, break green chillies over soup and add more brandy if desired.

Chicken in Coriander (Ayam Sio)

Cooking time: 40 minutes

This is a variation of the classic Itek Sio (Duck Sio) or duck braised in coriander and spices and takes a lot less time to cook. Substituting duck with chicken is perfectly acceptable. Since it requires assiduous watching over the kwali (wok) or whatever deep fry pan you use, it makes sense to adapt the recipe for chicken. A duck takes something like 1½ hours to cook.

What's important about this dish is the glaze on the fowl when it it is cooked. My mother would look her nose down at any attempt to do this dish if the gleam on the duck did not come up to scratch. But for many today, the gleam of hunger should suffice and if at first you don't succeed, why not glaze, glaze and glaze again?

1 chicken about 1.5 kg (3 lbs)
3 tbsp coriander powder, dry-fried in a clean pan until fragrant
2 tsp pepper
2 tbsp sugar
2 tsp salt
4 tbsp thick, black soy sauce
4 tbsp oil
20 shallots, sliced fine or roughly pounded
2 litres (3½ pints) water
5 cm (2 in) stick cinnamon
6 cloves
2 bunches fresh coriander leaves
2 stalks spring onions

Wipe chicken all over after cleaning with kitchen paper. Rub all over with coriander, pepper, sugar, salt and soy sauce.
Marinate for 30 minutes.

Heat oil in a non-stick pan if you have one and fry shallots until light brown but not crisp. Put in chicken and fry, turning constantly to make sure every inch of skin is brown.

Using a non-stick pan means less likelihood of burning and tearing the chicken skin. When chicken is well-sizzled, add water, cinnamon and cloves and simmer. Keep turning chicken and spooning gravy over while it is simmering.

Cover from time to time for the chicken to cook faster but this could rob chicken of some of its glaze eventually. Chicken should be ready when liquid is reduced by two-thirds.

Chop coriander leaves. Cut spring onions into 4 cm (1½ in) lengths and slit at both ends to make flower petals. Soak in ice-water. Serve chicken whole and let diners cut and come again. Garnish with fresh coriander and onions.

Mixed Vegetable Soup (Chap Chye) (illustrated opposite)

Cooking time: 40 minutes

30 lily buds or golden needles
3 tbsp tree fungus
30 g (1 oz) transparent vermicelli
6 Chinese mushrooms
300 g (10 oz) prawns, shelled
2 tbsp oil
5 tbsp oil
4 cloves garlic, pounded
2 tbsp preserved soy bean, mashed
300 g (10 oz) belly pork, cut into bite-sized
    pieces
¼ cabbage, cut into large pieces
2 tsp salt
2 litres (3½ pints) water

Soak lily buds, fungus, vermicelli and mushrooms in water for 10 minutes. Wash and shell prawns. Drain dried ingredients. Remove hard tails of lily buds and tie each into a firm knot.

Heat oil and fry garlic until brown. Add preserved soy bean and fry for 1 minute.

Add pork, cabbage and lily buds and fry for 2 minutes. Add remaining ingredients and fry for 1 minute more. Transfer to large pot. Add water, salt and simmer for 30 minutes.

Minced Pork and Crab Soup (Bakwan Kepiting)

Cooking time: 20 minutes

2 large crabs or
300 g (10 oz) crab meat
200 g (7 oz) prawns
300 g (10 oz) minced pork
2 bunches coriander leaves, chopped fine
1 tsp salt
5 tbsp oil
10 cloves garlic, crushed
1 tbsp cornflour
1 small can bamboo shoots
2 litres (3½ pints) water
2 tsp salt
1 bunch coriander leaves, chopped
1 tsp pepper

If using live crabs, wash and steam for 5 minutes until they change colour. Remove meat and reserve row. Keep shells for stuffing mixture into later.

Obviously if you are using ready-flaked crab meat you won't have shells but make mixture into meat balls. Chop prawns roughly and mix with minced pork, crab meat, chopped coriander leaves and 1 tsp salt.

Heat oil and fry garlic until light brown. Scoop out about 2 tbsp and add to mixture. Add cornflour and knead well.

Cut bamboo shoots into fine shreds and add to mixture.

Stuff crab shells with some of the mixture, reserving the rest to make into meatballs. Bring water to the boil. Add crab shells and meat balls and simmer for 4 minutes.

Season to taste and garnish with fresh coriander leaves and fried garlic.

Melon Soup (top, recipe on p. 280).
Mixed Vegetable Soup.

Fried Noodles (Nonya Mee Teochew Style)

Cooking time: 25 minutes

Visitors to Singapore and Singaporeans themselves are no doubt familiar with the well-known Nonya Mee — noodles fried in a preserved bean gravy and garnished with egg and cucumber. This version was one my family prepared often and which I enjoy as much. It's simpler if less rich because the Teochews were not overly fond of rich sauces which perhaps accounts for their beautiful complexions.

My mother was from the Teochew stock of Straits Chinese and though my father often sniffed at her Teochew cooking, nevertheless enjoyed the dishes. My mother, of course, could cook the entire range of Straits Chinese dishes and, thankfully, passed on the knowledge to me before she passed on.

200 g (7 oz) belly pork, skinned
2 litres (3½ pints) water
300 g (10 oz) prawns
5 tbsp oil
4 cloves garlic
250 g (½ lb) fresh yellow noodles
200 g (7 oz) beansprouts, tailed
300 g (10 oz) mustard greens, cut into pieces
2 tsp salt
1 tsp monosodium glutamate

INGREDIENTS FOR GARNISH
10 shallots, sliced fine
1 cucumber
2 eggs
1 bunch fresh coriander leaves, chopped
3 red chillies

Boil belly pork in 2 litres (3½ pints) water for 20 minutes. Remove and reserve stock. Shell prawns but leave tails on. When pork is sufficiently cooled, cut into thin slices or strips.

Heat oil and fry sliced shallots until brown and crisp. Dish up and set aside. In remaining oil fry crushed garlic until brown and add beansprouts and mustard greens.

Fry for 1 minute and add noodles to stir for 3 minutes. Add stock and bring to the boil. Simmer for 3 minutes and add pork and prawns to simmer for 2 minutes more. Add seasoning and dish up onto large serving platter.

GARNISHES
Skin cucumber with a sharp knife and cut into paper-thin strips. Beat eggs and fry in a little oil to make an omelette. Shred finely.

Slice red chillies. Garnish fried noodles with cucumber, egg, coriander, fried onions and chillies and serve with a side dish of sambal belacan.

Chicken Opor (illustrated on p. 218)

Cooking time: 30 minutes

1 chicken about 1 kg (2 lbs)
1 coconut, grated
500 ml (16 fl oz) water
1 stalk lemon grass, bruised or grated lemon
   rind
2 tsp salt
2 tbsp tamarind powder or lemon juice
200 ml (7 fl oz) water

SPICES
3 red chillies
10 skinned almonds
1 large onion
3 cloves garlic
2 tbsp coriander powder
1 tsp aniseed powder
1 tbsp shrimp paste powder

Cut chicken into 8 pieces. Squeeze coconut with water for milk. Pound spices till fine and blend with coconut milk. Bring to the boil and add chicken joints.

Simmer for 20 minutes add lemon grass and salt. Add tamarind mixed with water at this stage. Simmer for 10 minutes more and serve with crusty French bread.

Chicken with Bamboo Shoots

Cooking time: 30 minutes

3 pieces canned bamboo shoot
1 chicken about 1 kg (2 lbs)
300 g (10 oz) prawns, shelled
1 coconut, grated
1.5 litres (2¼ pints) water
4 tbsp oil
2 tsp salt
1 tsp sugar

SPICES
10 dried chillies, soaked till soft
4 red chillies
2 tsp lemon grass powder or grated lemon rind
2 tsp shrimp paste powder
1 tsp pepper
1 tsp turmeric powder
2 tbsp coriander powder

Slice bamboo shoots into ½ cm (¼ in) thick pieces, wash and drain. Cut chicken into 8 joints or smaller bite-sized pieces if you wish. Squeeze coconut with water for milk.

You should get about 2 litres (3½ pints) of milk. Pound or blend spices till fine. Heat oil and fry until fragrant. Add chicken pieces and fry until they are completely coated with spice mixture. Add coconut milk and simmer for 15 minutes. Add bamboo shoots and simmer for 10 minutes.

Thai-style Cucumber Salad

Cooking time: 5 minutes

This is a variation of the Straits Chinese Sambal Timun or cucumber salad but it could just as well be the source from which the latter version evolved. Straits Chinese cooking, especially in north Malaysia, has been influenced by Thai cooking for many decades.

2 cucumbers
1 large onion
1 big bunch coriander leaves
2 red chillies

SEASONING
3 tbsp dried shrimps
1 tbsp fish sauce — in this instance only Thai fish sauce will do. It's called Nam Pla and is sometimes available in Chinese emporiums
3 limes or more if necessary
1 tbsp sugar

Peel cucumbers and, using a vegetable slicer, shred cucumber thinly.

Cut again to get fine strips. Finely shred onion and mix with cucumbers.

Set aside in a refrigerator to chill slightly. Soak dried prawns in a little hot water and pound till fine.

Mix with lime juice, fish sauce and sugar just before serving so it won't become watery.

Grey Mullet Curry (Masak Pedas)

Cooking time: 10 minutes

3 tbsp oil
1 stalk lemon grass, bruised or grated lemon rind
2 tbsp tamarind powder
750 ml (1¼ pints) water
1 grey mullet
1 tsp salt
1 tsp sugar
1 tsp black soy sauce

SPICES
1 large onion
8 almonds
1 tbsp shrimp paste powder

Pound or blend spices until fine. Heat oil and fry spices until fragrant. Add lemon grass and fry for 1 minute more. Mix tamarind with water and add to pan.

Bring to the boil. While gravy is simmering, gut grey mullet and cut into large chunks; add to gravy and simmer for 5 minutes, then add salt, sugar and soy sauce.

Fish in Pepper Gravy (Ikan Kuah Lada) (illustrated on p. 219)

Cooking time: 10 minutes

500 g (1 lb) mackerel
2 aubergines
4 tbsp oil
1 stalk lemon grass, bruised or grated lemon rind
4 tbsp tamarind powder
750 ml (1¼ pints) water
1 tsp salt

SPICES
2 red chillies
4 almonds
2 cloves garlic
12 shallots
1 tsp turmeric powder
2 tbsp pepper

Pound or blend spices till fine. Cut fish into large steaks.

Half aubergines lengthwise. Remove stalk and make a cut right down two-thirds of each half.

Heat oil and fry pounded spices until fragrant. Blend tamarind with water and add to fried spices. Bring to the boil and add fish and salt. Simmer for 2 minutes and add aubergines. Simmer for 5 minutes more and serve with sambal belacan.

Roast Chicken in Coconut Milk

Cooking time: 20 minutes
Grilling time: 10 minutes

1 chicken, about 1.5 kg (3 lbs)
½ coconut, grated
500 ml (16 fl oz) water
5 tbsp oil
3 fragrant lime leaves or grated lemon rind
1 tsp salt

SPICES
1 tsp chilli powder
1 stalk lemon grass or grated lemon rind
3 almonds
1 large onion
½ tsp turmeric powder
1 tbsp coriander powder
1 tsp cumin powder
1 tsp aniseed powder

Wash chicken and leave whole, removing only claws. Squeeze coconut with water for milk. Pound or blend spices fine and fry in hot oil until fragrant. Add lime leaves and fry for 30 seconds. Add coconut milk and salt and bring to the boil. Put chicken to simmer for 15 minutes.

Turn oven grill to high. Remove chicken from gravy and place in a roasting tin. Put half the gravy in the tin and reserve the rest for basting. Grill chicken for 10 minutes turning occasionally to brown evenly. Baste occasionally so chicken is moist but with charred bits here and there. Serve chicken whole with gravy on the side.

CLAY-POT COOKING

While Cantonese cooking is undoubtedly the premiere cuisine among the five major schools of Chinese — in sheer range alone it is reputed to have something like half a million dishes — relatively little has been written about the "Clay Pot" style. Since it is an established fact that Chinese food in general and Cantonese food in particular may be eaten with impunity be it bull's testicles or roasted python, it can be safely assumed that utensils are regarded in much the same light.

Perhaps the only pot available then was a mishapen clay basin and from this humble beginning evolved a style of cooking that is much loved today. Called Sar Po (literally sand pot) the utensil — an unglazed or glazed pot with a stumpy handle and fitting lid which some believe to have been used by early Chinese herbalists to brew medicinal tea, lends itself very well to a wide range of stir-fried and stewed dishes.

It combines particularly well with another Cantonese cooking style called "Hong Siew" which literally means "Red Roasting". This is simply a method of cooking meat, fish, bean curd or poultry rendering it a rich burgundy-like glaze. When a dish is cooked thus and then transferred to a clay pot for a final touch, the results are ambrosial.

Actually clay pot cooking is one of those peculiarly Chinese styles that appears more pretentious than it really is. There are two ways to cook clay pot dishes. One is to stir-fry food in a wok and transfer it to a clay pot previously heated until it almost glows. The whole pot is served sizzling with goodness. The other, more authentic way, is to heat a clay pot gently on the range and begin cooking when the temperature is sufficiently high for stir-frying or sauteeing.

But clay pots have a propensity to crack when overheated, so the first method is by far safer and easier. The one thing that remains subjective is whether food actually tastes different and better when cooked in a clay utensil. It's no more or less a fallacy than that hot dogs taste infinitely better at a beach barbecue than when served at a fast-food joint.

But one thing that is certainly not subjective is the fact that serving a sizzling clay pot at table, when you have guests, sets you apart as a host with more than fine flair. That said, you can proceed to experiment with this method of cooking without any distraction.

But use the pre-heated clay pot method as it's not only easier, it produces much the same results as you would if you used the other method. The dishes in this section are typical examples of clay pot cooking but virtually any stir-fried dish can be adapted to this method of cooking.

Chicken and Mushroom Shreds (illustrated opposite)

Cooking time 15 minutes

4 Chinese mushrooms
2 tbsp oil
3 slices stem ginger, shredded
1 clove garlic, crushed
1 chicken breast, cubed
1 tsp salt
400 ml (13 fl oz) water
1 tbsp cornflour
1 tbsp sesame oil
1 tsp pepper
Spring onions for garnish

Soak Chinese mushrooms in hot water for 10 minutes. Drain and squeeze out liquid. Cut into thin strips. Heat oil (not sesame oil) in wok until smoking and add crushed garlic and ginger to fry for 30 seconds.

Add cubed chicken and fry for 2 minutes then add mushroom to fry for further 2 minutes. Add water and simmer for 5 minutes or until chicken is cooked.

Dissolve cornflour in a little water and add to wok. When gravy thickens add sesame oil and give it a good stir. Transfer to clay pot and garnish with pepper and spring onions.

Beef and Broccoli

Cooking time: 10 minutes

3 tbsp oil
1 clove garlic, crushed
200 g (7 oz) fillet steak
200 g (7 oz) broccoli
500 ml (16 fl oz) boiling water

MARINADE
1 tbsp oyster sauce
1 tbsp Chinese wine or sherry
1 tsp black pepper
1 tbsp cornflour
150 ml (¼ pint) water

Cut broccoli into florets and scald in boiling water for 1 minute. Refresh under cold running water to blanch broccoli and retain its colour. Drain and set aside. Slice beef into bite-sized pieces and marinate for 10 minutes. Drain and set aside marinade. Heat oil in wok until smoking and fry crushed garlic until brown and fragrant.

Add broccoli and beef and fry for 30 seconds. Add marinade and bring to quick boil. Liquid should be thickish. Adjust with a little salt if you find the oyster sauce not salty enough. Transfer to clay pot and serve with boiled rice.

Liver with Ginger and Spring Onions (illustrated opposite)

Cooking time: 4 minutes

3 tbsp oil
6 thin slices ginger
2 stalks spring onions
2 tbsp Chinese wine or sherry
100 ml (3½ fl oz) water
2 tbsp oyster sauce
2 tbsp sesame oil
1 tbsp dark soy sauce
1 tsp sugar
350 g (¾ lb) fresh pig liver
Parsley or fresh coriander for garnishing

Wash, dry and chill liver until it is just firm. Cut into thin bite-sized slices and marinate in a mixture of soy sauce, wine, oyster sauce and sugar for 10 minutes.

Cut ginger into fine strips and spring onions into 4 cm (1½ in) lengths. Heat oil in wok until smoking. Fry ginger until light brown add drained liver. Fry for 30 seconds and add spring onions. Fry for another 20 seconds and add marinade and water.

Bring to a brisk boil and dish up immediately into heated clay pot. Garnish and serve on a heat-proof mat.

Clay Pot Rice

Cooking time: 20 minutes

250 g (½ lb) rice
800 ml (1 ¼ pints) water (water level should be 3 cm (¼ in) above level of rice in pot)
3 tsp oil
1 wedge cod
2 tbsp sesame oil
1 knob ginger, bruised
2 cloves garlic, crushed
2 Chinese sausages, diced
3 tbsp dark soy sauce
1 tbsp oyster sauce
4 tbsp diced chicken breast (optional)
1 tbsp salt

Wash rice and cook in water over slow heat until fluffy. It should take about 12 minutes depending on the type of rice used. While rice is cooking during the last five minutes, heat wok with oil. Fry cod until brown and lift out to cool. Fry ginger and garlic for a minute or two and put in diced sausages.

Shred the cod and add to the wok together with chicken if you are using it. (This is a good way to use up leftover roast chicken).

Add oyster sauce, soy sauce and salt and stir well. When rice is practically dry but still steaming transfer ingredients from wok to rice pot and add the sesame oil.

Give the pot a good stir to distribute all ingredients and cover. Just before serving transfer to pre-heated clay pot and garnish with cut chillies, fresh coriander or whatever small greens that strike your fancy.

NOTE: When using sesame oil in any dish add it in last and never over heat or it will turn bitter.

Mixed Vegetables

Cooking time: 4 minutes

4 tbsp oil
2 cloves garlic, crushed
8 young corn cobs, tinned or fresh
15 mange tout
6 Chinese mushrooms
6 straw mushrooms, tinned
10 button mushrooms
150 g (5 oz) medium-sized prawns
10 thin slices (canned) bamboo shoots
1 tbsp light soy sauce or fish sauce
1 tbsp salt
250 ml (8 fl oz) water
1 tsp cornflour

If you are using fresh young corn cobs remove husk and stalk and boil in water for 3 minutes and drain. Soak Chinese mushrooms in hot water until soft and leave whole or quarter if you like. Assemble all vegetables in a large plate but in individual groups.

Heat wok with oil and fry crushed garlic until light brown. Put mange tout in first and stir-fry over high heat for 30 seconds. Add all other vegetables and stir-fry for 30 seconds more.

Remember, the success of stir-fried dishes depends on the heat. If it's not hot enough you will end up with not only insipid vegetables but a mushy mess.

High heat seals in the vegetable juices and cooks them through without losing their crunch. Dissolve cornflour in water and add to vegetables. Bring to a quick boil and add soy sauce. Serve in clay pot immediately.

Liver and Kidney in Soy Sauce

Cooking time: 4 minutes

3 tbsp oil
1 large onion sliced into rings
4 slices ginger
2 tbsp black soy sauce
1 tsp salt
200 g (7 oz) fresh pig liver
1 kidney
150 ml (¼ pint) water

Wash kidney thoroughly under running tap and gently force water into side aperture. The kidney will swell a little bit but the ammonia smell will have been reduced. Slice kidney lengthwise and remove every trace of white membrane. Score across and cut into bite-sized pieces. Soak in water while you prepare liver.

Wash liver and slice thinly. Heat wok with oil and fry sliced onions until they are soft but not brown. Add ginger and fry for 1 minute. Add liver and kidney and stir fry for 30 seconds over high heat. Add soy sauce, salt and water and bring to the boil. Transfer to clay pot and serve with rice.

Braised Beancurd

Cooking time: 25 minutes

5 tbsp oil
400 g (13 oz) soft beancurd or tofu
200 g (7 oz) minced pork
2 cloves garlic
2 tbsp shredded ginger
1 tbsp black soy sauce
2 tbsp Chinese wine or sherry
2 tbsp sesame oil
1 tbsp hoisin sauce
300 ml (½ pint) water
2 stalks spring onions

Heat oil and fry beancurd until brown skin forms. Lift out with slotted spoon and remove all but 3 tbsp of oil. Crush garlic and fry in hot oil for 1 minute. Add ginger and stir until light brown. Add minced pork and stir well to break up lumps. Add all other ingredients except spring onions and simmer for 2 minutes.

Heat a claypot and transfer beancurd. Pour sauce over beancurd and garnish with spring onions. Serve with a dash of pepper and sliced red chillies for extra zest.

THE INDISPENSABLE EGG

Nature's most blessed food the egg must rank as the humble wonder of the culinary world. But not for Singaporeans the usual boiled poached or fried versions. Egg cookery reaches great heights in Asia and there must be literally thousands of ways to prepare it if one takes the trouble to see beyond its breakfast potential and explore its remarkable versatility. This section has but a few of the endless variety of egg dishes but they can be the basis for your own innovation and invention.

Hard-boiled Egg Sambal

Cooking time: 30 minutes

4 eggs
6 dried chillies, soaked till soft
2 large onions, sliced
2 cloves garlic
10 almonds
1 tbsp tomato puree
1 tbsp tamarind paste
5 tbsp water
1 tsp sugar
½ tsp salt
3 tbsp oil

Hard boil eggs and peel when cool. Pound onions, almonds, garlic and chillies till fine. Heat oil and fry paste until fragrant. Add puree and tamarind water (squeeze paste with 5 tbsp water), sugar and salt and simmer for 2 minutes. Cut eggs into halves and spoon sambal over. Serve with plain or coconut rice.

Tamarind Eggs (illustrated on p. 80)

Cooking time: 15 minutes

3 tbsp oil
12 shallots, sliced
4 dried chillies, soaked and sliced fine
5 hard-boiled eggs
2 tbsp palm sugar or brown sugar
1 tbsp tamarind paste
8 tbsp water
1 tsp lime juice
2 fragrant lime leaves, sliced or ½ tsp grated
   lemon rind
1 stalk spring onions chopped
1 tsp salt

Heat oil and fry shallots and sliced dried chillies till brown. Remove and drain. In remaining oil quickly fry hard-boiled eggs until skin turns brown and bubbles. Remove and drain. Mix palm sugar, tamarind paste with water (remove pulp), lime juice, lime leaves, spring onions and salt and bring to the boil. Pour over fried eggs and serve with plain boiled rice.

Stuffed Egg Roll

Cooking time: 20 minutes

2 tbsp oil
1 clove garlic, crushed
200 g (7 oz) minced pork
1 tsp cornflour
½ tsp salt
½ tsp pepper
1 tsp chilli powder
1 tsp sugar
3 eggs
2 tbsp cornflour
2 tbsp water
3 tbsp oil
Fresh coriander leaves
3 red chillies, sliced into strips

Heat oil and fry garlic until brown. Add minced pork mixed with cornflour, pepper, salt, chilli powder and sugar. Stir well and sprinkle a few drops of water if mixture is too dry. Remove and cool. Mix eggs with cornflour and water and stir well. Lightly oil a flat pan and fry thin omelettes. Remove and cool. Wrap each omelette with pork mixture and fold into parcels. Garnish each with chilli strips and coriander leaves and serve with chilli sauce.

Stewed Eggs with Beef

Cooking time: 30 minutes

3 tbsp oil
1 tbsp coriander powder
1 tsp garlic powder
1 tsp pepper
1 large onion, pounded
200 g (7 oz) fillet beef, cut into thin strips
1 tsp salt
1 tbsp palm or brown sugar
500 ml (16 fl oz) water
4 hard-boiled eggs

Heat oil and fry coriander, garlic, pepper and pounded onion until fragrant. Add beef and fry for 2 minutes. Add salt, palm sugar and water and simmer for 20 minutes. Add eggs and simmer for 10 minutes more.

Egg Drop Soup with Ginger and Brandy

Cooking time: 10 minutes

2 tbsp oil
1 tbsp shredded green ginger
1 clove garlic, crushed
1 cucumber
800 ml (1¼ pints) water
2 eggs
1 tsp salt
1 tsp fish sauce
½ tsp pepper
1 tbsp brandy

Heat oil and fry ginger and garlic until brown. Peel cucumber and remove inner pith. Cut into diamond shapes. Add to pan and fry briefly. Add water and bring to the boil. Dribble eggs in one by one and add fish sauce, salt and pepper. Just before serving add brandy and serve at once.

Fried Stuffed Eggs

Cooking time: 10 minutes

6 eggs
100 g (3 oz) minced pork
1 tsp cornflour
100 g (3 oz) minced prawns
100 g (3 oz) minced scallops
2 tbsp coconut cream
1 tsp salt
½ tsp pepper
1 tsp fish sauce
1 stalk spring onions, chopped
1 stalk coriander leaves, chopped
Oil for deep frying

BATTER
75 g (2½ oz) flour
300 ml (½ pint) water
2 tbsp oil
½ tsp salt

Hard boil eggs for 5 minutes. Cool, shell and scoop out yolk and mix with pork, cornflour, prawns, scallops, coconut cream and all seasoning.

Fill hollow egg whites with mixture until each half is shaped like a whole egg. Add a little flour if mixture seems too wet. Mix batter ingredients and dip each egg in before deep-frying. Keep filling side down when frying as they require longer frying than the cooked egg half.

Crispy Eggs

Cooking time: 5 minutes

4 tbsp oil
2 fish steaks
6 shallots, sliced
2 red chillies
1 tsp salt
4 eggs
1 tbsp fish sauce
1 tsp pepper

Rub fish with salt and fry in 4 tbsp oil until cooked. Remove to cool and flake. In remaining oil fry sliced shallots and chillies for 2 minutes. Remove and drain. Mix fried ingredients with egg and seasoning. Heat oil and fry 1 tbsp at a time until golden brown. Flatten egg mixture with ladle as you fry to get thin fritters.
Serve with any piquant sauce.

Onion Omelette (illustrated opposite)

Cooking time: 5 minutes

4 tbsp oil
2 large onions, sliced fine
2 red chillies, deseeded and sliced
½ tsp salt
4 eggs

Heat oil and fry onions light brown. Add chillies, salt and lightly beaten eggs. Fry until brown and cut up into rough pieces. Serve with rice.

Curried Eggs (illustrated opposite)

Cooking time: 15 minutes

6 hard boiled eggs
3 tbsp oil
2 slices green ginger, shredded
1 medium onion, chopped
2 tbsp curry paste
125 g (4 oz) coconut cream
300 ml (½ pint) water
1 tsp fish sauce
1 tsp salt

Heat oil and fry ginger and onion until light brown. Add curry paste and fry for 2 minutes more. Add coconut cream, water and all seasoning and bring to the boil. Add eggs and simmer for 5 minutes. Serve with plain rice or bread.

Chinese Sausage Omelette

Cooking time: 5 minutes

4 tbsp oil
3 eggs
2 Chinese sausages
½ tsp salt
Fresh coriander leaves

Slice Chinese sausages fine. Beat egg lightly and add salt. Heat oil and fry sausages for 1 minute. Add beaten egg and cook until set. Turn over once and continue cooking. Cut up roughly and serve with fresh coriander leaves.

Steamed Egg and Spinach

Cooking time: 15 minutes

I learnt this dish from a neighbour who says the classic way to cook it is to use the type of spinach with purple stalks. This has richer taste than the ordinary green spinach and also looks very nice for service.

2 eggs (raw)
1 head purple spinach
1 tsp pepper
Pinch monosodium glutamate
1 tbsp oil

Wash spinach thoroughly and arrange on a deep steaming plate. Overlap leaves if necessary. Crack eggs on top of this and sprinkle with pepper, monosodium glutamate and dribble oil all over. Steam for 10-15 minutes until egg yolks are set. Serve with plain porridge.

Steamed Egg with Minced Beef

Cooking time: 15 minutes

3 eggs
200 g (7 oz) minced beef
1 tsp salt
½ tsp pepper
1 tsp cornflour
1 tsp oil
1 tbsp water

Lightly beat eggs and mix with all other ingredients. Place in a small enamel dish or deep bowl and cover with a piece of foil or muslin. Steam for 15 minutes until mixture is well set. Serve with pickles and plain porridge.

Egg Pickle

2 eggs
4 shallots
1 stalk spring onions
1 tbsp shredded ginger
1 tbsp vinegar
1 tbsp sugar
2 red chillies

Boil eggs for 10 minutes in plenty of water. Remove to cool and remove shells. Cut each egg into eight pieces. Mix vinegar with sugar and stir until sugar melts. Slice spring onions and chillies fine and mix with ginger. Sprinkle over eggs and pour vinegar and sugar mixture over.

Steamed Egg and Minced Pork

Cooking time: 25 minutes

3 eggs
150 g (5 oz) minced pork
1 tsp cornflour
3 tbsp water
1 tbsp salted winter vegetable
½ tsp pepper

Beat eggs lightly and put in deep pyrex or oven-proof dish. Mix pork with cornflour and water and stir into egg. Wash salted winter vegetable and add to mixture. Sprinkle with pepper and steam for 25 minutes until set.

Salted Vegetable Omelette

Cooking time: 5 minutes

4 tbsp oil
1 clove garlic
150 g (5 oz) salted vegetable
2 red chillies

Wash and drain salted vegetable. If you are using canned vegetable, do not soak in water but simply wash and drain. Salted vegetables bought off market stalls need to be soaked in cold water for at least 10 minutes to reduce saltiness.

Slice red chillies and crush garlic. Beat eggs lightly. Heat oil, fry garlic for 1 minute. Squeeze out all moisture from salted vegetable and add to pan. Fry for 1 minute until fragrant and pour beaten egg in. Spread around to form omelette. Sprinkle sliced chillies on top and cook till set. Cut up roughly and turn over to cook egg through. When slightly brown dish up and serve.

A NOTE ON INDIAN CURRIES

While I do not profess to be any hot stuff about cooking Indian curries, I have had some of the most memorable lessons from Indian colleagues and friends. The French may have developed their cuisine to a remarkably sophisticated degree and the Chinese stand unique in having a bewiltering range of food from the most esoteric to the most imperial, no other cuisine can quite match Indian curries for their spicy complexity.

Often too, it is a misconception that curry per se is the sum total of Indian cuisine. The Indian sub-continent has as many different types of cooking as there are regions and provinces — and even villages. Since the Indian community in Singapore are largely descended from South Indians who first came here some 200 years ago, it is south Indian curries that we are most familiar with.

And like in French or Chinese regional cooking, South Indian cuisine relies heavily on one particular ingredient, in this case the coconut. Chillies, of course, come into their own as any one who has eaten curry fish head can testify.

Singaporeans, over the decades, have learnt to appreciate the hottest, spiciest Indian curries with equanimity and many are more than an authority on which restaurant serves the best mutton curry or beryani. For my part I find the cuisine so fascinating the greatest joy must come from attempting to try out the recipes given to me by my friends.

Deep-fried Spiced Fish

Cooking time: 20 minutes

6 white fish fillets about 2 kg (4 lbs) weight
2 tsp salt
1 tsp pepper
Oil for deep frying

BATTER
6 tbsp plain flour
3 tbsp chick-pea flour (besan or gramplant)
2 tsp turmeric powder
300 ml (½ pint) water

Cut each fish fillet into manageable pieces and rub all over with salt and pepper. Set aside. Combine batter ingredients adding water a little at a time until you get the consistency of thick cream.

Heat oil until smoking. Dip each fish fillet into batter and deep fry until golden brown. Drain on absorbent towels and serve as appetisers.

Fish Curry with Tomatoes

Cooking time: 15 minutes

3 tbsp oil
1 large onion, sliced
3 cloves garlic, sliced
1 bunch coriander leaves, chopped
1 tsp cumin powder
1 tsp turmeric powder
2 tbsp chilli powder
2 large tomatoes, chopped
2 tsp salt
1 tbsp garam masala
1 lemon
300 ml (½ pint) water
500 g (1 lb) mackerel steaks

Wash fish and pat dry. Fry onions, garlic and coriander in hot oil until soft but not brown. Add cumin, turmeric and chilli powder and continue frying for 1 minute.

Add tomatoes, salt and garam masala and fry until tomatoes turn mushy. Add water and lemon juice and fish and simmer for 4 minutes over gentle heat. If gravy is too dry, add more water and adjust with more lemon juice and salt if necessary.

Fish Masala

Cooking time: 15 minutes

2 large plaice
1 tbsp salt
1 tsp turmeric
Juice of 2 limes
6 tbsp oil

SPICES
1 large onion
1 tsp powdered turmeric
3 red chillies
2 tsp garam masala
2 cloves garlic
4 slices green ginger
3 tbsp water

Wash and clean fish with salt. Rub all over with turmeric and lime juice and set aside. Pound spices, except onion which should be sliced, fine. Heat 2 tbsp oil and gently fry pounded spices for 2 minutes.

Add 3 tbsp water and remove from pan. Make deep slit in fish and also along the sides. Stuff fish with pounded, fried spices making sure the side slits are liberally rubbed with spices as well. Heat the remaining oil (add more if neccessary) and shallow fry for 4 minutes on each side.

Spiced Mullet (Ikan Belanak)

Cooking time: 15 minutes

And Indian friend, somewhat of a culinary purist, insists that the fish used for this dish must be marinated for some five hours. I feel a little compromise is necessary here for few of us have the inclination or time to wait this long for our dinner. I have simplified the dish to a great degree so many more people can learn how to cook it.

2 large mullet about 400 g (13 oz) each
1 lemon
5 tbsp melted butter
2 tsp cumin powder

MARINADE
5 tbsp plain yoghurt
3 cloves garlic, crushed
1 2 cm (¾ in) piece green ginger, finely chopped
1 tbsp coriander powder
1 tsp garam masala
1 tbsp chilli paste

Wash and clean fish and make slits diagonally along each side. Sprinkle lemon juice all over and set aside. Combine marinade ingredients and stir well.

Spoon all over fish and leave for half an hour turning each fish once. Pre-heat a grill and lay fish on wire rack or foil. Mix melted butter with cummin and baste fish. Grill for 8 minutes on each side. Serve with lemon wedges.

Fish Head Curry

Cooking time: 20 minutes

2 large fish head about 1 kg (2 lbs)
1 tbsp salt
3 cloves garlic
2 large onions
5 tbsp tamarind paste
600 ml (1 pint) water
1 coconut, grated
750 ml (1¼ pints) water
2 eggplants or aubergines
2 tsp mustard seeds
1 large knob ginger, shredded
4 stalks curry leaves
2 large onions, sliced
3 tomatoes, quartered
Salt to taste
5 tbsp oil

SPICES
3 tbsp chilli powder
4 tbsp coriander powder
2 tbsp cumin powder
1 tbsp aniseed powder
2 tsp turmeric powder
2 tbsp pepper
5 cardamoms

Wash fish head with salt and clean thoroughly. Drain and put aside. Pound the 3 cloves garlic and 2 large onions coarsely. Mix tamarind with 600 ml (1 pint) water and squeeze coconut with 750 ml (1¼ pints) water.

Cut off stalks of aubergines and slice each into two lengthwise. Slice each half again but only halfway through.

Leave to soak in water to prevent them turning black. Pound spices fine and moisten with a few tbsp of coconut milk or tamarind liquid. Heat oil in a kwali or wok, and fry mustard seeds for 1 minute.

Add onions and garlic, shredded ginger and fry until light brown. Add pounded spices and fry for 3 minutes. Add both liquids and bring to the boil. Add fish head, tomatoes and aubergine. Simmer for 5 minutes and adjust taste with salt. Serve with plain boiled rice.

Mutton Kurmah (illustrated opposite)

Cooking time: 35 minutes

I find this an excellent dry curry dish to serve those not used to very hot dishes. Kurmah is spicy without burning your mouth off and reheats extremely well. In fact the gravy gets richer after a day or two.

5 tbsp ghee or cooking oil
2 large onions, chopped
3 cloves garlic, chopped fine
2 stalks lemon grass, bruised or grated lemon rind
2 kg (4 lbs) mutton, cubed into 5 cm (2 in) squares
2 tsp salt
4 potatoes, peeled and cut into quarters
400 ml (13 fl oz) evaporated milk
2 tbsp lime juice
1 coconut
500 ml (16 fl oz) water

SPICES
2 tbsp coriander powder
2 tsp aniseed powder
2 tsp cumin powder
2 tsp pepper
10 almonds
1 large knob ginger
1 tbsp fenugreek

Blend spices except fenugreek. Heat ghee and fry onions, garlic and bruised lemon grass for 2 minutes. Add spices and fenugreek and fry for 2 minutes more. Add mutton and stir until meat is well coated.

Squeeze coconut with water for milk and add half to mutton. Bring to the boil and add evaporated milk and lime juice. Simmer for 20 minutes and add potatoes. Simmer for 15 minutes more and add salt. Adjust with more salt if necessary.

Dry Lamb Curry

Cooking time: 25 minutes

This is the perfect dish for entertaining friends who prefer mild curries to hot ones. It also reheats well and served the next day with bread, will win you new legions of fans.

3 tbsp ghee or cooking oil
2 tbsp oil
2 large onions, sliced
3 cloves garlic, chopped
3 tbsp shredded stem ginger
4 tbsp curry paste
1 kg (2 lbs) lean lamb, cubed
1 large carrot, cubed
1 coconut, shredded
600 ml (1 pint) water
2 tsp salt
1 stalk curry leaves

Squeeze coconut with water for milk. Add $1/2$ tsp salt and set aside. Heat a nonstick or heavy-bottomed pot with oil and ghee and fry onions, ginger and garlic until golden brown.

Add meat curry paste moistened with 2 tbsp of coconut milk and continue frying until oil seeps out again. Add cubed lamb and fry for a few more minutes until well-steeped with spices.

Add half the coconut milk and simmer for 15 minutes. Add carrots and remaining coconut milk and simmer for 10 minutes more. You could simmer it even longer until gravy is reduced by half and the lamb so tender it melts in your mouth.

Personally, I like my meat with some "give." Serve on a bed of fluffy white rice as a dinner centrepiece. When reheating this dish, add a little more water.

Chicken Vindaloo (illustrated opposite)

Cooking time: 45 minutes

I learnt how to cook this dish from a Eurasian colleague who married an Indian and had lived in India for many years. In fact it was Mrs Chelvam who first introduced me to this delicious chicken dish with its curiously hot and sour taste, coming from the use of good malt vinegar and chillies. It is actually Portuguese in origin.

5 tbsp oil
1 large onion, finely sliced
1 tsp turmeric powder
1 chicken about 1 kg (2 lbs), cut into 8 pieces
2 tsp chilli powder or paprika
Juice of 1 lemon
2 tsp salt
1 chicken stock cube
750 ml (1¼ pints) water

SPICES
2 tbsp malt or wine vinegar
3 dried chillies, soaked in hot water till soft
3 tbsp shredded ginger
1 tsp cumin powder
2 tbsp coriander powder
1 tsp pepper
1 tsp cinnamon powder

Rub chicken pieces with salt, chilli powder and lemon juice and set aside. Pound or blend spices with vinegar. Heat oil and fry sliced onion until soft and light brown. Add turmeric and pounded spices and fry for about 4 minutes. Add chicken pieces and stir thoroughly until well mixed. Add water and stock cube and simmer for 30 minutes. Serve with crusty French bread.

Aubergine and Mutton Curry

Cooking time: 35 minutes

5 tbsp ghee or cooking oil
1 large onion, sliced
1 kg (2 lbs) mutton, cubed
3 aubergines, cut into 4-cm (1½ in) chunks
1 coconut
750 ml (1¼ pints) water
2 tsp salt

SPICES
2 tbsp coriander powder
1 tbsp cumin powder
½ tsp cinnamon powder
1 tsp aniseed powder
1 tbsp chilli powder
4 cloves garlic
1 thumb-sized piece ginger
½ tsp turmeric powder
10 almonds

Pound or blend spices till fine. If you use a blender, you can throw in the whole lot of whole and powder spices to save time. Heat ghee and fry onions till soft and transparent. Add spices and fry till oil seeps out again. Add diced mutton and fry for 5 minutes till well coated. Squeeze coconut with water for milk.

Add to mutton and bring to the boil. Simmer for 25 minutes and add aubergines and salt. Simmer for 20 minutes more until gravy thickens. Serve with rice or bread.

Mutton Curry (Mild)

Cooking time: 30 minutes

4 tbsp oil
3 tbsp curry paste
1 knob ginger about 3 cm x 2 cm (1 ¼ x ¾ in)
4 cloves garlic, sliced
1 tsp cinnamon powder
5 cardamoms, lightly bruised
400 g (13 oz) mutton cubed
250 ml (8 fl oz) yoghurt
1 large carrot, diced
600 ml (1 pint) water
2 large onions, sliced
1 lime

Traditionally, mutton curry is cooked with ghee but this is a very fatty oil and may not be to everyone's taste. Using corn or vegetable oil will produce a curry that's only slightly less rich but none the less authentic.

This is derived from an Indian mutton curry which uses yogurt instead of coconut milk. Heat oil in a non-stick casserole or wok. Fry ginger and garlic until light brown.

Add curry paste and stir fry until oil seeps out again. Add cinnamon, cardamoms and mutton and continue to fry for several minutes. Add carrots and yoghurt and water. Bring to the boil and simmer in covered pot over slow flame. Add water if curry dries up before mutton reaches consistency you want.

Add sliced onions in the last 10 minutes of cooking and squeeze juice of lime over curry just before serving. If you use lamb, it'll take a shorter time to cook but there is a little difference in flavour between mutton and lamb especially in curries.

Sri Lankan Curry

Cooking time: 45 minutes

This is a devilishly hot curry as I found out once when invited to a friend's home for Deepavali dinner. You might temper it by replacing what my friend used (some 25 red chillies!) with either a little tomato puree or red food colouring but the taste isn't quite the same.

1 chicken about 1.5 kg (3 lbs)
3 tbsp ghee or cooking oil
2 large onions, sliced
4 cloves garlic, sliced
1 tbsp grated ginger
1 stalk curry leaves
2 tbsp curry powder
2 tsp chilli powder
2 tsp salt
2 tbsp lime juice
3 tomatoes, quartered
4 cardamoms
1 5 cm (2 in) stick cinnamon
2 stalks lemon grass, bruised or grated lemon rind
1 coconut, grated squeezed with
400 ml (13 fl oz) water

Cut chicken into bite-sized pieces or small joints. Heat ghee or a mixture of half and half of ghee and oil and fry onions, garlic and ginger until light brown. Add curry leaves, curry powder and chilli powder moistened with some water or coconut milk and fry until fragrant.

Add salt, lime juice, tomatoes, cardamoms, cinnamon and lemon grass and stir-fry for 2 minutes.

Add coconut milk and bring to the boil. Add chicken and simmer for 20 minutes.

Yoghurt Chicken

Cooking time:

I came to yogurt rather late in life, the years before my culinary experiments with this ingredient being rather restricted to things Straitsborn. But once introduced to yogurt as an item in cooking I became a great fan. In fact, after an Indian friend taught me how to use yoghurt in savoury dishes, I went through something like a month of yogurt-based dishes.

My friend, the kind soul, kept me well supplied with her mother's home-made yogurt from which I replenished by making my own from powdered milk. Besides providing good taste, yogurt really is about the healthiest thing you can eat or cook with.

1 small 150 ml (¼ pint) cup yoghurt
3 cloves garlic, chopped finely
5 slices preserved ginger, minced
1 chicken about 1 kg (2 lbs)
1 tsp salt
1 tsp turmeric powder
2 tsp lemon juice
4 tbsp oil or butter

Wash chicken and rub with salt, lemon juice and turmeric powder. Set aside for 20 minutes. Combine yogurt, ginger and garlic and marinate chicken for 15 minutes. Brush a roasting rack with a little oil and place chicken on it.

Roast in a medium oven for 30 minutes and increase heat to high for 10 minutes to brown. Baste frequently with oil mixed with marinade. Serve whole with extra basting liquid which should have been caught by roasting pan and fragrant by the time the chicken is ready.

NOODLES

Fried noodles, boiled noodles, noodles in soup, in curry, in sugar syrup and — the small miracle of modern times — instant noodles are all steeped in symbolism. To the Chinese, to eat noodles means to have longevity because all noodles never seem to end. As the star dish in any festive occasion noodles, from their humble beginnings as strands of wheat or rice flour, are elevated to near reverence.

I remember my parents disallowing anyone at the table to cut noodles even if, transferring from main centre dish to individual plate, they slopped all over the place. We each had to take all of the forkful of fried noodles at grandpa's birthday and wish him in hushed tones, "umor panjang" (long life).

Ritual over, it was a feast of the most slurping kind. To our noodle dishes would be added prawns, pork, vegetables, fragrant herbs and fried onions. We ate noodles fried Hokkien style, Teochew style, in preserved soy beans, in laksa, in tamarind juice Penang style or plain boiled in sugar syrup for more symbolism and a sweet life.

There was also Cantonese noodles from hawker stalls, Shanghainese noodles with minced beef and Indian noodles with lots of chilli and mutton. Symbolism aside, noodles not only make excellent eating they are one-dish meals that take the chore out of entertaining.

Noodles are made either from plain flour, rice flour, mung bean flour or wheat flour. The types most commonly used in Singapore are:

Yellow noodles (mien) which is sold fresh and used in fried Hokkien noodles, Indian Mee Goreng and Malay Mee Rebus. It is also used for frying Nonya Mee and by Teochew noodle hawkers. Should not be stored longer than a day or they turn bad.

White rice flour noodles (hor fun) which are flat 1 cm (1½ in) wide noodles with a bland flavour much like plain rice. Excellent for noodle dishes with plenty of thick gravy as it absorbs liquid well. Can be fried, boiled or steamed.

Dried wheat flour noodles (sang mien or ee fu mien) are sold in packets or small mounds. Some contain egg and all have to be boiled in hot water for several minutes before they can be cooked.

Chinese vermicelli (mi fun) are dried rice-flour noodles sold in oblong packets and resemble brittle white threads all coiled up. These have to be soaked in hot water for several minutes depending on the size of vermicelli. There are three varieties. Thin, medium or very thick which the Cantonese use for their famous fish head mi fun.

Dried wheat flour noodles (fine) or Mee Sua come in little skeins tied with red thread and some six or eight skeins in a box. This is, of all the noodles, most revered as the longevity symbol and served to the birthday person in a sweet syrup with boiled eggs first thing in the morning. They have to be briefly boiled before being added to soup. Does not fry well.

Cellophane noodles or Transparent noodles (fun see). Made from mung bean flour into fine transparent strands, they come dry and have to be soaked in cold or warm water for a few minutes before being cooked.

Instant noodles, especially in Western countries where fresh noodles are hard to come by, make very good substitutes in practically all the noodle dishes in Asian cuisine.

Noodles in Sweet Potato Gravy (Mee Rebus)

Cooking time: 45 minutes

500 g (1 lb) fresh yellow noodles
200 g (7 oz) beansprouts, scalded

GARNISH
4 hard-boiled eggs, quartered
4 tbsp sliced shallots
4 tbsp oil
1 stalk celery
4 green chillies, sliced
2 squares hard beancurd or tofu
4 limes
2 tbsp black soy sauce

GRAVY
10 dried chillies, soaked till soft
8 almonds
2 large onions
2 tbsp coriander powder, dry fried for 3
   minutes
1 tbsp preserved soy beans, washed and
   mashed
400 g (13 oz) sweet potatoes, boiled and
   mashed fine
3 tbsp oil
4 litres (7 pints) beef stock (see p 276)

Prepare gravy first. Pound or blend chillies, almonds and onions until fine. Fry in oil until fragrant and add coriander powder, preserved soy beans and fry for 2 minutes until well mixed. Add stock and bring to the boil. Add mashed sweet potato and stir well until gravy thickens. Set aside and keep warm.

Heat 4 tbsp oil and fry hard beancurd until brown. Slice or dice into large crumbs. Fry sliced shallots until brown and crisp. Set aside in a large plate with other garnishes.

Heat a large pot of water and scald noodles and beansprouts, one service portion at a time for a minute. Put in individual bowl or deep soup plate and pour gravy over. Garnish with eggs, celery, sliced chillies, beancurd, fried onions, lime juice and black soy sauce if preferred.

If you are feeling affluent, you could use 250 g (½ lb) beef to make stock and diced beef as extra garnish.

Fried Hor Fun (illustrated on p. 250)

Cooking time: 15 minutes

5 tbsp oil
400 g (13 oz) rice flour noodles (hor fun)
2 tbsp black soy sauce
2 cloves garlic, crushed
200 g (7 oz) prawns, shelled
2 chicken livers, boiled and sliced
100 g (3 oz) liver, sliced
150 g (5 oz) mustard greens (canned)
150 g (5 oz) squid, sliced
300 ml (½ pint) water
1 tbsp cornflour
2 tsp salt
1 tsp pepper
2 tbsp pickled green chillies
3 tbsp pork fat chips

Heat oil until hot and smoking. Put hor fun in to singe for 2 minutes. Add soy sauce and stir until hor fun is dark brown. Remove from pan and in remaining oil fry garlic until brown. Add prawns, chicken livers, mustard greens and squid and fry for 1 minute. Add water mixed with cornflour and seasoning and bring to the boil. Add fried hor fun and simmer until gravy is thick. Serve with chillies and fried pork fat chips.

Fried Chicken Noodles

Cooking time: 15 minutes

Though this is a fried dish the basis is good meat stock, and a lot of it, as the fresh yellow noodles and white vermicelli soak up quite a bit. Traditionally lard is used but any vegetable oil will do because the meat stock is already rich in lard. Prepare the stock by boiling the pork, prawns and squid in 3 litres (5½ pints) water.

5 tbsp oil
200 g (7 oz) beansprouts
250 g (½ lb) fresh yellow noodles, scalded
 briefly
250 g (½ lb) rice vermicelli, soaked for 5
 minutes in hot water
200 g (7 oz) sliced belly pork without skin
200 g (7 oz) boiled prawns
100 g (3 oz) boiled squid, sliced
4 eggs
6 cloves garlic, chopped fine
3 tbsp fish sauce
2 tsp pepper

STOCK
5 tbsp chives, cut into 4 cm (1½ in) lengths
6 limes
4 red chillies, sliced
Fresh coriander leaves

Heat oil in a large kwali (or wok) and add beansprouts, both types of noodles and fry for 2 or 3 minutes. Add about ¼ stock and cover briefly to cook noodles. Stir well for 2 or 3 minutes and push noodles to one side. Add 2 tbsp oil and fry chopped garlic until brown. Crack eggs in and break up yolk. When eggs set, add prawns, sliced ingredients and the rest of the stock and stir well. Add seasoning and chives and stir well. Dish up and serve garnished with sliced chillies, lime juice and coriander leaves.

Fried Noodles Teochew Style

Cooking time: 10 minutes

4 tbsp lard from 300 g (10 oz) fresh lard
150 g (5 oz) beansprouts, washed and drained
250 g (½ lb) fresh yellow noodles
150 g (5 oz) rice noodles (hor fun)
4 eggs
4 Chinese sausages, sliced fine diagonally
200 g (7 oz) fresh mussels, shelled
1 bunch Chinese chives, cut into 4 cm (1½ in)
 lengths
4 tbsp sweet sauce
2 tbsp chilli paste or bottled chilli sauce
2 tsp fish sauce
250 ml (8 fl oz) water
1 tsp pepper

Render lard down and reserve lard chips. Reheat oil and fry beansprouts, and both types of noodles for 1 minute. Sprinkle a few drops of water to cook noodles and stir well. Add more lard if pan is dry. Your heat must be at high for this dish.

Push noodles aside and crack eggs in. Stir well and add sausages and fish sauce. Add more water and stir well. Add sweet sauce, chilli sauce, the rest of the water, pepper, chives and mussels last and stir for 2 minutes. Noodles should be black, richly oily and fragrant.

Rice Noodles in Coconut Gravy (Laksa Lemak)

Cooking time: 40 minutes

This is a one-pot noodle dish that is the favourite of the Straits Chinese. Although most hawker centres have at least one stall selling it, there are few who make it properly giving rise to snorts of derision that it is not laksa but curry noodles. Some like the traditional laksa lemak with fragrant laksa leaves, fish meat and prawns and others like a handful of mussels, clams or even chicken meat in the gravy. There's no accounting for taste but the gravy remains basically the same.

GRAVY
4 tbsp oil
8 dried chillies, soaked till soft
2 stalks lemon grass or strips lemon rind
2 large onions
1 tsp powdered turmeric
10 almonds
1 tsp shrimp paste
4 tbsp dried prawns, soaked till soft
1 coconut, grated
2 litres (3½ pints) water
2 tsp salt

Pound or blend chillies, lemon grass, turmeric, almonds, onions, and shrimp paste till fine. Pound dried prawns separately until fine. Heat oil and fry prawns for 3 minutes. Add pounded spices and fry until oil seeps out again. Squeeze coconut with water for milk and add to fried spices. Bring to the boil and simmer for 15 minutes. Add salt.

MAIN INGREDIENTS
500 g (1 lb) fresh laksa noodles or fresh yellow
   noodles if preferred
250 g (½ lb) beansprouts, scalded
3 large fish cakes (available from Chinese
   grocers), fried and sliced thin
300 g (10 oz) chicken meat
200 g (7 oz) fresh mussels or clams
1 cucumber, peeled and shredded fine

To serve laksa, simply place as much noodles (scalded first) together with beansprouts, fish cakes, prawns or other garnishes and pour hot gravy over. Drain back into gravy pot and top up again. This is to infuse the spiciness with the noodles. Serve with shredded cucumber. Add pounded fresh red chilli for extra kick.

Chicken and Mushroom Noodles

Cooking time: 25 minutes

3 tbsp lard
1 clove garlic, crushed
1 chicken breast, sliced into strips
4 Chinese mushrooms, soaked till soft
1 tbsp black soy sauce
1 tsp salt
1 tsp pepper
250 ml (8 fl oz) water
2 tsp cornflour
200 g (7 oz) rice noodles (hor fun)
1 tbsp sesame oil
1 stalk spring onions, cut into 4 cm (1½ in)
   lengths

Heat lard and fry crushed garlic until light brown. Add chicken meat and mushrooms either whole or cut into strips and fry for 2 minutes. Add soy sauce, salt, pepper and water mixed with cornflour and bring to the boil. Add noodles, sesame oil and spring onions and simmer for 2 minutes. Serve with pickled green chillies.

Shanghainese Noodles (Char Chian Mien) (illustrated on p. 254)

Cooking time: 35 minutes

Among the many tenants who lived in our house was a Shanghainese family who made pianos for a living. Mrs Liew was a robust, jolly woman who loved to cook for her five sons and in the three years they shared our roof, we got to eat many Shanghainese dishes. This is one she prepared often for afternoon snacks.

400 g (13 oz) wheatflour dried noodles or fresh yellow noodles
1 tbsp light soy sauce
1 tbsp lard
3 tbsp oil
2 cloves garlic, crushed
2 red chillies, chopped
1 square hard beancurd or tofu
300 g (10 oz) minced pork
2 tsp cornflour
1 tbsp light soy sauce
1 tsp black soy sauce
200 ml (7 fl oz) water
200 g (7 oz) beansprouts, scalded
100 g (3 oz) Chinese chives
4 tbsp finely shredded cucumber

Boil water an scald noodles for 1 minute. Drain and mix with soy sauce and lard. Set aside. Heat oil and fry garlic and chillies for 1 minute. Roughly chop bean curd and add to pan. Fry until mixture is brown. Add minced pork mixed with cornflour and fry for 2 minutes. Add black and light soy sauces and water and simmer for 5 minutes.

To serve Shanghainese noodles arrange on a large plate, noodles to one side, minced pork in the centre and scalded beansprouts, chives and cucumber lining the side. Each diner helps himself to ingredients and makes his own mix. Minced beef can also be used for this dish with other green garnishes like coriander, celery or spring onions.

Cantonese Dried Chilli Noodles (illustrated on p. 251)

Cooking time: 20 minutes

2 litres (3½ pints) water
150 g (5 oz) whitebait
1 tsp salt
½ tsp monosodium glutamate
300 g (10 oz) canned mustard greens, washed and cut into 5 cm (2 in) lengths
250 g (½ lb) sliced barbecued pork
15 won ton dumplings (see page 317)
400 g (13 oz) egg noodles or instant noodles
4 tbsp peanut oil
2 tbsp sesame oil
2 tbsp black soy sauce
1 tbsp light soy sauce
3 tbsp fresh chilli paste
3 tbsp tomato ketchup

Put whitebait in water and simmer for 15 minutes. Strain and season soup. Scald mustard greens and dumplings and set aside. Boil a large pot of water and scald individual portions of noodles for 1 minute. Mix with a little peanut oil, sesame oil, soy sauces, chilli paste and tomato ketchup and stir well. Serve with mustard greens, sliced pork and dumplings or put dumplings in individual bowls of soup.

Cantonese Noodle Soup (Hor Fun Sap Gum)

Cooking time: 10 minutes

2 tbsp oil
1 clove garlic
1 litre (1 ¾ pints) water
100 g (3 oz) squid, sliced
5 prawns, shelled
6 slices plaice fillets
1 stalk mustard greens (or chinese cabbage)
200 g (7 oz) rice flour noodles (hor fun)
1 tsp salt
1 tsp fish sauce
Pinch monosodium glutamate
1 tsp pepper

Heat oil and fry garlic until brown. Add water and bring to boil. Add squid, prawns, fish and mustard greens cut into short lengths and simmer for 1 minute. Add noodles, seasoning and simmer for 2 minutes more. Serve with pickled green chillies.

Indian Fried Noodles (Mee Goreng) (illustrated on p. 257)

Cooking time: 10 minutes

3 tbsp oil
2 tbsp sliced shallots
1 large onion, sliced
1 stalk mustard greens, (or chinese cabbage) cut into short lengths
150 g (5 oz) beansprouts
2 tomatoes
200 g (7 oz) fresh yellow noodles
1 boiled potato, diced
2 green chillies, sliced
1 tbsp chilli oil (see p 289)
1 tbsp tomato ketchup
1 tsp salt
2 eggs

Heat oil and fry shallots until brown. Lift up and drain. In remaining oil fry sliced onion, mustard greens and beansprouts for 1 minute. Add tomatoes and noodles and continue frying for 3 minutes adding a little more oil if necessary. Cut up noodles a little and push to one side.

Add a few drops of oil and crack eggs in. Stir well with noodles and add the rest of the ingredients to stir for 3 minutes. This is a dryish dish and the order in which you put ingredients in is not particularly important. Noodles must be well-fried and reddish. Serve with sliced cucumbers.

Special Birthday Noodles

Cooking time: 20 minutes

2 tbsp oil
1 large onion, sliced
200 g (7 oz) beansprouts
300 g (10 oz) egg noodles, scalded and drained
3 eggs
4 tbsp diced roast pork
200 g (7 oz) small prawns
1 tsp salt
1 tbsp fish sauce
1 tsp pepper
¼ head lettuce finely shredded

Heat oil and fry sliced onion until soft. Add beansprouts and noodles and stir over high heat for 3 minutes. Push noodles to one side and crack eggs in. When eggs are almost set, break up and stir well with noodles.

Add roast pork and prawns and stir for 3 minutes. Add seasoning and stir until mixed and noodles cooked. Serve garnished with shredded lettuce.

Shanghainese Noodles (recipe on p. 253).

Home-made Teochew Noodles

Cooking time: 35 minutes

Few people can be bothered to recreate this typical hawker noodle soup at home as it calls for a large variety of items and garnishes. It is also not worth the bother to make it for one or two or even three people so I tend to prepare this dish whenever the family and siblings gather round for weekend feasts. The amounts specified here should serve 8 people.

5 or 6 litres (9 pints) stock or water
300 g (10 oz) pork fillet
400 g (13 oz) prawns
2 large squid
20 fishballs (available from Chinese grocers)
2 fish cakes (from Chinese grocers) about 150g (5 oz) each
5 tbsp oil
300 g (10 oz) minced pork
3 tbsp fish sauce
1 tsp salt or more if necessary
400 g (13 oz) fresh yellow noodles
200 g (7 oz) white rice flour noodles
300 g (10 oz) beansprouts

GARNISHES
3 bunches coriander leaves
3 stalks spring onions, chopped
8 tbsp fried lard chips from 300 g (10 oz) fresh lard (pork fat)
4 red chillies, sliced
pepper
individual dips of fish sauce

You can also eat noodles in a dry form by mixing scalded noodles with the following:
(For one serving)
1 tbsp garlic chilli sauce
1 tbsp tomato sauce
1 tbsp vinegar
1 tbsp lard (from rendered lard chips)
Serve garnished either in a separate bowl of soup or with the dried chilli noodles.

Put stock to boil and add cleaned pork fillet, unshelled prawns and squid. Simmer for 10 minutes and remove prawns and squid. Shell prawns and cut each into two lengthwise. Slice squid into bite-sized pieces.

Continue to simmer pork fillet for 10 minutes and dish up to cool. Slice fine and arrange on a side plate with prawns and sliced squid. Boil a separate pot of water and cook fishballs until they float to the surface. Drain and remove.

Fry fish cakes in 5 tbsp oil until brown and wrinkled. Drain and cool. Slice thin. Skim any froth from stock and season with fish sauce and salt. Reheat and when boiling again, stir minced pork in to simmer for 4 minutes. Keep soup hot. In a separate large pot, bring water to the boil and let guests take as much of noodles and beansprouts as they want.

Scald each serving in boiling water with a wire mesh ladle for 1 minute. Run under cold tap to remove starch and dip into hot water again. Drain and place in soup bowl.

Pour soup into each bowl and garnish with cooked fish, prawns, pork and cuttlefish and other garnishes to taste.

Vegetarian Noodles

Cooking time: 15 minutes

250 g (½ lb) rice noodles soaked till soft
1 carrot
¼ cabbage
10 French beans
15 mange tout
150 g (5 oz) beansprouts
400 ml (13 fl oz) water
2 tsp salt
5 tbsp oil

SPICES
5 red chillies
2 cloves garlic
4 slices green ginger
2 tbsp preserved soy beans

Peel and shred carrot as for coleslaw. Shred cabbage fine and slice French beans into diagonal strips. Wash and tail beansprouts. Pound spices together but wash preserved soy beans and drain first before pounding. Heat oil and fry spices for 2 minutes.

Add carrot, beans and mange tout and fry for 2 minutes. Add water and salt and simmer for 3 or 4 minutes. Add drained noodles and beansprouts and stir well until mixed. Rice noodles have a tendency to soak up liquid alarmingly so add a little more and adjust seasoning if necessary.

Transparent Noodles and Fishball Soup

Cooking time: 15 minutes

700 ml (1¼ pints) water
10 cooked fishballs (available from Chinese grocers)
150 g (5 oz) noodles
1 tbsp salted winter vegetable (canned)
1 stalk spring onion, chopped
1 tsp pepper
2 red chillies, sliced
1 tbsp fish sauce
½ tsp lard

Bring water to the boil and add fishballs. Soak noodles in hot water for 5 minutes until soft. Add to soup together with all other ingredients and serve hot.

Crisp Transparent Noodles

Cooking time: 10 minutes

200 g (7 oz) transparent noodles
Oil for deep frying
2 tbsp oil
1 clove garlic, crushed
150 g (5 oz) prawns, shelled
150 g (5 oz) crab meat
4 Chinese mushrooms, soaked and sliced
150 g (5 oz) beansprouts
1 stalk spring onions, cut into 3 cm (1¼ in) lengths
2 red chillies, sliced into strips
1 tbsp light soy sauce
1 tsp sugar
1 tsp vinegar
1 tsp fish sauce

Heat oil and fry raw noodles a few handfuls at a time. They will puff up nicely if the oil is hot. Drain well and set aside. Heat 2 tbsp oil and fry garlic until brown. Add prawns, crab meat, mushrooms, beansprouts, spring onions, chillies and fry for 1 minute. Add seasoning and stir for 2 minutes more. Add a few drops of water if mixture is dry. Dish up and serve with fried noodles heaped on top.

Fried Transparent Noodles

Cooking time: 15 minutes

200 g (7 oz) transparent noodles
6 Chinese mushrooms, soaked till soft
20 shredded lily buds, tailed and soaked
200 g (7 oz) prawns
3 tbsp oil
2 tbsp sliced shallots
2 cloves garlic, crushed
1 tbsp light soy sauce
½ tsp salt
1 tbsp black soy sauce
½ tsp sugar

Soak noodles in hot water for 5 minutes or until soft. Remove and drain. Cut mushrooms into strips. Heat oil and fry shallots until brown. Remove and set aside. In remaining oil fry garlic until brown. Add mushrooms, lily buds, prawns and stir for 1 minute. Add seasoning and noodles and stir well to heat through. Dish up and garnish with fried shallots.

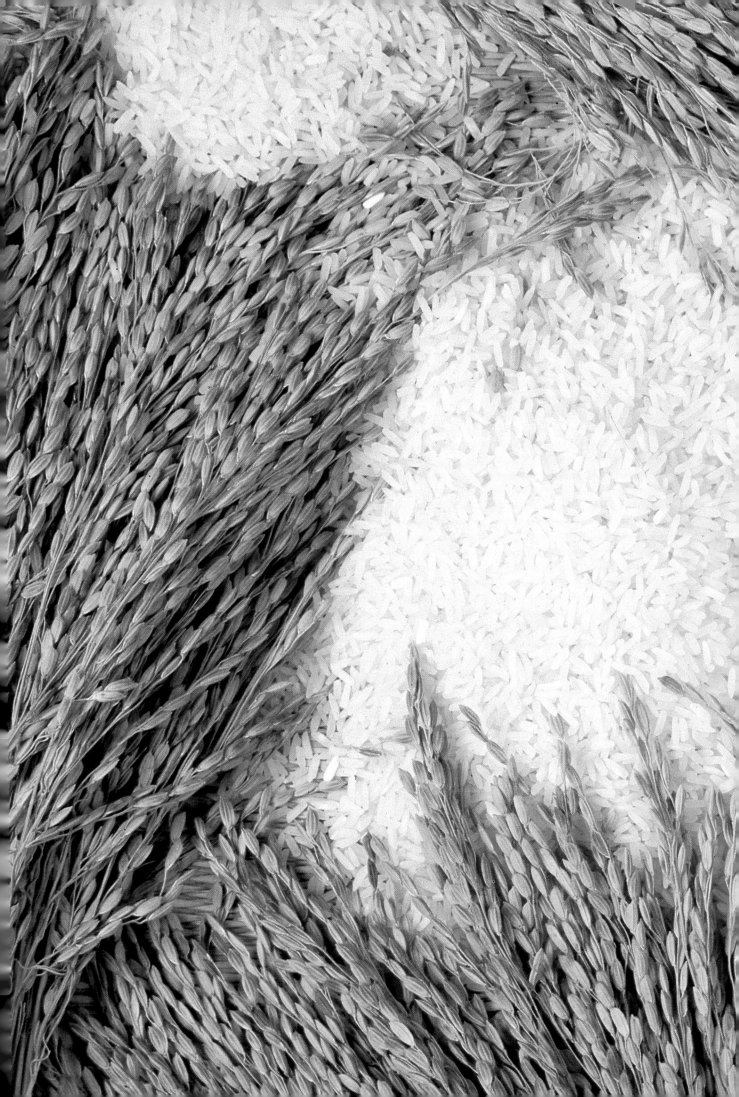

RICE

Rice is the staple in most Asian countries but this precious grain is by no means confined to being boiled and eaten unadorned with savoury dishes. Indian cooking has elevated rice to taste heights unmatched by any other for spicy ingenuity. Yellow saffron biryani, pilau with ghee, steamed, boiled, fried and stirred rice in a bewilthering number of dishes.

And there are as many varieties of rice as there are different nationalites who eat it every day of the year. On the Indian subcontinent long-grained rice that can be cooked to fluffy perfection is preferred. In the Asean countries shorter-grained rice is plain boiled and eaten a little dry. Japanese and Koreans prefer their rice sticky and almost lumpy to be perhaps shaped into innumerable sushis.

It is one of Singapore's glories of being at the crossroads of the world and where so many types of rice are available. And never is rice treated with anything but reverence. It is considered bad luck that one's rice bin become completely empty.

It is one of the simplest jobs to boil rice yet there is some mystique that floors the novice cook. How much water should I add? When will I know if it's cooked? Thanks to the electric rice cooker, much of the agonising has been eliminated. The important thing to remember is to top up water to no more than 4 cm above the level of rice however big a pot you cook. It takes an average of 20 minutes for rice to be completely cooked and dry.

In the following rice recipes I have referred to the watery rice gruel cooked and eaten by most Chinese as porridge. This has nothing to do with the Scottish oats and milk breakfast and the term "congee" somehow brings to mind a picture of regurgitated cud.

Biryani and Mutton Curry

Cooking time: 45 minutes

RICE
5 saffron threads
150 ml (¼ pint) water
500 g (1 lb) Basmati or American long-grain
   rice
3 tbsp ghee or cooking oil
1 large onion, sliced
1 small can evaporated milk
1 litre (1¾ pints) water
1 tsp salt
2 packets raisins

MUTTON CURRY
½ coconut, grated
400 ml (13 fl oz) water
150 ml (¼ pint) evaporated milk
5 tbsp ground almonds
Juice of 2 limes
3 tbsp ghee or cooking oil
2 tbsp ground ginger
5 cm (2 in) stick cinnamon
5 cardamoms
4 green chillies, split lengthwise
1 bunch fresh coriander leaves, chopped
600 g (1 lb 2 oz) mutton, cut into large chunks
2 tsp salt

SPICES
4 cloves garlic
1 tbsp coriander powder
1 tsp turmeric powder
1 tsp cumin powder
1 tsp aniseed powder
2 tsp chilli powder

Wash rice and drain. Soak saffron in a little water until you get a golden yellow liquid. Heat ghee and fry sliced onion until light brown. Add rice and fry over gentle heat so rice does not stick to pan surface.

Add first amount of evaporated milk, water and salt and transfer the whole lot to a heavy-bottomed pot. Cook over slow heat for about 15 minutes or until rice is almost dry. Scoop out about half the amount and mix with saffron water. Remove threads first. Put back into pot and stir gently so there is a good mixture of both white and yellow grains.

Actually it doesn't make any different if you make the entire amount of rice yellow. For presentation purposes, a contrast of colours is more attractive.

Add raisins and finish cooking for about 5 minutes.

Squeeze coconut with water for milk and mix with evaporated milk and ground almonds. Add lime juice to mixture and leave for 5 minute to curdle slightly.

Heat ghee and fry ground ginger for 2 minutes. Add pounded or mixed spices, cinnamon, cardamoms, green chillies and coriander leaves and fry for 1 minute more. Add cubed mutton and fry well until all meat is well-covered with spices. Add the milk mixture and simmer for 20 minutes. Add salt.

Do not cover and stir occasionally to prevent meat from sticking. When liquid is reduced by almost half the mutton should be ready. Whether you cook it longer depends on how you like the consistency of your meat. Scoop up and spread over rice burying about half just below surface of rice. Cover and let steep for a few minutes.

Teochew Fish Porridge

Cooking time: 45 minutes

This dish has a special place in my heart for it recalls a very colourful childhood. Some 20 years ago street operas or Chinese wayangs were a common sight especially during festival months. Some operas would perform as many as five nights in a row and the entire road leading up to where the wayang stage was would be lined with hawker stalls selling food of every hue and taste.

I would make a beeline for the Teochew Fish Porridge stall for its delicious compote of mackerel, grainy rice (it's quite different from the broken up Cantonese rice porridge) in fish stock, crackly dried sole and dried prawns.

200 g (7 oz) rice
4 litres (7 pints) water
600 g (1 lb 2 oz) mackerel
6 tbsp oil
2 or 3 dried sole or any unsalted dried fish
10 shallots, sliced
150 g (5 oz) dried prawns
2 tbsp light soy sauce or fish sauce
1 tsp pepper
2 tbsp salted winter vegetables (optional)
4 stalks spring onions

Wash rice in several changes of water and put to boil with water. Heat oil and fry dried fish until brown. Remove and drain. When cool to the touch crush with a rolling pin coarsely.

In the remaining oil fry sliced shallots until brown and crisp.

Check rice, and when grains are cooked but still whole, turn off heat.

Just before doing this add fish sliced into small pieces, dried prawns, fish sauce and pepper and simmer for 3 minutes before turning heat off. Serve garnished with salted winter vegetable, spring onions, fried fish, shallots and a side dish of cut red chillies for those with a taste for it.

Chicken Porridge

Cooking time: 50 minutes

1 litre (1¾ pints) water
1 chicken about 1 kg (2 lbs)
2 tsp salt
300 g (10 oz) rice (broken grains)
3 litres (5½ pints) water
1 chicken stock cube
2 tsp fish sauce
4 tbsp oil
10 shallots, sliced
4 tbsp shredded ginger
2 stalks spring onions, chopped
Pepper
2 tbsp sesame oil

Wash and clean chicken and put to the boil with 1 litre (1¾ pints) water. Boil for 30 minutes and turn off heat. Lift out Chicken and allow to cool.

Wash rice in several changes water and put to the boil with stock cubes, fish sauce and chicken stock. Simmer for 20 minutes and add shredded chicken meat.

Fry sliced shallots in oil and dish up to drain. Add sesame oil to porridge and serve garnished with spring onions, fried shallots, ginger and pepper.

Rice and Coddled Eggs

Cooking time: 20 minutes

200 g (7 oz) rice
600 ml (1 pint) water
3 eggs
1 tsp salt
1 tsp pepper
2 tomatoes
2 red chillies

Wash rice and cook with water till almost dry. Remove from heat and keep covered. Lightly beat eggs and mix with salt and pepper. Stir into still-steaming rice and put back on heat to dry off rice grains for 5 minutes. Heat must be very low or rice will burn. Chop tomatoes and chillies and sprinkle over rice for service. Add more salt if necessary.

Fried Rice and French Beans

Cooking time: 10 minutes

3 tbsp oil
400 g (13 oz) cold, cooked rice
1 large onion
2 French beans
2 eggs
2 tbsp boiled prawns (optional)
2 tsp salt
1 tsp pepper
1 egg
1 tbsp oil
2 red chillies
1 stalk fresh coriander leaves
Sliced cucumber

Cut French beans into small dice and slice onion fine. Heat oil and fry onions for 1 minute. Add French beans and fry for 1 minute more. Add rice and stir for 2 minutes. Push rice aside and crack eggs into centre of wok or frying pan. Stir well for 3 or 4 minutes and add prawns and seasoning. Dish up and clean wok.

Heat wok and fry egg until yolk just sets (bullseye or sunny side up). Serve rice with egg on one side and sliced chillies, coriander leaves and sliced cucumber garnished on the other.

Butter Rice

Cooking time: 25 minutes

250 g (½ lb) rice
4 tbsp butter
2 cloves garlic
4 whole cardamoms
1 stalk fresh coriander leaves
1 tsp salt

Cook rice as usual. Before rice is completely dry melt butter over low heat in a pan. Crush garlic and fry in butter gently. Add whole cardamoms and fry until fragrant. When rice is almost dry with still a little moisture on surface stir in butter and mix well. Chop coriander leaves fine and mix in together with salt. Finish cooking rice and allow to cool slightly. Pack into rice bowls tightly and unmould as individual portions to be served with plain meats and fish.

Dried Oysters and Scallop Porridge (illustrated on p. 268)

Cooking time: 1 hour

One of my first memories of scallop porridge was, morbidly enough, at a funeral. One of my uncles had died and it was customary in those days to have the body lying in state for several days. The kitchen help cooked huge pots of a tasty porridge that I found out later contained nothing more than dried scallops. Of course you don't have to wait for any special occasion to cook this porridge. Porridge for dinner is light and does not give you a feeling of surfeit.

4 litres (7 pints) water
300 g (10 oz) rice
6 dried oysters
6 dried scallops
2 tsp salt
2 tbsp sesame oil
3 tbsp chopped spring onions
1 tsp pepper

Wash rice in several changes of water and put to the boil with water. More or less water depends on whether you like your porridge thin or thick. Wash oysters and scallops and add to porridge. Simmer for an hour, stirring occasionally until rice grains are completely broken up. Stir in sesame oil for a smooth flavour and salt and serve with spring onions and pepper.

Rice and Chinese Cabbage Stew (Wei Fun)

Cooking time: 30 minutes

I used to think this dish rather peasant-like on account it was of the most unlikely combination. Then I was called up for national service and wei fun became a source of comfort amid all that square bashing and hill-charging. Just outside our camp was this make-shift stall selling fried noodles and the kind old man would dish up his wei fun at any time of the day or night when foot-weary soldiers preferred his mosquito-infested stall to the camp food. I cook it today not so much to remind me of those days but because it is very tasty.

2 tbsp oil
¼ Chinese cabbage, cut into 4 cm (1½ in) pieces
Few slices of cooked pork
2 tbsp small prawns, peeled
200 ml (7 fl oz) water
1 tbsp cornflour
1 tsp pepper
1 tsp salt
100 g (3 oz) cooked rice

Cook rice as you would normally. Just before rice is cooked, heat oil and fry Chinese cabbage for 1 minute. Add pork and prawns and stir for 1 minute. Mix cornflour with water, pepper and salt and add to pan. When gravy thickens dish up onto rice spread on deep plate. Gravy should be just thick enough and sufficient to soak through rice.

Cantonese Fish Porridge (illustrated on p. 268)

Cooking time: 30 minutes

400 g (13 oz) cod or haddock fillets
300 g (10 oz) rice (broken grains)
3 litres (5½ pints) water
3 tsp salt
1 tsp monosodium glutamate
1 tsp fish sauce
3 tbsp shredded ginger
5 tbsp oil
10 shallots, sliced
1 bunch transparent vermicelli
1 tsp pepper

Wash fish fillets and cut into thin slices. Marinate in a little oil and leave aside. Wash rice in several changes of water and put to the boil with water. While porridge is simmering prepare other ingredients.

Heat oil and fry sliced shallots until brown and crisp. Dish up and set aside. Fry vermicelli until they puff up. This takes a few seconds. Drain on absorbent paper. Pour two spoonfuls of oil into simmering porridge. Add salt and monosodium glutamate and fish sauce.

Add fish during last 5 minutes of cooking and serve in individual bowls with shredded ginger, fried shallots, fried vermicelli and a dash of pepper.

Fried Rice with Corned Beef and Cabbage (illustrated on p. 161)

Cooking time: 6 minutes

This is a simple savoury dish that not only uses up leftover food but with a little fillip and imagination can be turned into a star item.

3 tbsp oil
¼ cabbage, shredded fine
5 tbsp corned beef (about ¼ can)
200 g (7 oz) cold cooked rice
1 tsp chilli powder
1 tsp salt
1 tsp fish sauce
2 eggs

Heat oil and fry shredded cabbage for 2 minutes. Mash corned beef with a fork and add to pan. Stir well and add rice. Stir for 3 minutes and add chilli powder. Add other seasoning and stir for 3 minutes more. Dish up onto an oval plate to serve. Fry eggs sunny side up and garnish fried rice.

Yang Chow Fried Rice (illustrated on p. 264)

Cooking time: 6 minutes

4 tbsp oil
1 large onion, sliced
200 g (7 oz) shelled prawns
5 tbsp cubed luncheon meat or ham
3 eggs
300 g (10 oz) cold cooked rice
2 tsp salt
1 tsp pepper
½ chicken stock cube
1 small can green peas
1 stalk spring onions, chopped

Sprinkle a little water over rice and break up any lumps. Heat oil and fry sliced onions until soft but not brown. Add prawns, luncheon meat and fry for 1 minute.

Push aside and crack eggs in breaking up yolks. Stir when egg is almost set and add rice. Stir well over high heat for 5 minutes until well combined. Break up chicken stock cube and add to rice together with salt and pepper. Just before serving add peas and spring onions.

Tomato Rice (illustrated on p. 242)

Cooking time: 25 minutes

300g (10 oz) rice
600 ml (1 pint) water
1 tbsp tomato puree
1 tbsp tomato ketchup
1 tsp sugar
½ tsp salt
4 tbsp flaked tuna fish or
boiled prawns
Fresh coriander leaves

Wash rice and cook with water until almost dry. Stir in tomato puree, ketchup, sugar and salt and finish cooking for about 5 minutes until rice is dry. Serve with flaked fish or boiled prawns and fresh coriander leaves.

Fried Rice with Dried Prawns

Cooking time: 10 minutes

4 tbsp oil
1 large oil, chopped
4 tbsp dried prawns, soaked till soft and
  pounded
650 g (1¼ lbs) cold, cooked rice
4 eggs
300 g (10 oz) cooked prawns
150 g (5 oz) frozen green peas
1 tbsp fish or light soy sauce
1 tsp pepper
1 chicken stock cube
4 tbsp hot water

Heat oil and fry onion until soft but not brown. Add pounded dried prawns and continue frying for 3 minutes and until prawns are fragrant. Oil will be completely absorbed by the prawns for a few minutes but it will seep out again.

When it does, add rice and stir for 1 minute. Crack eggs in the middle of the wok one by one. Push rice aside briefly to do this. Stir well and add peas, fish sauce, pepper and stock cube dissolved in hot water. Stir until rice is completely mixed with ingredients. Serve with sliced cucumber or pineapple.

Beef Rice

Cooking time: 35 minutes

250 g (½ lb) rump or sirloin steak
4 slices green ginger, pounded for juice
1 tbsp cornflour
1 tbsp black soy sauce
1 tbsp sesame oil
½ tsp pepper
300 g (10 oz) rice
1 tsp salt
Fresh coriander leaves

Cut steak into strips and marinate in ginger juice, cornflour, soy sauce, sesame oil and pepper. Cook rice with salt until almost dry. Toss marinaded beef in a dry, non-stick pan for 1 minute and pile on top of rice. Cover and cook for 5 minutes until rice is dry. Just before serving, loosen rice grains by stirring with a pair of chop-sticks. This also allows the juices from the beef to soak in thoroughly. Garnish with fresh coriander leaves or cut fresh red chillies. If you want more flavour add a tablespoon of oyster sauce to the marinade.

White Fish Rice (illustrated on p. 272)

Cooking time: 30 minutes

300 g (10 oz) rice
4 tbsp oil
100 g (3 oz) cod
2 Chinese sausages, diced
2 tbsp black soy sauce
1 tbsp oyster sauce
½ tsp pepper
Large knob green ginger, bruised
Chopped spring onions

Wash rice and cook as per normal until almost dry. While rice is cooking heat oil and fry cod until fragrant. Remove to cool and shred a little. In remaining oil fry diced sausages and add all seasoning except spring onions.

Pile on top of rice including oil and add the knob of ginger. Stir well and allow to finish cooking on low heat. Serve with spring onions.

Chicken in Glutinous Rice

Cooking time: 45 minutes

350 g (¾ lb) glutinous rice
6 tbsp oil
2 chicken thighs
4 Chinese mushrooms
100 g (3 oz) diced roast pork (optional)
2 Chinese sausages, diced
1 tbsp cornflour
1 tbsp light soy sauce
1 tbsp black soy sauce
2 tbsp oyster sauce
1 tbsp sesame oil
½ tsp pepper

Soak rice for four hours or overnight and drain. Debone chicken thighs and cut meat into small pieces. Soak mushrooms in hot water for 5 minutes and cut into strips. Marinate chicken in cornflour, soy sauces, oyster sauce, sesame oil and pepper. Heat oil and fry mushrooms, roast pork and sausages for 2 minutes. Remove and drain.

In remaining oil fry chicken for 2 minutes until cooked. Steam rice (do not add any more water) for 25 minutes until fluffy. You can do this in individual bowls. When rice is almost cooked pile chicken and mushroom mixture on top and give it a good stir. Alternatively place a portion of chicken and mushrooms at the bottom of each individual bowl and pile rice on top. Upturn and serve each bowl with chopped spring onions.

Savoury Glutinous Rice

Cooking time: 45 minutes

300 g (10 oz) glutinous rice
10 dried oysters
5 Chinese mushrooms
2 Chinese sausages, diced
2 tbsp diced roast pork
4 tbsp oil
10 shallots, sliced
2 tbsp black soy sauce
1 tbsp oyster sauce
1 tbsp sesame oil
1 tsp salt
400 m (13 fl oz) water
Chopped spring onions

Soak glutinous rice overnight or for at least four hours. Rinse and drain well. Soak dried oysters and mushrooms in hot water for 15 minutes. Remove mushroom stalks and cut into strips. Leave oysters whole if small and cut each into two if large.

Heat oil and fry shallots until brown. Remove and set aside. In remaining oil fry oysters, mushrooms, diced sausages and roast pork. Add glutinous rice and stir well. Add soy sauce, oyster sauce, sesame oil and salt and water. Cook over low heat stirring rice every so often to prevent sticking. This is unnecessary if you use a nonstick pot. Garnish with browned onions and spring onions.

Compressed Rice (Nasi Empet) (illustrated on p. 164)

Cooking time: 30 minutes

This is the basis for one of the most delicious Malay meals that I have eaten. Of course the Straits Chinese borrowed it and refined it to suit their tastes which means to say they really couldn't improve upon it but merely adopted it as part of their own cuisine.

It's possibly the nicest form of plagiarising practiced, for the Straits Chinese actually increased the number of dishes that went with the rice. The Malays cooked it for birthday parties, their New Year and other religious festivals. The Straits Chinese, at least my family, cooked it like every other weekend! And what a spread there would be.

350 g (¾ lb) broken rice
650 ml (1 pint) water
½ tsp salt
2 screwpine leaves or vanilla pods

Wash rice and combine with water up to 4 cm (1½ in) above rice level. Add salt and screwpine leaves, knotted. Cook for about 20 minutes until all water is absorbed. Stir to break up rice further and transfer rice to a shallow tray.

Pat down firmly and cover with a piece of muslin. Use a heavy object to weight rice down preferably as close fitting to the sides of the tray as possible. Leave in refrigerator overnight and cut into cubes for service.

Compressed rice is ideally served with sayur lodeh (page 166) fried coconut (page 295) mutton or beef rendang (page 143) and fish in thick tamarind gravy (page 212).

Thai Fried Rice

Cooking time: 10 minutes

I cooked this dish rather once too often when two Thai students were staying with us for a time. There was always leftover rice which, time being rather short, invariably ended up in the wok being fried one way or another. Since Nik and Wan had taught me how to cook Thai food I naturally tried to make them feel less homesick.

4 tbsp oil
1 large onion, sliced
4 tbsp diced cooked pork
200 g (7 oz) prawns, shelled
½ packet crab meat or diced lobster
2 eggs, lightly beaten
1 tsp salt
1 tsp nam pla or fish sauce
1 tbsp tomato puree
1 stalk spring onions, chopped
1 bunch fresh coriander leaves
200 g (7 oz) cold cooked rice

Heat oil and fry onions until soft. Add prawns, pork and crab meat and fry for 1 minute. Push to side of pan and crack eggs in. Cook until almost set and add rice. Stir well and add seasoning and tomato puree. Stir for 1 minute more and serve garnished with spring onions and coriander leaves.

Steamed Glutinous Rice

Cooking time: 1 hour

600 g (1 lb 2 oz) glutinous rice, soaked
  overnight and drained
5 Chinese mushrooms
2 Chinese sausages
4 tbsp lard
15 shallots, sliced
2 cloves garlic, crushed
2 tbsp shredded ginger
600 ml (1 pint) stock
1 tsp pepper
2 tbsp black soy sauce
1 tbsp sesame oil
1 tsp salt

Soak mushrooms until soft and dice. Dice sausages. Heat wok with lard and fry crushed garlic and ginger for 1 minute. Add diced ingredients and fry for 1 minute more. Add drained rice and stir well. Pour in stock and stir well. Add pepper, soy sauce, sesame oil and salt and simmer covered for 5 minutes till all liquid is absorbed. Remove rice and press in individual bowls. Steam bowls covered with foil for 15 minutes. Serve hot or cold.

Savoury Rice Rolls

Cooking time: 40 minutes

1 kg (2 lbs) glutinous rice
1 coconut grated
1 tsp salt
2 screwpine leaves, washed and knotted
4 tbsp oil
150 g (5 oz) dried prawns, soaked and pounded
400 g (13 oz) fresh prawns, minced
½ coconut, grated without skin
12-14 banana leaves (or foil) 12 cm x 8 cm
  (5 in x 3 in) scalded

SPICES
4 dried chillies, soaked till soft
2 large onions
1 tsp pepper
3 cloves garlic
8 macadamias or almonds
1 tbsp coriander powder
1 tbsp shrimp paste powder
1 tsp salt
1 tbsp sugar

Soak glutinous rice overnight or for at least four hours. Drain and mix with coconut cream squeezed from 1 coconut without water. Combine with salt and screwpine leaves and steam in a flat tray for about 15 minutes.

Grind all spices together and fry in 4 tbsp oil. When oil seeps out again add dried and fresh prawns and fry until cooked. Remove from pan and clean pan. Dry-fry white coconut until light brown and pound lightly. Add to prawns mixture and stir well.

On each piece of banana leaf place about 3 tbsp of steamed rice and pat into flat squares about 1 cm (½ in) thick. Spoon 1 tablespoon of filling onto each rice square and roll up leaf. Secure both ends either with tooth picks or staples. Grill over charcoal or under electric grill for 5 minutes or until leaf is slightly charred. Serve hot or cold as snacks.

SOUPS

It is rare that a typical Chinese meal, especially Cantonese, would not include a soup. The premise that "four plates and a bowl" on which Chinese meals are built is indeed a sensible one for it is only when you have a meat, vegetable, fish and sweet around a steaming bowl of soup that a balance of taste and nutrition is possible.

Soup in a Chinese meal is usually served from a central bowl and every diner helps himself. Modern Singaporeans are less likely to follow this eating pattern eschewing the soup and perhaps one or two other dishes and making do with only two dishes. Most Chinese soups are light and meant to refresh the palate for what's to come, hence the reason for it appearing nearly at the end of a full-course Chinese meal at weddings.

Like the provincial French tradition of boiling some half a dozen cloves of garlic in water and not much else for soup, Singaporeans are rather ingenious in creating tasty soups from simple stocks and a few vegetables.

I never throw away chicken heads, necks, legs and claws or blade and shin bones as they are an excellent source of flavour for meat stocks. As for fish stock, clean fish heads, prawn shells and dried anchovy give a delicate flavour.

Soup Stocks

MEAT
2 litres (3½ pints) water
1 kg (2 lbs) pork or beef bones
1 tbsp lard
2 cloves garlic, crushed
2 tsp salt

FISH
4 shallots
2 tbsp oil
Fish heads or prawn shells
2 litres (3½ pints) water

Fry the crushed garlic in lard for 3 minutes and add water. Bring to the boil and add the rest of the ingredients. Simmer for an hour or so and you have a stock that has much more flavour than if you simply used stock cube or monosodium glutamate. Allow to cool if refrigerating and when fat congeals on the surface, skim off with a spoon.

Fry shallots in oil until soft and add cleaned fish heads (cut up) or prawn shells. Fry for 2 minutes and add water. Simmer for 30 minutes and skim off any froth floating on top. Use for seafood soups or as stock for fish porridge.

Won Ton Soup

Cooking time: 15 minutes

It was with bemusement that I encountered won ton soup in Australia. It was called short soup which made sense as long soup could not be anything else but noodle soup.

2.5 litres (4½ pints) water
100 g (3 oz) dried anchovies
1 tsp salt
1 tbsp fish sauce
20-30 won ton skins (available from Chinese grocers)
200 g (7 oz) minced prawns
150 g (5 oz) minced pork
½ tsp salt
1 tsp sesame oil
1 tsp cornflour
250 g (½ lb) mustard greens (canned)
1 tsp pepper
Chopped spring onions

Put water and dried anchovies to boil for 10 minutes and strain. Put anchovies in muslin and tie firmly. Put back into stock and allow to simmer while you prepare other ingredients. Add seasoning. Mix prawns, pork, salt, sesame oil and cornflour well and place one heaped teaspoonful of mixture onto one won ton skin.

Fold over diagonally to form a triangle and seal sides with a little water. Finish making won tons and bring a small pot of water to boil.

Cut mustard greens into 6 cm (2¼ in) pieces and put in to boil for 1 minute. Remove and drain and boil won ton for 2 minutes. Drain and set aside. To serve, place a few won ton in an individual soup bowl, top up with soup and mustard greens, spring onions, pepper and whatever seasoning desired.

Rich Beef Soup

Cooking time: 30 minutes

1 coconut grated
750 ml (1¼ pints) water
300 g fillet beef
1 stalk lemon grass or slice lemon rind
2 fragrant lime leaves or grated lemon rind
1 tbsp fish sauce
2 red chillies, sliced and deseeded
1 tbsp lime juice
½ tsp salt
1 stalk fresh coriander leaves

Squeeze coconut with water for milk and bring to the boil. Cut beef into thin slices. Bruise lemon grass. Add all ingredients to soup and simmer for 25 minutes or until beef is tender.

Liver and Kidney Soup with Ginger

Cooking time: 5 minutes

750 ml (1¼ pints) water
200 g (7 oz) liver
1 small kidney
4 slices green ginger
2 cloves garlic, crushed
4 tbsp oil
1 tbsp fish sauce
½ tsp pepper
1 stalk spring onions, chopped

Slice liver thinly and remove white part of kidney. Wash in several changes of water to reduce ammonia smell and cut into slices. Score a few cuts into each kidney slice. Heat oil and fry garlic. Remove and drain. Bring water to the boil. Add all ingredients to boiling water and simmer for 1 minute. Do not overboil or liver and kidney will be tough. Serve with fried garlic.

Beancurd and Minced Pork Soup

Cooking time: 10 minutes

1 litre (1¾ pints) water
250 g (½ lb) minced pork
1 tbsp cornflour
½ tsp salt
½ tsp pepper
1 tsp sesame oil
200 g (7 oz) soft beancurd or tofu
1 tbsp light soy sauce
1 tsp salt
2 tbsp chopped spring onions
2 cloves garlic, crushed
3 tbsp oil

Put water to the boil. Mix minced pork with cornflour, salt, pepper and sesame oil and shape into small balls. Put into boiling water and add beancurd cut into large cubes. Add soy sauce and salt. Fry garlic in hot oil until brown and serve soup garnished with spring onions and garlic.

Radish and Dried Cuttlefish Soup

Cooking time: 30 minutes

Dried cuttlefish lends a rich smoky flavour to soup if you simmer it for at least 30 minutes. This soup has been a good family standby for most of my life and I still enjoy it today.

6 shallots, sliced
2 tbsp oil
2 litres (3½ pints) water
1 small dried cuttlefish
1 white radish
100 g (3 oz) lean pork
100 g (3 oz) prawns
1 tsp salt
1 tsp fish sauce
1 stalk Chinese parsley

Heat oil and fry shallots until brown. Add water and bring to the boil. Transfer to a deep pot and simmer after adding cuttlefish cut up into small pieces. Slice pork into thin pieces and add to soup after it has simmered for 20 minutes. Add prawns and seasoning and simmer for 5 minutes more. Serve garnished with chopped Chinese parsley.

Mustard Greens and Squid Soup

Cooking time: 10 minutes

2 tbsp oil
2 cloves garlic, crushed
2 litres (1¾ pints) water
200 g (7 oz) mustard greens (canned)
3 small fresh squid
1 tbsp fish sauce
1 tsp pepper
6 shallots, sliced
3 tbsp oil

Wash greens and cut into 6 cm (2¼ in) pieces. Separate stalks from leaves. Wash squid and remove thin membrane. Cut into 4 cm by 3 cm (1½ × 1in) pieces and using a sharp knife, score criss-cross cuts on each piece.

Heat 2 tbsp oil and fry garlic until brown. Add water and bring to the boil. Add squid and mustard greens stalks and simmer for 1 minute. Add leaves and simmer for 30 seconds. Fry shallots in oil until crisp and brown. Serve garnished with sliced shallots and pepper.

Corned Beef and Potato Soup (illustrated on p. 118)

Cooking time: 15 minutes

I have a particular fondness for this rather odd concoction for an even stranger reason. Whenever I was sick my mother would brew this up and ladle spoonfuls down my reluctant and sore throat. It had something to do with the Ying Yang philosophy as beef and the ingredients in the soup were considered "heaty" and my illnesses were generally of the cold variety. To put it simply, I had to have a heavy case of the sniffles to earn this hearty soup.

2 litres (3½ pints) water
200 g (7 oz) corned beef
2 large potatoes, diced
1 large onion
1 tsp pepper
1 tsp salt

Combine all ingredients and bring to the boil. Simmer for 15 minutes or longer and serve with an additional dash of pepper.

Szechuan Vegetable and Pork Soup

Cooking time: 20 minutes

2 litres (3½ pints) water or stock
150 g (5 oz) Szechuan preserved vegetable
150 g (5 oz) lean pork
1 tsp salt
1 tsp fish sauce
1 tsp pepper

Wash Szechuan vegetable and cut into thin slices. Cut pork into strips. Put all ingredients in water or stock and simmer for 20 minutes. If using stock, use a little less seasoning to taste.

Boil Okra top, recipe on p. 157),
Stuffed Squid Soup (recipe on p. 281).

Lotus Root and Pork Rib Soup

Cooking time: 35 minutes

1 can lotus root
250 g pork ribs
2 tsp salt
1 tbsp fish sauce

Wash lotus root of all traces of mud and scrape skin a little. Boil a little water and scald root to remove some of the sap. Allow to cool and slice lotus root into 1 cm (½ in) thick pieces. Combine root, pork ribs, water and seasoning and simmer for 35 minutes. Serve with fried rice as a refresher.

Double-boiled Winter Melon, Chicken Soup (illustrated on p. 214)

Cooking time: 40 minutes

500 ml (16 fl oz) water
1 large winter melon about 1.5 kg (3 lbs)
1 chicken breast
1 chicken liver
4 Chinese mushrooms, soaked till soft
1 tsp salt
1 tsp fish sauce
Pinch monosodium glutamate
1 tsp pepper
1 tsp lard

Choose an evenly rounded melon. Cut off top about 5 or 6 cm (2 in) exposing flesh and a cavity large enough to accommodate the rest of the ingredients. In other words transform melon into a pot. Make jagged cuts along rim of melon for style.

Scoop out melon pith and a little of the pale green meat. Discard pith and cut meat into large chunks. Slice off a bit of the melon bottom so it can sit. Dice chicken breast and liver. Remove stalks from mushrooms and leave mushrooms whole.

Put all ingredients into scooped-out melon and place in container. Place container in a second container half-filled with water. Bring to the boil and double-boil for about 45 minutes. Use kitchen gloves to remove melon carefully. Serve as a centrepiece for a special occasion.

Spinach and Anchovy Soup

Cooking time: 15 minutes

2 tbsp oil
3 tbsp anchovy or whitebait, washed and
  drained
250 g (½ lb) spinach, washed and cut into
  small pieces
600 ml (1 pint) water
2 tsp salt
Pinch monosodium glutamate
1 tsp pepper

Heat oil and fry anchovies until brown. This not only enriches the soup it is one of the most nutritious foods available. Fry spinach for 1 minute and add water. Transfer to soup pot and add seasoning. Simmer for 15 minutes and serve as a clear in-between-courses soup.

Peanut and Pork Rib Soup

Cooking time: 45 minutes
20 minutes in pressure cooker

2 litres (3½ pints) water
200 g (7 oz) peanuts
250 g (½ lb) pork ribs
2 tsp salt
1 tsp fish sauce
1 tsp pepper

Soak raw peanuts in hot water until skins can be easily peeled or rubbed off. Put all ingredients except pepper in pot and simmer for 45 minutes. If you are using a pressure cooker, cook nuts in 1.5 litres (2¾ pints) of water without any seasoning or pork ribs for 15 minutes. Release pressure and add the rest of the ingredients and cook under 15 pounds pressure for 5 minutes more. The peanuts should be nice and tender by then.

Stuffed Squid Soup (illustrated on p. 278)

Cooking time: 10 minutes

2 litres (3½ pints) stock or water
6 medium-sized squid
250 g (½ lb) minced pork
1 tbsp cornflour
1 stalk spring onions, diced
2 tsp salt
1 tsp pepper
Fresh coriander leaves

Wash and clean squid and remove eyes and ink sac. Mix minced pork with cornflour, spring onions and 1 tsp salt and stuff each squid with mixture. Do not stuff too full as squid shrinks when cooked and is likely to eject some of the stuffing. Secure tentacles back with toothpicks. Bring water or stock to the boil and put squid in. Add salt and pepper and simmer for 3 minutes. Serve with chopped coriander leaves.

Tripe and Pepper Soup

Cooking time: 45 minutes

It is always better to use prepared tripe available at most supermarkets as raw tripe takes hours to boil down.

500 g (1 lb) tripe, cut into pieces
2 litres (3½ pints) water
3 tbsp peppercorns
2 tsp fish sauce
1 tsp salt
3 tbsp shredded ginger
4 tbsp oil

Wash tripe and put to the boil with peppercorns. Simmer for 30 minutes and remove peppercorns. If you put them in a small muslin bag it will be easier to remove them. Add fish sauce, salt and serve with shredded ginger fried in hot oil.

Chicken and Abalone Soup

Cooking time: 25 minutes

3 litres (5½ pints) water
1 chicken about 1 kg (2 lbs)
1 can abalone
1 tsp salt
1 tbsp light soy sauce
1 tsp pepper
1 bunch coriander leaves

Put water to boil. Wash chicken and cut into bite-sized pieces. Slice abalone thinly. Put in water to simmer for 20 minutes or so. Allow to cool and skim off fat from surface of soup. Reheat and simmer for 10 minutes more. Add seasoning and garnish with chopped coriander leaves. This is a delicate soup served usually during special occasions.

Kale and Pork Rib Soup

Cooking time: 30 minutes

2 litres (3½ pints) water
500 g (1 lb) pork ribs
200 g (7 oz) kale or broccoli
2 tsp salt
1 tsp fish sauce
1 tsp monosodium glutamate (optional)
5 tbsp sliced shallots
4 tbsp oil

Bring water to the boil. Have your butcher cut pork ribs into 5 cm (2 in) pieces. Buy only the ribs without the accompanying spinal bone which has more gristle than meat and also takes longer to cook. Wash ribs and add to water to simmer for 25 minutes.

Cut kale into short lengths and add to soup. Add all seasoning and simmer for no more than it takes to soften the kale — about 3 minutes. Meanwhile, fry sliced shallots in hot oil until brown and serve soup garnished with fried shallots. Serve a side dish of sambal belacan to go with the kale.

Bitter Gourd and Pork Bone Soup

Cooking time: 30 minutes

1 litre (1¾ pints) water
400 g (13 oz) pork ribs
1 large bitter gourd about 250 g (½ lb)
1 tbsp salt
2 tsp light soy sauce
5 shallots, sliced fine
4 tbsp oil
1 tsp pepper

Bring water to the boil and add pork ribs to simmer for 20 minutes. A pressure cooker will do it in half the time. Cut gourd into half lengthwise and remove pith and seeds. Cut diagonal slices about 2 cm (¾ in) thick and sprinkle with 1 tsp salt.

Set aside for 10 minutes and squeeze out all moisture. Add to soup and simmer for 10 minutes or so. Add seasoning and turn off heat. Heat oil and fry sliced shallots until brown and garnish soup with it before serving.

Mutton Soup (illustrated on p. 282)

Cooking time: 1 hour

1 kg (2 lbs) mutton, cut into small pieces
3 litres (5½ pints) water
18 cm (7 in) piece cinnamon
15 cardamoms, bashed
1 star anise
4 tbsp shallots, fried till crisp
Fresh coriander leaves

SPICES
10 shallots
3 cloves garlic
4 slices ginger
½ piece nutmeg
1 tsp turmeric powder
1 tsp cumin powder
2 tbsp coriander powder

Blend spices together and marinate mutton in it for 20 minutes. Bring water to the boil and add cinnamon, cardamoms and anise. Add marinated meat and boil for 25 minutes over high heat. Lower heat and simmer for 35 minutes until mutton is tender. Serve garnished with coriander and slices of French bread.

Hot Pot Soup

Cooking time: 25 minutes

The origin of this dish is rather obscure and no one in the family even knew what it was really called. In fact we had a rather amusing name for it — "leftover soup" — as it indeed seems like something conjured from last night's leftovers. It has, however, magnificent taste.

100 g (3 oz) chicken meat
100 g (3 oz) boiled, lean pork
100 g (3 oz) boiled prawns
100 g (3 oz) roast pork
3 tbsp oil
2 cloves garlic, crushed
750 ml (1¼ pints) water or stock
¼ Chinese white cabbage, shredded
10 French beans, sliced
6 Chinese mushrooms, soaked till soft
2 tbsp tree fungus, soaked
2 eggs
1 tsp pepper
1 tbsp light soy sauce

Slice or dice all cooked meats. Heat oil and fry garlic until brown. Add water and bring to the boil. Add all other ingredients except eggs and simmer for 15 minutes. Just before serving crack eggs in, swirling it around a bit. Serve with chopped spring onions or Chinese parsley.

Spicy Snapper Soup

Cooking time: 15 minutes

400 g (13 oz) snapper fillets
750 ml (1¼ pints) water
2 stalks lemon grass, bruised or grated lemon
  rind
3 fragrant lime leaves or 1 tsp grated lemon
  rind
1 tbsp fish sauce
1 tsp pepper
1 tsp lemon juice
1 tsp salt

Cut snapper fillets into serving pieces. Bring water to the boil and add lemon grass, lime leaves, fish sauce and pepper. Simmer for 3 minutes and add fish fillets. Simmer for 2 minutes and add lemon juice and salt. You can substitute the snapper with any kind of seafood.

Chicken, Mushroom and Quail's Egg Soup

Cooking time: 30 minutes

2 litres (3½ pints) water
2 chicken breasts, cubed
8 Chinese mushrooms
15 quail's eggs
1 tsp salt
1 tsp light soy sauce
1 tbsp Chinese wine or sherry
1 tsp pepper
1 stalk fresh coriander leaf

For stock if you are using this instead of water:
2 litres (3½ pints) water
2 large pork blade bones
Chicken carcass
150 g (5 oz) belly pork

To make stock boil all ingredients in a deep pot for 45 minutes and allow to cool. Skim off fat and remove all bones. Slice belly pork thinly and leave in stock for next step of preparation.

Bring stock to the boil. Add chicken and simmer for 15 minutes. Soak mushrooms in water for 10 minutes until soft and remove stalks. Boil quail's eggs for 10 minutes and remove shell when cooled. Add mushrooms and eggs to simmering chicken and continue cooking for 15 minutes more.

The traditional method for this clear soup is slow cooking in a double boiler. The Cantonese swear this method produces much more nutrition in any dish but I cannot see the logic in it. Of course, during more languid times, people had more hours on their hands to man slow-cooking dishes but this is impractical today.

SAMBALS, SAUCES AND SIDE DISHES

Far from casting a disdainful eye on these co-starring dishes, I have a healthy regard for them. In Singapore cuisine at least, they are prepared with as much tender loving care as the main dishes. Indeed, some Singapore sambals take on starring roles in spite of their secondary role as you'll find out why when you prepare them from yourself.

But whatever is prepared, the principle remains constant. A sharp or tart sambal to counteract an oily soup; a fragrant and crunchy fried anchovy to balance coconut rice. There are any number of fruits and vegetables that lend themselves to sambals (chutney is probably the closest western counterpart) with the addition of chillies, shrimp paste or limes. They are fun to prepare, take very little time and can transform an otherwise mundane dish.

Chilli and Soy Sauce with Lime (illustrated on p. 292)

5 bird chillies or
3 red chillies
3 tbsp black soy sauce
2 limes
1 tsp sugar

Crush chillies roughly with the back of a spoon and mix with soy sauce. Squeeze lime juice over and remove lime pulp. Slice lime skin into thin slivers and mix with sauce. Add sugar and serve as a dip for fried fish.

Sambal Belacan (Shrimp Paste Dip) (illustrated on p. 292)

1 large square shrimp paste 1 cm x 4 cm
  (½ in x 1½ in) square
4 or 5 red chillies
2 fragrant lime leaves or grated lemon rind
  (optional)
1 tsp water

Toast shrimp paste over charcoal or gas flame until slightly charred. Pound in pestle and mortar or wooden grinding bowl with chillies. Chillies can either be ground coarsely or fine depending on your taste. Slice lime leaves hair-fine and mix with paste. Add a few drops water if sambal is to dry. Serve as a dip for fried fish or raw greens.

Mango Sambal

3 green mangoes
2 tsp sambal belacan (see above)
2 tbsp sugar
Pinch of salt

Grate mangoes with skin and mix with sambal belacan. Add salt and sugar only just before serving or it will become watery.

Pineapple Sambal

1 small pineapple
2 tsp sambal belacan (see above)
2 tsp sugar
1 tbsp black soy sauce

Skin pineapple and dice fine. Drain off juice. Mix with sambal belacan and sugar and pour soy sauce over just before serving.

Cucumber and Dried Prawn Sambal

2 cucumbers
4 tbsp dried prawns
1 tbsp sambal belacan (see above)
1 tbsp sugar
2 limes

Peel cucumbers and cut into four lengthwise. Remove pith and cut into diamond shapes. Soak dried prawn in water until soft and pound until fine. Mix all ingredients with lime juice and serve slightly chilled.

Ginger and Vinegar Sauce

3 slices green ginger
3 tbsp vinegar

Slice ginger fine and mix with vinegar. This is a traditional dip for Peking Dim Sum dishes and dumplings.

Pickled Green Chillies (illustrated on p. 292)

30 fat green chillies
1 litre (1 ¾ pints) malt vinegar
1 tsp salt

Slice green chillies and discard any loose seeds. Do not wash chillies or they will not keep well. Boil half the vinegar and scald sliced green chillies. Drain chillies and discard vinegar. Pickle scalded slices in remaining half of vinegar and salt and eat a few days later.

Pickled Green Papaya (Pawpaw)

1 large green papaya
500 ml (16 fl oz) malt vinegar
1 tbsp salt

Skin papaya and cut into thin slices. Sprinkle with salt and set aside to "sweat." Squeeze out all moisture with a muslin cloth. Boil vinegar and allow to cool. Pickle papaya slices in this for few days. Before serving, drain and sprinkle with brown sugar.

Pickled Raw Crab

3 large crabs about 1.5 kg (3 lbs) total weight
500 ml (16 fl oz) wine vinegar
1 tbsp black soy sauce
1 tbsp salt
4 tbsp chopped peanut brittle
Fresh coriander leaves

Wash and clean crabs. Remove fibrous matter and main shell. Cut remaining crab into small pieces, shell and all. Drain and dry as much as possible. Boil vinegar and allow to cool. Mix with soy sauce and salt and place crab pieces in mixture. Transfer to a glass jar and seal tightly. Pickle for two days and serve with chopped peanut brittle and fresh coriander leaves.

Note: This is very much an acquired taste as blue cheese is.

Chilli Oil

30 dried chillies
10 almonds
4 large onions
4 cloves garlic
2 tbsp sugar
2 tbsp tamarind paste
5 tbsp water
6 tbsp oil

Soak dried chillies in hot water until soft. Deseed for milder flavour. Pound together with onions, garlic and almonds until very fine. Heat oil and fry paste over slow fire for 10 minutes. Squeeze tamarind with water and add to paste. Add sugar and simmer until thick. Allow to cool and serve as extra sambal for coconut rice, mee siam and lontong.

Preserved Beancurd Dip

2 squares red preserved bean curd
4 shallots
2 red chillies
2 limes
2 tbsp sugar

Mash bean curd squares lightly and drain off a little of the liquid. Slice shallots and chillies and mix with mash. Squeeze juice of two limes and sprinkle with sugar just before serving with steamed fresh anchovies.

Preserved Soy Bean Sauce (illustrated on p. 292)

3 tbsp preserved soy beans
2 red chillies
4 shallots
2 limes
2 tbsp sugar

Wash and drain soy beans. Slice red chillies and shallots and mix with beans. Squeeze lime juice over and sprinkle with sugar before serving.

Thick Coconut Milk and Sambal Belacan

1 coconut, grated
3 tbsp water
1 tbsp cornflour
1 tsp salt
1 tsp sambal belacan (see page 288)

Knead coconut with water and squeeze for thick milk. Dissolve cornflour with water and add to milk. Simmer gently over low heat and add salt until sauce thickens. Allow to cool. Mix with sambal belacan and pour as sauce over boiled okra, fresh cucumber, courgettes or other raw greens.

Simple Cod Tempera

Cooking time: 15 minutes

4 tbsp oil
150 g (5 oz) cod fillet
3 cloves garlic
2 red chillies
2 green chillies
1 stalk lemon grass or grated lemon rind
1 knob green ginger
1 tsp powdered turmeric
1 tbsp sugar
1 tbsp vinegar
4 tbsp water
Juice of 2 limes

Fry cod until fragrant and cut into small pieces. Remove to cool. Slice garlic, chillies and lemon grass. Fry all sliced ingredients in remaining oil until fragrant and add all other ingredients. Simmer for 2 minutes and add cod. Simmer for 1 minute more and serve with saffron rice or steamed rice.

Pickled Radish and Carrot

1 white radish
1 carrot
2 red chillies
2 tsp salt
3 tbsp malt vinegar
2 tbsp sugar

Peel radish and skin carrot. Cut into matchstick sizes and sprinkle with salt. Set aside for 15 minutes and squeeze out moisture. Slice chillies and deseed. Mix all ingredients and serve with sweet-sour pork or fish.

Anchovy Sambal (illustrated on p. 292)

Cooking time: 15 minutes

6 tbsp oil
5 tbsp dried anchovy
2 large onions
3 red chillies
15 macadamia nuts or almonds
1 tbsp tamarind paste
1 tbsp sugar
6 tbsp water
½ tsp salt

Fry anchovy in hot oil until crisp. Drain and set aside. Pound onions, chillies and almonds until fine. Fry in remaining oil until fragrant. Squeeze tamarind with water and add to pan. Simmer for 2 minutes and add sugar and salt. Add fried anchovies and serve with coconut rice.

Chilli Garlic Sauce

5 red chillies
3 cloves garlic
½ tsp salt
3 tbsp malt vinegar
1 tsp sugar

Pound chillies and garlic till fine. Mix with salt, vinegar and sugar and serve with plain boiled chicken.

Peanut Brittle Sauce

3 red chillies
2 dried chillies
2 cloves garlic
3 pieces peanut brittle
1 tsp sugar
3 limes
1 tbsp black soy sauce

Soak dried chillies until soft. Pound with fresh chillies and garlic and remove from pestle and mortar. Pound peanut brittle separately and mix with chilli, sugar, lime juice and soy sauce. Serve with deep-fried prawn fritters.

Ginger and Garlic Salt Sauce

1 large knob green ginger
1 tsp garlic salt
1 tbsp oil
1 tsp sesame oil
1 tsp sugar

Pound ginger until fine and mix with all other ingredients. Put in a glass bottle and shake well to combine oil and ginger juice. They will separate again when allowed to settle. This is served with plain boiled meats.

Fried Coconut with Fermented Beans (Tempe)

1 coconut, grated without skin
2 pieces fermented beans
2 chillies, sliced
5 shallots, sliced

Cut fermented beans into small pieces. Fry coconut in dry wok over slow fire for 5 minutes. Add beans, chillies and shallots and continue frying for 10 minutes or until coconut is brown.

Fried Garlic Slices (illustrated on p. 292)

10 cloves garlic
6 tbsp oil

Slice garlic and fry in hot oil until brown. Cool and store in airtight bottle for use as garnish for noodle soups and stews.

Fried Croutons

3 slices white bread
10 tbsp oil

Cut bread into 1 cm (½ in) cubes and fry in hot oil until brown. Remove wok from heat when croutons are light brown as they will continue to brown in residual heat. Cool and store in airtight bottle for use as garnish in chicken and macaroni soup and oxtail stew.

Belimbing Sambal

Cooking time: 10 minutes

Belimbing is a sour fruit the size of dates and found only in tropical and sub-tropical climates. Substitute with green mango or any other firm, sour fruit.

250 g (½ lb) belimbing
300 g (10 oz) prawns, shelled
4 cloves garlic, sliced fine
2 stalks lemon grass, sliced or lemon rind
½ coconut
200 ml (7 fl oz) water
1 tsp salt
1 tsp sugar
4 tbsp oil

SPICES
5 macadamia nuts or almonds
1 large onion
3 red chillies
1 tbsp shrimp paste powder

Slice belimbing into two lengthwise and remove bitter core. Sprinkle a little salt on them and set aside. Squeeze coconut with water for milk. Pound spices till fine. Heat oil and fry sliced garlic and lemon grass until golden brown.

Remove and drain. In remaining oil fry spices until fragrant. Add belimbing and prawns and stir for 1 minute or 2. Add coconut milk and simmer for 3 minutes. Add seasoning and serve with fried garlic and lemon grass sprinkled on top. You can also fry shallots, sliced green and red chillies for garnish of variation.

*Clockwise from top, right: Fried Coconut (recipe on p. 295),
Anchovy Sambal (recipe on p. 291),
Fried Garlic Slices (recipe on p. 293), Preserved Soy Bean
Sauce (recipe on p. 290), Sambal Belacan (recipe on p. 288), Chilli and Soy
Sauce with Lime (recipe on p. 288), Pickled Green Chillies (recipe on p. 289).*

SAMBALS, SAUCES AND SIDE DISHES   293

Salted Fish Roe Sambal

Cooking time: 8 minutes

3 salted fish roe about 200 g (7 oz)
4 tbsp oil
12 shallots, sliced
2 red chillies, sliced fine
2 limes
1 tbsp sugar

Wash fish roe and drain well. Heat oil and fry until brown and cooked. Be careful when frying fish roe as the little eggs tend to pop all over the place. Use a cover for your wok.

Remove and drain on absorbent paper. In remaining oil fry sliced shallots until crisp and brown. Discard oil. Cut up fish roe into smaller pieces and mix with all ingredients. Squeeze lime juice and remove the lime pith. Slice the skin and add to sambal for extra crunch.

Simple Coconut Sauce

Cooking time: 5 minutes

1 coconut, grated
¹/₂ tsp salt
2 pieces peanut brittle or
2 tbsp crunchy peanut butter
1 tbsp light soy sauce
2 tbsp lime juice

Squeeze coconut without water for very thick milk. You might have to add a few tbsp of hot water to the coconut if it has been left in refrigerator for some time. This is quite alright. Bring the thick milk to the boil and mix with all other ingredients. Serve as a dip for raw cucumbers, bean curd, cold roast beef or green salad.

Nam Prik (Thai Prawn Sauce)

Thanks to our Thai friends this delicious sambal is now very much a part of our kitchen. It's not only extremely easy to prepare it goes well with so many things. Eat it with raw vegetables, fried fish, fried chicken or hard boiled eggs.

4 tbsp dried prawns
1 tbsp dried shrimp paste, toasted
6 cloves garlic
3 red chillies
2 tbsp palm (or brown) sugar
1 tbsp fish sauce
4 tbsp water
3 tbsp lime juice
4 red chillies, crushed ·

Soak dried shrimps in hot water, drain and pound till fine. Pound toasted dried shrimp, garlic and chillies and mix with pounded dried shrimps and palm sugar. Add all other ingredients and adjust taste with more sugar or lime juice to taste.

Dried Prawn Sambal

Cooking time: 10 minutes

200 g (7 oz) dried prawns, soaked and pounded
½ coconut, grated without skin
2 fragrant lime leaves, sliced fine or grated
   lemon rind
1 tsp coriander powder
½ tsp chilli powder
2 tbsp sugar
½ tsp salt
½ tsp pepper

Mix all ingredients and stir-fry in a wok over low heat. Do not add oil as the coconut will exude sufficient to keep the sambal moist when cooked. The important thing to remember is you cannot rush this dish. The heat must be low and the frying action non-stop. Leave out the chilli if you prefer a mild dish.

Fried Coconut

Cooking time: 25 minutes

2 coconuts, grated without skin
10 shallots, sliced
4 green chillies, sliced fine
2 red chillies, sliced
1 tbsp lime juice
1 tbsp sugar

SPICES
1 tsp turmeric powder
3 slices green ginger
2 red chillies
2 cloves garlic
3 tbsp oil

Grind spices and fry in hot oil until fragrant. Add shallots and chillies and fry for 2 minutes. Add all other ingredients except lime juice and fry over low heat for 20 minutes or until coconut turns a rich brown. Add lime juice and serve sprinkled over compressed rice.

DESSERTS

Though Asians are not known to have a sweet tooth, we do have a fantastic range of desserts. Unlike western desserts and cakes where the basis is diary products most Asian — especially Straits Chinese — desserts use rice flour, bean paste, eggs, screwpine leaf flavouring and coconut milk. Certainly no cream or diary product, aside from a little butter, is used which perhaps explains why Asian cakes do not leave one with a feeling of surfeit.

Egg simply steamed with sugar and served with glutinous rice, bean paste wrapped with rice flour dough and steamed, or simple cookies made from rice flour and sesame seed — most are easy to prepare if you follow instructions. It is not an exact a science as making a souffle or cream cake — but a few are elaborate. These latter are generally relegated to the festive seasons but more and more people are eating the traditional cakes out of season. And why not?

Many of the desserts in this book do not have English names and those within brackets are merely descriptions. The word "kuih" means cake or cookie and is a prefix for most Straits Chinese desserts.

Rice flour and rice flour dough are sold at most markets and even in delicatessens in western countries. But the essential ingredient in Asian desserts is coconut milk. Coconut cream in cans can be used but this tends to have a slightly oily flavour. If you can be bothered, buy fresh coconut and grate them either manually or with a food processor and squeeze out milk by mixing with the stipulated amount of water.

Deep-fried Bean Paste Pancakes

Cooking time: 30 minutes

PANCAKE BATTER
100 g (3 oz) plain flour
½ tsp salt
2 eggs
50 ml (1 fl oz) milk
100 ml (3½ fl oz) water
1 tsp oil

Sift flour with a pinch of salt into mixing bowl. Make a well in centre and crack two eggs in. Combine milk and water and dribble about half into flour, drawing in from the sides. Beat well with wooden spoon and add oil. Add the rest of the liquid and set aside for 20 minutes.

Heat a flat-bottomed pan or cast iron griddle with raised sides. Grease very lightly with oil. Pour in enough batter to form a small round pancake. When underside is brown turn over and do other side.

Spread bean paste onto one side of pancake, fold over to form a rectangle. Deep fry each pancake or grill for 5 minutes if you don't like it oily. The amount specified makes about 4 medium-sized pancakes.

Cut into squares and serve as dessert.

BEAN PASTE
Making this yourself is laborious if you don't have a pressure cooker. Ready made bean paste is sold in cans at most Chinese food emporiums and specialist food shops.

Lima Beans in Sugar Syrup (Lek Tow Suan)

Cooking time: 25 minutes

One of these days this favourite breakfast, lunch and dinner item of Singaporeans is going to disappear together with other vanishing or vanished foods. It has never been the tradition to cook hawker dishes, especially the breakfast ones, at home but it looks like we might have to as fewer hawkers feel inclined to sell them. Thank goodness for supermarkets that sell pre-prepared lima beans that would otherwise take hours to soak and boil. Actually this is a very easy, and delicious, dessert to make at home if you can get the beans from your nearest supermarket. What's even better some come with a little sachet of sweet potato flour in each 250 g (½ lb) packet.

4 packets prepared lima beans, shelled and
   split
700 g (1 lb 6 oz) sugar
2 litres (3½ pints) water
6 screwpine leaves, knotted (or vanilla pods)
4 tbsp sweet potato flour

Wash beans thoroughly and put to boil with sugar, water and screwpine leaves. You need not boil for too long, only until sugar melts completely as beans are already soft from long soaking. If they are too hard for your taste, boil them first without adding sugar. Simmer for 30 minutes or so and then add sugar.

Just before serving, dissolve sweet potato flour in a little water and add to beans. The consistency should be like thin starch.

NOTE:
If you are using dried lima beans, soak 600 g (1 lb 2 oz) overnight and remove all skins. Boil in a large amount of water for 15 minutes and drain. They should be ready for the next step of cooking.

Bubor Cha Cha (illustrated on p. 304)

Cooking time: 30 minutes

400 g (13 oz) yam
400 g (13 oz) sweet potatoes
4 ripe bananas
2 screwpine leaves, washed and knotted (or
  vanilla pods)
650 ml (1 pint) water
1 coconut, grated
200 g (7 oz) sugar
½ tsp salt
4 tbsp palm sugar or golden syrup

Dice yam and sweet potatoes into 2 cm (¾ in) cubes and steam or boil until cooked. Drain and cool. Slice bananas into thick chunks. Squeeze coconut with water for milk. Put to the boil and add sugar, salt, palm sugar and screwpine leaves. Simmer for 5 minutes and add yam and sweet potatoes. Simmer for 3 minutes and add bananas.

Simmer for 3 minutes more and serve hot or cold.

Rainbow Layer Cake (Kuih Lapis) (illustrated on p. 306)

Cooking time: 40 minutes

1 kg (2 lbs) glutinous rice
2 tbsp sago flour
150 g (5 oz) plain flour
700 g (1 lb 6 oz) sugar
1½ coconuts, grated
1.5 litres (2¼ pints) water
½ tsp salt
Red, blue, green, yellow and purple food
  colouring

Mix three types of flours well. Squeeze coconuts with water for milk and stir into flour mixing well. Add sugar and salt and stir until sugar is melted. Divide into as many portions as you are using colours. Grease a square baking tray 18 cm (7 in) squared and pour a thin layer of batter into it. The thickness or thinness depends on the presentation you want.

The thinner it is the more work involved of course. Steam each layer for about 6 minutes. Alternate with different coloured batters until all are used up. Remove to cool and cut into squares or oblongs. A nice way to eat this is to peel off the kuih lapis layer by layer.

Lotus Seed Dessert (Lien Chee Suan) (illustrated on p. 300)

Cooking time: 40 minutes

This is another vanishing food — in fact it has practically disappeared from the scene — and basically the same as Lek Tow Suan except lotus seeds are used in place of beans. It's one of the most delicious desserts eaten cold or hot and well worth the trouble to prepare. Some Chinese supermarkets sell prepared and boiled lotus seeds that need no other preparation. Failing this lotus seeds in cans can be used but these tend to be rather mushy.

300 g (10 oz) or 2 packets lotus seeds
1.5 litres (2¼ pints) water
4 screwpine leaves, knotted (or vanilla pods)
250 g (½ lb) sugar
3 tbsp potato flour
5 tbsp water

Put all ingredients except flour and 5 tbsp water to boil. Simmer for 30 minutes and remove screwpine leaves. Dissolve sweet potato flour with water and add to mixture. Serve hot. This is a simple way to make Lien Chee Suan.

NOTE: The traditional way is to caramelize a small amount of sugar, about 4 tbsp, in a small pot until golden brown. Add this to the rest of ingredients for a light brown colour that makes it look more appetising and imparts a honeyed tang.

Fried Bananas in Batter (Goreng Pisang)

Cooking time: 10 minutes

150 g (5 oz) self-raising flour
1 tbsp Farine flour
200 g (7 oz) rice flour
450 ml (14 fl oz) water
1 tsp lime paste or grated lemon rind
3 tbsp water
2 tsp sugar
12-15 bananas
Oil for deep-frying

Sift self-raising, Farine and rice flours into a large bowl. Make a well in centre and pour in 450 ml (14 fl oz) water gradually. Mix well until batter reaches consistency that will coat bananas well. Adjust with more or less water and rice flour. Mix lime paste with 3 tbsp water. Add to batter together with sugar and stir well.

Peel bananas and cut into two lengthwise if large. Heat oil until smoking. Coat each banana with batter and gently slide into oil. Fry a few at a time so you won't lower the oil temperature too much. Fry till golden brown. Remove and drain on absorbent paper or in a wire mesh colander. You can also fry slices of sweet potato, yam bean, and tapioca this way.

Steamed Sponge Cake

Cooking time: 45 minutes

500 g (1 lb) sugar
10 eggs
1 coconut
500 ml (16 fl oz) water
1 tsp salt
1 tsp vanilla essence
500 g (1 lb) plain flour

Whisk eggs and sugar until light and frothy. This could take quite a while and it's always wiser to employ a son or daughter with nothing better to do for the chore. I was one of the unfortunate sons who had to whisk not 10 but 100 eggs at one go.

Squeeze coconut with water and add to eggs and sugar. Add vanilla essence and salt. Stir in flour gently and incorporate until mixture is absolutely smooth. Pour into ring mould or deep tins and steam covered. Steamer lid should have holes to release steam or cake will be damp. Steam for about 45 minutes or until cake has risen.

Sweet Potato Fritters

Cooking time: 20 minutes

600 g (1 lb 2 oz) sweet potatoes
150 g (5 oz) glutinous rice or ordinary flour
1 tsp salt
Extra flour for dusting
Oil for deep-frying
100 g (3 oz) icing sugar

Skin and boil sweet potatoes for 5 minutes or until soft. Mash and mix with sifted flour. Add salt and shape into small balls the size of walnuts. Dust each with a little flour and deep fry until golden brown. Roll in icing sugar until all are coated. Serve as tea-time snack.

Lotus Seed Dessert (recipe on p. 299).

Pineapple Tarts

Cooking time: 30 minutes

This delicious treat deserves more attention than the once-a-year binge by Singaporeans before Chinese New Year. I guess, on reflection, it is better to relegate it to a festive occasion so all can enjoy it more. Deprivation, after all, makes the palate more sensitive to good things.

800 g (1 ¾ lbs) flour
1 tsp salt
3 tbsp fine sugar
500 g (1 lb) butter
1 egg
75 ml (2 ½ fl oz) cold water
2 tsp vanilla essence
2 drops yellow food colouring

FILLING
4 or 5 large pineapples
600 g (1 lb 2 oz) sugar
4 cloves
1 4 cm (½ in) piece cinnamon stick

Sift flour with sugar and salt into a mixing bowl. Rub butter into flour mixture until it resembles breadcrumbs. Lightly beat eggs in a separate container and add to crumbed flour. Add cold water, vanilla essence and food colouring.

Mix well to form a thick dough. Cover with a muslin cloth and refrigerate for 45 minutes. Roll pastry to ½ cm (¼ in) thickness on a floured board or marble table top if you have one. Cut with a pastry cutter or a thin rimmed cup to the size you want.

Fill pastry with 2 tsp of pineapple filling and pinch edge for a frill pattern. Decorate top with pastry bits as desired.

Another way is to completely. cover pineapple filling with pastry and shape into little ovals. Snip with scissors to resemble stylised strawberries and stick one clove at the narrow end to form a stalk.

Place tarts on a greased tray and bake in hot over 180 Degrees C (gas mark 4) for about 15 minutes. Reduce heat and bake for 10 minutes till light brown and fragrant. Cool completely before storing in air-tight tins. Try and keep until Chinese New Year!

FILLING
Remove skin from pineapple. Nowadays, most fruit sellers will do this efficiently. Use a vegetable grater and grate pineapples coarsely. Squeeze out a little juice but not until pineapple mash is completely dry. Chop until really fine. Add all other ingredients in a heavy-bottomed pot or non-stick pan and cook over low heat until mixture is thick and resists the ladle. Cool and store. Filling should ideally be made the day or two before.

Chilled Sago Pudding

Cooking time: 25 minutes

250 g (1 lb) sago
200 g (7 oz) sugar
1 litre (1 ¾ pints) water
Pinch of salt
1 egg white
½ tsp vanilla essence
½ tsp salt
½ coconut, grated

Soak sago in water for an hour and drain. Boil water and sugar for a few minutes and pour in sago to cook over a low fire until sago turns transparent. Drain in a fine mesh sieve. Beat egg white with salt and stir in sago with vanilla essence. Pour into a tray or individual moulds and chill for several hours to set. Cut into squares or unmould sago and roll in grated coconut with salt.

Pengat (Stewed Bananas in Coconut Milk)

Cooking time: 20 minutes

10 large bananas
1 coconut, grated or
1 (packet) coconut cream
1.5 litres (2¼ pints) water
400 g (13 oz) palm sugar or golden syrup
2 screwpine leaves or vanilla pods
4 tbsp sugar

Peel bananas and cut into diagonal wedges. Steam them for a few minutes to remove any raw sap that might be lingering. This is not necessary if you use very ripe, almost mushy bananas. Bring water to the boil and add palm sugar and screwpine leaves to melt slowly.

If sugar has foreign matter, strain this liquid through fine muslin. Bring to the boil again and add coconut milk (obtained by squeezing grated coconut with a little water) or cream. Add bananas and simmer for 5 minutes and add sugar. Simmer until sugar melts and allow to cool. Serve chilled after removing screwpine leaves.

Fried Sweet Potato Slices

Cooking time: 10 minutes

200 g (7 oz) self-raising flour
2 tbsp rice flour
2 tbsp Farine flour
400 ml (13 fl oz) water
1 tsp lime paste (optional)
5 tbsp water
1 tbsp sugar
12 slices peeled sweet potato each 1 cm
   (½ in) thick
Oil for deep frying

Sift all flours into a large bowl and make a well in the centre. Add water gradually blending as you go along. Batter should be thick enough to coat sweet potato slices without flowing off completely. Dissolve lime paste in 5 tbsp water and add sugar. Add to batter and mix well. Heat oil until smoking hot and dip each slice of sweet potato into batter. Fry in batches until golden brown. Drain on absorbent paper or colander before serving.

NOTE:

You can use slices of yam, sliced or whole bananas, pumpkin wedges or boiled and mashed mung bean cakes in the same way.

Pulot Hitam (Black Glutinous Rice Dessert)

Cooking time: 2 hours (45 minutes in pressure cooker)

If you have a pressure cooker this dessert will take no more than 45 minutes to cook. Boil the rice in enough water to cover to 5 cm (2 in) above rice level but do not add sugar or they will not cook.

250 g (½ lb) black glutinous rice
4 litres (7 pints) water
250 g (½ lb) sugar
2 screwpine leaves or vanilla pods
1 coconut, grated
5 tbsp water
½ tsp salt

Wash rice thoroughly and put to the boil with water. Boil for a good hour over stove and top up with more water if necessary. Black glutinous rice soaks up liquid at a tremendous rate so adjust accordingly.

Add sugar and screwpine leaves and continue simmering until rice grains are completely fluffed up. Squeeze coconut with water for thick milk and add salt. Serve pulot hitam in individual bowls with a tbsp of coconut milk in each bowl.

Kuih Bangket

Cooking time: 45 minutes

I grew up helping my mother and grandmother make this delicious Chinese New Year sweet-meat by the thousands. We did not only make them for the festive season we had to make batches on order as it was a good source of income. It was my task after the tins were filled to deliver them all over the town we lived in. 30 years on I still love this crispy, melt-in-the mouth cake that has no western equivalent.

2 kg (4 lbs) Farine flour
2 large coconuts, grated
450 ml (14 fl oz) water
450 g (14 oz) sugar
1 tsp salt
3 screwpine leaves or vanilla pods
6 egg yolks
4 egg whites
1 tsp vanilla essence
4 tbsp sesame seeds
3 egg whites, lightly beaten
Flour for dusting

In the old days we used to dry the tapioca flour in the sun for days before the cooking began. One effective short cut is to fry the flour in a dry, warm wok for 10 minutes or so. Allow to cool.

Knead coconut with water and squeeze for milk. Add salt and put in a pot to cook with sugar, screwpine leaves. Simmer until sugar dissolves completely. Allow to cool.

Beat egg yolks and whites until creamy and pour into coconut milk. Add vanilla essence and continue beating gently. Fold in flour a little at a time and knead with hands until it becomes a smooth pliable dough for about 8 minutes.

Roll out to ½ cm (¼ in) thickness and use pastry cutters to make pretty shapes. Any cutter shaped into flowers, birds and insects will do. Dust with flour and sprinkle with sesame seeds or pinch some with designs.

Brush others with beaten egg whites and bake for about 20 minutes in a moderate oven until light brown. Cool and keep in airtight tins.

Coconut Candy

Cooking time: 1 hour

This used to be my favourite home-made candy though it takes some assiduous stirring over a hot stove. But the result is worth the effort as there is really nothing quite like it.

4 coconuts, grated without skin
1 kg (2 lbs) sugar
500 ml (16 fl oz) evaporated milk
200 ml (7 fl oz) condensed milk
2 tbsp butter
½ tsp salt
1 tsp vanilla essence
1 egg white, beaten
Red, green or yellow food colouring

Mix coconut with sugar, milk, butter and salt. Put mixture in a heavy-bottomed pot (preferably a non-stick pan) and stir constantly over very low heat until it boils. Add essence and continue cooking until mixture is dry and resists movement of your ladle.

This may take quite a while so be prepared to sweat over the fire! Stir in beaten egg white at this stage and pour candy mixture into a square biscuit tray. Press firmly down with a spoon or wax paper and allow to set and cool. Cut into shapes when still a little warm and separate pieces when completely cool. If using colouring add to a little water and stir into mixture while it's still soft.

*Bubor Cha Cha (in bowl, recipe on p. 299),
Banana Fritters (recipe on p. 308).*

Sargon (Coconut and Rice Granules)

Cooking time: 30 minutes

As a child, I used to love this treat that my mother and her sisters would make mountains of during Chinese New Year. She would take the trouble to make little paper cones and fill each one with the crunchy coconut, sugar and rice mixture and we would spend happy afternoons knocking back cones of the stuff.

I use the term "knocking back" in its literal sense as one, in order to enjoy sargon, had to tilt the head back, aim the cone at one's throat and tap all the contents into the back of the throat. One swallow made a whole Chinese New Year then.

But helping to make it wasn't so much a pleasure as my mother insisted on milling her own rice that went into the mixture. I suggest you use commercially packaged milled rice or, if you have a pestle and mortar, process the rice yourself.

500 g (1 lb) good quality rice, milled or ground till fine
3 coconuts, grated without skin
½ tsp salt
¼ tsp smooth lime paste or grated lemon rind
2 eggs, lightly beaten
300 g (10 oz) sugar
Paper cones

Wash rice and soak overnight for at least six hours. Dry thoroughly and mill till fine. Mix salt, lime paste and coconut well and pour eggs over mixture. mix evenly and add rice flour, a little at a time till well incorporated.

Here comes the hard part. Heat a wok or non-stick pan (my mother used nothing but her beloved "gerenseng" or brass pan proclaiming that anything else might just as well be mud) and fry mixture over low heat till dry. Purists might swear that a charcoal fire is the only heat you can fry sargon over but this is impractical in flats.

Turn your gas flame or electric plate to its lowest intensity and fry away. You must not, on any account, stop frying or the mixture will turn lumpy before complete evaporation of moisture sets in. Once this happens the granules will be brittle and fragrant. Add sugar last and stir for a few minutes as it must not melt. Leave to cool and fill paper cones as treats for kids (and adults please!).

Steamed Yam and Coconut

Cooking time: 20 minutes

This is a very easy dessert that can be made ahead and just mixed when you're ready to serve. Be generous with your grated coconut as this is what makes the dish.

1kg (2 lbs) yams
2 coconuts, grated without skin
300 g (10 oz) sugar
1 tsp salt

Peel yams and cut into large chunks for steaming. There is an easy was to peel yams. Cut right round the brown skin at 8 cm (3 in) intervals and cut again right down the length of each yam. When you peel the skin it then comes apart easily in even pieces.

Steam for 15 minutes or until soft. Let cool and cut into 2 cm (¾ in) cubes. Steam coconut for 2 minutes to prevent it going rancid overnight if you intend keeping some for the next day. Mix with salt and sugar and serve well-mixed in individual dessert bowls of cubed, steamed tapioca.

Clockwise from top: Rainbow Layer Cake (recipe on p. 299), Yam and Banana Rolls (recipe on p. 309), Pawpaw Rice Dessert (recipe on p. 308).

Pawpaw Rice Dessert (illustrated on p. 306)

Cooking time: 20 minutes

This is an excellent way to use up extra pawpaws or mangoes.

1 kg (2 lbs) glutinous rice
3 screwpine leaves, knotted (or vanilla pods)
1 coconut, grated
500 ml (16 fl oz) water
1 tsp salt
300 g (10 oz) yam meat, lightly mashed
200 g (7 oz) palm sugar (or golden syrup)

Soak glutinous rice for several hours or overnight. Place in steamer with screwpine leaves well buried and steam without any water for 10 minutes. Remove from heat and mix with half the coconut milk obtained from 1 coconut squeezed with 500 ml (16 fl oz) water. Steam for 5 minutes more and remove to cool.

Put remaining coconut to the boil and add pawpaw meat. Simmer for 5 minutes and add sugar. Put one screwpine leaf in pawpaw mixture if you like extra fragrance. Allow to cool and serve rice with a few scoops of pawpaw gravy. It tastes even better chilled.

Basic Agar-Agar

Cooking time: 15 minutes

2 litres (3½ pints) water
4 screwpine leaves, washed and knotted (or vanilla pods)
50 g (1½ oz) Japanese agar-agar, soaked for 5 minutes
250 g (½ lb) sugar
100 g (3 oz) castor sugar

Drain agar and remove any foreign matter. Put to the boil with water, screwpine leaves and both types of sugars. Simmer until agar-agar is completely dissolved. Pour into jelly moulds or steaming trays and allow to cool completely before refrigerating. Cut into diamond shapes or unmould and serve jelly whole with fruit cocktail or ice cream. To this basic jelly can be added food colouring, coconut milk and chopped fruits.

Banana Fritters (Jemput-Jemput) (illustrated on p. 304)

Cooking time: 10 minutes

I used to love the jemput-jemput a Malay woman hawker used to sell early every morning. She would use very ripe bananas and if she was feeling generous towards us kids, she would add an extra sprinkle of fine sugar over the delicious brown fritters. She also taught me how to make it.

1 coconut, grated
400 ml (13 fl oz) water
3 eggs
300 g (10 oz) sugar
1 tsp salt
250 g (½ lb) self-raising flour
12 ripe bananas (pisang rajah), mashed
Oil for deep-frying

Squeeze coconut with water for milk. Beat eggs and sugar till creamy. Sift in flour gradually, add mashed bananas and coconut milk. Stir lightly until well incorporated. Mixture must be of consistency you can drop in oil with a spoon. Heat oil and fry a few tablespoons at a time until dark brown. Drain on absorbent paper and serve sprinkled with fine sugar.

Yam and Banana Rolls (illustrated on p. 306)

Cooking time: 30 minutes

This dessert has a rather fascinating history in that it dates back to the Japanese Occupation of Singapore between 1942 and 1945. I was still a toddler then but years later my parents never let us forget what hard times they were and just about the only thing available for eating were yams.

The plant grew wild everywhere and Singaporeans used every ounce of their ingenuity to steam, boil, bake and shape the yam into a multitude of delicious desserts. This one was resuscitated by my mother-in-law who does not claim it as her original (others have cooked it too) but who makes it a mouth-watering sight.

She remembers the war years too but the memories are tempered with bemusement that she ate so many yams she began to feel she was putting down roots! It's not only very easy to make it's one of the most attractive desserts to present at table.

1 ½ kg (3 lbs) yams, peeled
8 bananas (pisang rajah)
1 coconut, grated without skin
400 ml (13 fl oz) water
2 tbsp cornflour
2 tbsp sugar
½ tsp blue colouring
4 tbsp sugar

Cut peeled and washed yams into chunks. You have to do this in order to remove the central root which is fibrous and unpalatable in older yams. Use a food processor to grind the yam fine. Put ground yam in a colander and drain off as much liquid as possible. There's usually quite a lot.

Squeeze one-third of the coconut with water for milk. Mix half of this coconut milk with yam mash, 2 tbsp cornflour and 2 tbsp sugar. Mix well and divide into two portions. Mix one portion with blue colouring and stir well. Peel bananas and leave whole. Wrap each banana with half white yam and half blue-tinged yam.

Shape into rolls with about 2 cm (¾ in) of yam around each banana. Steam for about 20 minutes. Cut each yam roll into thick slices and roll liberally in steamed coconut mixed with 4 tbsp sugar.

Note: It is not necessary to steam coconut if you are serving immediately. Coconut tends to go rancid rapidly if uncooked amd unrefrigerated. Steam it if you are serving later or even the next day.

Lima Bean Fritters

Cooking time: 30 minutes

300 g (10 oz) lima beans, soaked overnight
1 coconut, grated
750 g (1 ½ lbs) sugar
½ tsp vanilla essence
5 eggs, lightly beaten
Oil for deep frying

Wash beans thoroughly and rub away skins. Place in a pot of water when every bit of skin is removed and boil till soft. Reduce heat and continue stirring till dry while draining away water from time to time. Beat boiled beans with a wooden spoon till no lumps are visible.

Squeeze coconut for milk without adding water and add to mashed beans. Add sugar and essence and stir over low heat till mixture is thick and begins to leave the sides of the pan. It's much easier if you use a non-stick pot. Cool and roll out bean mash to small squares about 6 cm (2¼ in) squared x 2 cm (¾ in) thick. Dip each square in beaten egg and fry in hot oil till golden brown.

Coconut Milk Pudding (Kuih Talam)

Cooking time: 35 minutes

1 coconut, grated
200 ml (7 fl oz) water
6 tbsp rice flour
150 g (5 oz) palm sugar or golden syrup
75 ml (2½ fl oz) hot water
Pinch salt
Small ramekins or metal cups

Squeeze coconut for thick milk without adding water. Add water to used coconut and squeeze for second milk. Mix thick milk with 2 tbsp rice flour and blend well. Dissolve palm sugar in hot water and mix with thin coconut milk and salt.

Sift remaining rice flour into thin coconut milk mixture and stir well. Strain through fine muslin. Fill each ramekin two-thirds full and steam for 12 minutes till set. Spoon thick coconut milk mixture over, then continue steaming for 15 minutes more. Cool and turn out to refrigerate.

Tako (Thai Coconut and Water Chestnut Pudding)

Cooking time: 15 minutes

The first time I ate this was 16 years ago on the plane to Bangkok. It was love at first bite and I asked the Thai International stewardess what it was. She described the ingredients but could not tell me how it was made.

The delicious flavour lingered for many years and when my wife and I spent our honeymoon a few years later in Bangkok, we coaxed a friend's cook to part with the recipe. Since then my wife has made it hundreds of times and since her version is much better than mine I leave her to it.

The traditional way is to make little cups out of screwpine leaves which is not only for aesthetics but the leaves impart a lovely flavour to the dessert. An easier way is to use small metal or enamel ramekins and place a square of screwpine leaf in each cup to even up.

BOTTOM LAYER
4 tbsp arrowroot
4 tbsp rice flour
120 g (4 oz) sugar
16 water chestnuts, peeled and chopped
400 ml (13 fl oz) water
6 screwpine leaves (or vanilla pods)
4 screwpine leaves (or vanilla pods) cut into
  squares

TOP LAYER
5 tbsp rice flour
2 coconuts, grated without skin
350 ml (11 fl oz) water
½ tsp salt

BOTTOM LAYER

Mix arrowroot, rice flour, sugar and water. Cut up six screwpine leaves and pound. Squeeze out all the juice and mix with flours, sugar and water. Strain into a non-stick or enamel pot.

Heat over low flame and stir until mixture turns clear and thick like soft custard. Do not allow lumps to form. Add water chestnuts and stir for a minute or two.

Scoop up enough to fill ramekin, each containing a square of screwpine leaf.

TOP LAYER

Squeeze coconut with water for milk. Blend rice flour and salt and half the coconut milk. Cook over low heat till mixture thickens. Add the remaining milk and continue stirring until mixture is smooth and of pouring consistency.

Remove from heat and spoon over bottom layer. Chill and serve after an hour or so. This dessert can be refrigerated for up to two days without turning bad.

Fermented Rice (Tapeh Pulot)

Cooking time: 30 minutes

This is as near as anyone can get to making bootleg alcohol! I do not know if any law forbids the making of fermented rice though as it is not the fermented liquor that is consumed but the rice itself. When chilled, fermented rice makes a delicious, if slightly intoxicating, dessert.

I had an aunt who used to make barrels of it and it was somewhat mild agony trying to sleep with the pungent fumes coming from under her bed which was next to the communal one shared between my brothers and I.

I had seen her making it often enough to try it on my own. My first few attempts produced more mess than mash but later attempts were, I'm glad to say, as good as I would wish.

1 kg (2 lbs) glutinous rice
150 g (5 oz) rock sugar (or icing sugar), ground till fine
180 ml (6 fl oz) hot water
250 ml (8 fl oz) tepid water
100 g (3 oz) dried yeast ground till fine

Wash glutinous rice thoroughly and soak overnight. Dissolve rock sugar in hot water and set aside. Steam rice for 15 minutes and mix with 250 ml (8 fl oz) water. Stir well and continue steaming for another 10 minutes. Remove to a deep container.

Set aside about half the yeast and sprinkle the rest mixed with the rock sugar syrup over warm steamed rice and mix well but gently. Sprinkle half the remaining yeast on the base of another clean container, large enough to hold all the rice. Put rice over this and sprinkle the remaining yeast evenly on top.

Cover container tightly and seal round it with strips of clean cloth. Keep in a warm, dark place for about a week. Do not, on any account, remove lid before the 5th day. Serve with chipped ice and in small amounts at a time please.

Cendol

Cooking time:

If you ever come across a Thai recipe with the rather grandiose name of Vishnu In A Sea of Milk, it is one and the same as the humble Singapore Cendol (pronounced Chen — dole).

1 packet green pea or channa flour
750 ml (1¼ pints) water
4 screwpine leaves or vanilla pods
Few drops green colouring
200 g (7 oz) palm sugar or golden syrup
2 coconuts, grated
Crushed ice

Blend greenpea flour with water and stir over low heat until mixture turns opaque and thick. Remove from heat. Pound screwpine leaves and extract juice. Mix with food colouring to get the desired green and stir into mixture. Push through a colander while still warm into a bowl of cold water. You should get little curls of green. Leave till firm then drain and chill.

Dissolve palm sugar over another pan of boiling water and chill. Squeeze coconut for thick milk and chill. To serve, spoon some pea flour curls into a tall glass, top with 1 or 2 tbsp palm sugar and 4 tbsp coconut milk. Top up with crushed ice and serve.

Ang Koo Kuih (Steamed Glutinous Cake with Sweet Bean Paste)

Cooking time: 30 minutes

Much as I love this Straits Chinese dessert my memories of earlier encounters are not all sweet. The chief reason lies in my late mother's insistence for authenticity and tradition. There were usually two versions made; red and black. The red one presented no problem as cochineal food colouring was easily available. It was the Or Koo or Black Cake that sent me on a tailspin.

The only natural colouring that my mother would use was an extract from a wild leaf that grew in the most impossible places. It was a large leaf that resembled a grape leaf but was dark grey and velvety. After scaling fences and trespassing grounds I would have quite a haul of the leaves.

I would then dry them in the sun, tending to them every so often and when they were dry would soak them in hot water and pound them into pulp. It was from this pulp that the greyish black colouring was extracted. I do not think I want to go through the ordeal of leaf-gathering from inaccessible places when commercial food colouring does the job just as well.

Most cake-implement shops in Singapore sell Koo Kuih moulds which are basically wooden slabs hollowed out either in circle designs or paisley shapes. Indentations are of traditional motifs and one mould keeps practically forever if you look after it.

1 whole sweet potato about 150 g (5 oz)
2 coconuts, grated without skin
200 ml (7 fl oz) water
500 g (1 lb) glutinous rice flour
½ tsp red food colouring
4 tbsp sugar
½ tsp salt
Small dish of coconut or vegetable oil

FILLING
600 g (1 lb 2 oz) lima beans, soaked overnight
150 ml (¼ pint) water
10 screwpine leaves, knotted (or vanilla pods)
650 g (1¼ lbs) white sugar

Peel sweet potato and boil for 4 minutes. Mash well and remove any fibres. Squeeze coconuts with a few tablespoons of water for thick first milk. you should get about 300 ml (½ pint). Add remaining water to coconut and squeeze for second milk. Combine with sugar and salt in a bowl. Set aside.

Combine mashed sweet potato with half the glutinous rice flour. Bring the second milk to a boil over gentle heat and add red food colouring. Remove from heat and pour in the remaining glutinous rice flour. Stir well. Mix with the sweet potato and rice flour dough and add first milk. Mix well to form a dough.

Dust a board with more glutinous rice flour and knead dough lightly on this. Place in a deep bowl and cover with a damp cloth to prevent drying up.

FILLING

Remove all skin from the lima beans and steam for about 15 minutes until soft. Mash thoroughly. Boil 150 ml (¼ pint) water with screwpine leaves and sugar until liquid turns thick and frothy. Add mashed beans and cook mixture, preferably in a non-stick pot or brass container, till almost dry. Stir constantly with a wooden spoon and remove screwpine leaves after about 15 minutes.

Shape filing into small balls about the size of golf balls and set aside.

TO MAKE KOO KUIH MOULDS

Oil palms of hands and divide dough into equal portions each to size of a child's fist. Make a deep dent in each to contain a ball of mashed beans and reshape into a ball covering filling completely.

Press each ball of dough and filling into a lightly oiled mould till completely filled up. It is just as well to do one to see how much dough it needed for the size of mould and make adjustments. Turn out each cake on a piece of oiled banana leaf or foil and repeat process till all dough is used up.

Placed Ang Koo Kuih on a perforated metal steamer and steam over medium heat for about 10 minutes. Water must not be too hot or cakes will become mis-shapen. Remove cakes and brush lightly with oil while still warm. Trim banana leaves to shape when cooled.

Gula Malacca

Cooking time:

I discovered I need not bother with a translation for this dessert as it seems to be a much-loved dessert by the British and Australians. Probably the British Empire had its last sunset in Singapore with this sweet, and present-day attempts to resuscitate the good old curry tiffin of empirical days never fail to put this on the menu.

Actually the name Gula Malacca can be misleading as Gula Malacca is the name of the palm sugar or jaggery that goes into steamed or boiled sago. The local name for it, as it is with our propensity to simplify food names, is sago pudding.

200 g (7 oz) sago
750 ml (1¼ pints) water
250 g good (½ lb) Gula Malacca or brown
  sugar
1 tbsp sugar
1 coconut, grated without skin
6 tbsp hot water
Pinch of salt

Bring water to the boil. Wash and rinse sago and add to boiling water. Stir constantly until water bubbles again. When sago turns transparent and thick remove from heat and spoon into individual serving bowls.

Chill in refrigerator.

Met Gula Malacca in a small pot placed over a larger one with boiling water. Add plain sugar and stir until completely liquefied.

Do not chill sugar or it will turn too hard to pour. Squeeze coconut with hot water for thick milk and add salt. Chill. To serve, pour a tbsp of syrup on sago and top up with as much coconut milk as desired.

Apom Bekuah

PANCAKES
200 g (7 oz) rice flour
100 g (3 oz) wheat flour
2 eggs
300 ml (½ pint) water
250 ml (8 fl oz) boiling water
150 g (5 oz) coconut water
½ tsp salt

GRAVY
150 g (5 oz) palm sugar or brown sugar
250 g (½ lb) sugar
1 can coconut cream or
1 grated coconut squeezed with 200 ml
  (7 fl oz) water
3 screwpine leaves or vanilla pods
5 or 6 bananas sliced 2 cm (¾ in) thick
½ tsp salt
1 tbsp cornflour

Mix two flours and sieve into mixing bowl. Beat eggs lightly and add to flour. Add water and stir till batter is smooth and slightly thick. Add boiling water and stir well. Add coconut water and mix batter till no lumps appear.

Add salt. Heat a small cast-iron wok or pancake griddle with curved bottom and grease lightly. Pour two spoonfuls of batter for each pancake and cook on one side only until surface bubbles and pancake becomes pockmarked. Remove and keep warm.

Mix both types of sugar with coconut milk and bring to the boil over gentle heat. Do not use high heat or coconut milk will boil over and cause a burnt smell. Strain mixture through fine meshed sieve to remove any foreign matter in palm sugar.

Bring to the boil again and add screwpine leaves, sliced bananas and salt. When bananas are soft dissolve cornflour with a little water and add to gravy. Heat to thicken and remove from fire. To serve, pour 2 tablespoons of gravy with a few slices of banana over one pancake.

SINGAPORE SNACKS

And we do, all the time regardless of the time of day or night. Actually most Singaporeans do not regard snacks as mere bites to appease peckishness but meals in themselves or at least appetisers for what's to come an hour or two later.

Most are simple to prepare but a few require a lifetime's learning. And regardless of its ethnic origin, a snack is enjoyed by all whether from a coffee trolley in the office or at 2 am.

Many snacks have been elevated into the ranks of main meals but, thankfully, quite a few still hold their own as morsels of in-between pleasure.

Corn Fritters

Cooking time: 10 minutes

1 packet creamed corn
250 g (½ lb) self-raising flour
1 egg, lightly beaten
½ tsp salt
1 tsp pepper
Oil for deep-frying

Sift flour and mix with creamed corn. Add beaten egg and stir well. Consistency should be like thick batter but soft and flowing. Heat oil and fry one tablespoon at a time until golden brown. Serve with fresh coriander leaves.

Sambal Sandwiches

Cooking time: 10 minutes

This is a Singapore classic that used to make a regular appearance at birthday parties and other teenage hops when food was the last thing on young minds. Nevertheless, my mother never failed to insist we ate something substantial while the music was hot and we didn't need much persuasion to down her delicious sambal sandwiches.

SAMBAL
250 g (½ lb) prawns, shelled and minced
200 ml (7 fl oz) coconut cream
1 tsp salt
4 tbsp oil
1 tsp sugar

Blend spices until fine. Fry in oil until fragrant. Add prawns, coconut cream, salt and sugar and simmer until thick and oil seeps out again. Cool and spread over plain bread. Cut each sandwich into fingers and serve with sliced cucumber.

SPICES
1 stalk lemon grass or grated lemon rind
3 macadamia nuts or almonds
2 tsp chilli powder
1 large onion

Chicken Livers with Bacon (illustrated on p. 321)

Cooking time: 5 minutes

250 g (½ lb) chicken livers
500 ml (16 fl oz) water
3 cloves
16-20 rashers streaky bacon
3 tbsp flour
1 tsp pepper
½ tsp salt
Oil for deep frying

Wash chicken livers and boil in water with cloves until cooked. Lift out with slotted spoon and drain. Cut each liver into two if larger than bite-size. De-rind each bacon rasher and roll round one piece of liver. Secure with a toothpick and dust with flour seasoned with pepper and salt. Deep fry in hot oil until golden brown and drain on absorbent paper. Serve with the toothpicks still on.

Chicken Pie

Cooking time: 1 hour

1 packet flaky pastry
3 tbsp milk

FILLING
2 chicken breasts, boiled and diced (reserve
 200 ml (7 fl oz) stock)
3 tbsp butter
2 tbsp plain flour
1 large onion, sliced
1 carrot, diced
1 potato, diced
3 tbsp frozen green peas
2 hard-boiled eggs, sliced
1 tsp salt
1 tsp pepper

Roll out pastry and fill a 18 cm (7 in) pie tin with ½ cm (¼ in) thick round. Trim off excess and roll out again to form another round for pie crust. Heat pan with butter and fry onion until soft. Sprinkle flour over and cook over low heat to form a roux.

Add chicken, carrot, potato, green peas and seasoning and stock and simmer until thick. Allow to cool and fill pie shell with mixture. Arrange boiled egg on top and cover with pastry round.

Pinch sides moistened with milk and make ridged design. Cut a few small slits on top crust to allow steam to escape during baking. Brush with milk and bake for 45 minutes or until crust turns a golden brown.

Steamed Wonton Dumplings (illustrated on p. 321)

Cooking time: 25 minutes

I must confess making these delicious bites took some learning but with the patience of my mother-in-law I soon learnt to whip them up in a matter of half a morning — with her help of course. Although it is called bamboo shoot dumpling in Chinese it contains no bamboo shoot but sweet potatoes.

PASTRY DOUGH
20-30 wonton wrappers (available from
 Chinese supermarkets)

FILLING
4 tbsp oil
300 (10 oz) minced prawns
400 g (13 oz) sweet potato , finely shredded
2 stalks spring onions, chopped
6 shallots, sliced
1 tbsp light soy sauce
1 tsp sugar
1 tbsp sesame oil
1 tsp pepper
1 tsp salt
1 tbsp cornflour
1 tbsp water

Fry sliced shallots in hot oil until brown and add minced prawns. Stir well for 1 minute and add sweet potatoes, seasoning and cornflour mixed with water. Fry for 2 or 3 minutes more and add a little more water if mixture is too dry. Dish out and cool.

Place 1 tbsp of filling on wonton wrapper and fold into half-moon shape. Press sides down firmly to seal and brush each dumpling with a little oil. This will prevent them sticking to one another when steamed. Steam for 5 or 6 minutes and serve with bottled chilli sauce and black soy sauce.

Curry Puff *(illustrated opposite)*

Cooking time: 20 minutes

500 g (1 lb) flaky pastry
3 tbsp oil
1 large onion, sliced fine
2 tbsp curry paste
300 g (10 oz) minced beef or chicken
2 large potatoes, boiled and diced
1 tsp salt
1 tsp sugar
150 ml (¼ pint) milk

Allow pastry to thaw for about an hour. Meanwhile heat oil and fry sliced onions until soft but not brown. Add curry paste and fry for 2 or 3 minutes until fragrant. Add minced beef and diced potatoes and fry for 2 minutes.

If mixture seems too dry add a few drops of water or milk. Add sugar and salt and dish up to cool. Roll out pastry to ½ cm (¼ in) thickness and cut into squares 12 cm (5 in) square. Fill each square with cooled mixture and form into half-moons. Moisten edges with milk and seal firmly.

Pinch edges to form scallop pattern. Brush each curry puff with a little milk and bake in a hot oven for 15 minutes or until golden brown. If you are impatient, you could deep fry the curry puffs which takes a few minutes but they will be more greasy.

Chicken Kromeskies

Cooking time: 10 minutes

Kromeskies are nothing more than savoury fritters in spite of their strange-sounding name. The basic mixture is similar to that of a croquette except the use of bacon which is rolled up and dipped into the batter and then fried.

250 g (½ lb) cooked, diced chicken
3 tbsp butter
2 tbsp flour
250 ml (8 fl oz) milk
½ tsp salt
½ tsp pepper
1 egg
12 bacon rashes, without rind

BATTER
200 g (7 oz) flour
½ tsp salt
1 tsp yeast
150 ml (¼ pint) warm water

To make batter, sift flour with salt and dissolve yeast in a little warm water. Mix together and let stand for half an hour. Melt butter and sprinkle flour over to cook over low heat. Add milk, salt, pepper and egg and stir well. Remove from heat and allow to get completely cold.

Place one bacon rasher over another, slightly overlapping to form a wide rasher. Put one tablespoon of chicken mixture on bacon and roll up. Dip each kromesky into batter and lift out with slotted spoon to drop into hot oil. Fry a few at a time as batter expands when cooked. Fry until golden brown and drain on absorbent paper. Serve with hot sauce.

Samosas (left, recipe on p. 320),
Curry Puffs.

Crab Meat Pie

Cooking time: 1 hour

500 g (1 lb) puff pastry
150 ml (¼ pint) milk

FILLING
350 g (¾ lb) crab meat
3 tbsp boiled, diced carrots
3 tbsp frozen green peas
1 stalk spring onions, chopped
1 tsp pepper
1 tbsp sesame oil
1 tbsp cornflour
1 tsp salt
3 tbsp water
Oil for deep frying

Roll out thawed pastry and form into a large round about ½ cm (¼ in) thick. Place in a pie-tin about 15-18 cm (6 in-7 in) in diameter. Trim off excess and reshape into round. Roll out and set aside for pie cover. Mix all filling ingredients, adding water a little at a time until mixture is thickish.

Fill pie shell with mixture and cover with pastry. Dampen edge of shell with milk and press down firmly to seal. Pinch or cut into ridges. Brush with milk and bake in moderate oven for 45 minutes.

Lotus Seed Paste Dumpling

Cooking time: 10 minutes

400 g (13 oz) lotus seed paste (ground from lotus seeds)
500 g (1 lb) wheat flour
200 g (7 oz) lard
1 tsp bicarbonate of soda
150 ml (¼ pint) water
5 tbsp sugar

Sieve the flour, bicarbonate of soda and mix with lard and water. Knead into soft dough and divide into two portions. Knead each portion separately and divide into 25 portions. Form each portion into rounds and flatten with rolling pin.

Place one round on another and roll once more. You should have rounds each formed by two pieces of dough. Fill each round with 2 tbsp of lotus seed paste and roll into a ball. Use a sharp blade to cut criss-cross patterns at the top of each ball to form an open-petal shape without cutting into filling. Deep fry until brown and sprinkle each dumpling with sugar while hot.

Samosas (illustrated on p. 318)

Cooking time: 8 minutes

10 spring roll skins
Oil for deep frying
3 tbsp oil
1 clove garlic, chopped
1 tsp curry powder
3 potatoes, boiled and diced fine
150 g (5 oz) frozen green peas
1 large onion, finely sliced
2 red chillies, chopped
½ tsp salt
1 stalk fresh coriander leaves, chopped
1 tbsp lemon juice

Heat oil and fry onion until soft but not brown. Add chopped garlic and fry for 1 minute more. Add curry powder and fry for 2 minutes over gentle heat. Add potatoes and peas and stir for a few seconds then add all other ingredients. Stir well and dish up to cool

Cut each spring roll skin into 8 cm (3 in) squares. Place one level tablespoon of filling in each square and fold into small triangles. Seal with water and fry in hot oil until golden brown and crisp.

Chicken Livers with Bacon (right, recipe on p. 316),
Steamed Wonton Dumplings (recipe on p. 317).

Yam or Taro Puffs

Cooking time: 20 minutes

PASTRY
200 g (7 oz) yam
3 tbsp plain flour
2 tbsp lard
Pinch bicarbonate of soda
Pinch baking powder
1 tsp sesame oil
½ tsp pepper
1 tsp sugar
½ tsp salt
Oil for deep-frying

FRYING
200 g (7 oz) prawns, coarsely minced
150 g (5 oz) roast pork, diced
150 g (5 oz) frozen green peas
1 tsp sesame oil
½ tsp pepper
1 tsp salt
1 tsp sugar
2 tbsp oil

Peel yam and cut into manageable chunks. Steam for about 10 minutes till cooked through. Mash while still a little warm and add all other pastry ingredients. Knead with lightly floured hands until pastry dough is soft and pliable. Keep covered so it doesn't dry out and set aside. Heat oil and fry prawns till they turn pink. Add peas, diced roast pork, sesame oil, pepper, sugar and salt.

Fry well for a few minutes and add a few tbsp water. Simmer for 1 minute and remove to cool. Divide pastry into 10 or 12 portions. Form into rounds and put 1 tbsp filling into each round. Shape into a neat round puff with floured hands. Fry in hot oil till brown. Drain on absorbent paper and serve warm with chilli or tomato sauce.

Peanut Cream

Cooking time: 30 minutes

This used to be my favourite late-night dessert when the peanut cream hawker came along usually well after midnight! He also sold sesame cream and it was these two creamy, stomach-warming snacks that saw us through many a weekend mahjong session.

300 g (10 oz) peanuts
80 g (2½ oz) sesame seeds
1 litre (1¾ pints) water
150 g (5 oz) sugar
150 ml (¼ pint) evaporated milk
1 tbsp cornflour

Fry peanuts in a dry wok over very low heat for about 15 minutes until nut skins are slightly charred and nuts brown. Taste one to check. A cooked nut should not have any "raw" flavour but be crisp and crunchy. Remove nuts to cool. Dry fry sesame seeds for 2 minutes and remove.

Skin peanuts by rubbing hands over them and winnowing away skins. Blend nuts and sesame seeds with 300 ml (½ pint) of the water until smooth. If it is still grainy, strain through fine wire mesh. Mix with the rest of the water and bring to the boil. Add sugar and cornflour blended with a little water. Stir for a minute or two and remove from heat. Add evaporated milk and serve hot.

Crab Croquettes

Cooking time: 10 minutes

200 g (7 oz) cooked crab meat
2 tbsp butter
3 shallots, sliced
2 tbsp flour
150 ml (¼ pint) milk
½ tsp salt
½ tsp pepper
1 small egg, lightly beaten

COATING
1 egg, lightly beaten
White breadcrumbs

Heat butter in pan and fry shallots until soft but not brown. Sprinkle flour over butter and stir for 1 minute. Add milk to simmer for 1 minute. Add crab meat, salt, pepper and egg and blend over low heat. Remove to cool. When quite cold divide into rolls. Dip in beaten egg and roll in bread crumbs. Fry until golden brown.

Scallop Rolls

Cooking time: 8 minutes

200 g (7 oz) scallops
100 g (3 oz) minced pork
4 Chinese mushrooms, soaked till soft
2 tbsp chopped water chestnuts
½ tsp salt
1 stalk spring onions, chopped
1 tsp sesame oil
1 tsp fish sauce
15 spring roll skins
1 egg
2 tbsp plain flour
Oil for deep frying

Remove orange scallop beard and cut into small pieces. Chop mushrooms roughly removing stalks. Mix scallops, minced pork, chestnuts, salt, spring onions, sesame oil and fish sauce and stir well.

Cut each spring roll into quarters and fill each quarter with 1 heaped teaspoonful of mixture. Make into rolls tucking ends in firmly and seal with paste made from batter of beaten egg mixed with flour. Leave this out and seal with water if you are pressed for time. Deep fry rolls in hot oil until golden brown. Serve with oyster sauce.

Shepherd's Pie

Cooking time: 30 minutes

I learnt to make this from a Eurasian neighbour who took great pride in her version which was delicious. It's a good way to use up leftover minced beef and mashed potatoes.

2 tbsp lard
1 large onion, chopped
500 g (1 lb) minced beef
1 tsp salt
1 tsp pepper
½ beef stock cube
3 tbsp water
4 tbsp cooked, diced carrot
650 g (1¼ lbs) mashed potatoes

Heat lard and brown chopped onion for 2 minutes. Add minced beef and fry for 1 minute. Add seasoning, stock cube and water and stir for 2 minutes more. Add carrots and transfer mixture to overproof casserole or deep pie dish. Top with mashed potatoes and rake with fork to make rough design. Bake in hot oven for about 15 minutes or until potato topping is brown here and there.

Shanghainese Dumplings (Woh Tip) (illustrated opposite)

Cooking time: 8 minutes

PASTRY DOUGH
500 g (1 lb) wheat flour
250 ml (8 fl oz) water
1 tsp salt

FILLING
500 g (1 lb) minced pork
150g (5 oz) minced prawns, chopped coarsely
350 g (¾ lb) shredded Chinese cabbage
2 tbsp shredded green ginger
3 tbsp sesame oil
1 tbsp light soy sauce
1 tsp salt
½ tsp sugar
4 tbsp oil
300 ml (½ pint) water

Mix water with salt and stir into flour in mixing bowl. Mix well and knead into a soft dough. Cover with damp muslin and set aside for 20 minutes. Knead again on floured board until smooth and pliable. Divide into small portions to be rolled into rounds each about 8-cm (3 in) in diameter and ½ cm (¼ in) thick.

Mix all ingredients except oil and water. Fill each pastry round with 1 tbsp of filling and seal into oval or half-moon shapes. Heat a flat frying pan with oil and line pan with dumplings. Fry over hot fire for 1 or 2 minutes until brown and pour in water. Cover pan and cook until all water has evaporated. Alternatively you could boil dumplings for 30 seconds and then fry them. Serve with black vinegar.

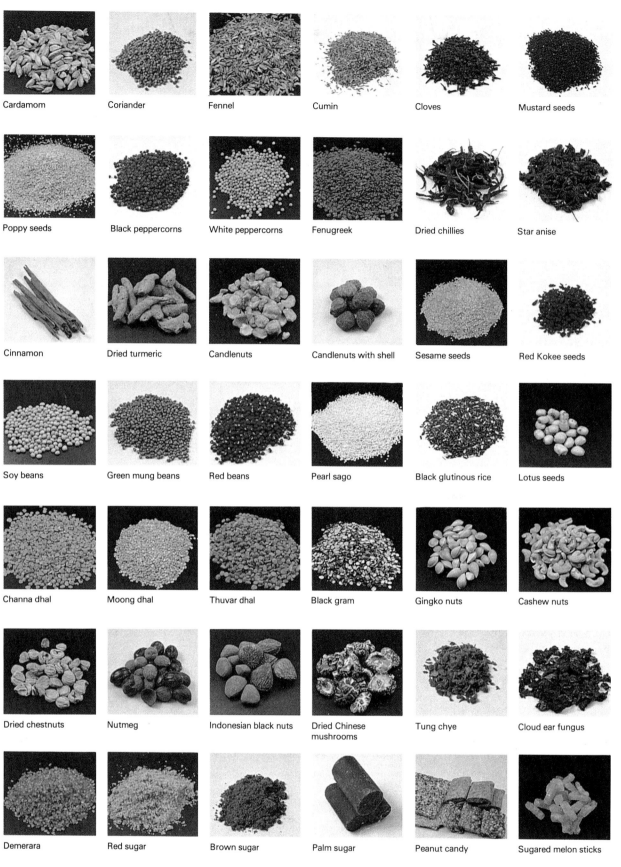

Cardamom

Coriander

Fennel

Cumin

Cloves

Mustard seeds

Poppy seeds

Black peppercorns

White peppercorns

Fenugreek

Dried chillies

Star anise

Cinnamon

Dried turmeric

Candlenuts

Candlenuts with shell

Sesame seeds

Red Kokee seeds

Soy beans

Green mung beans

Red beans

Pearl sago

Black glutinous rice

Lotus seeds

Channa dhal

Moong dhal

Thuvar dhal

Black gram

Gingko nuts

Cashew nuts

Dried chestnuts

Nutmeg

Indonesian black nuts

Dried Chinese
mushrooms

Tung chye

Cloud ear fungus

Demerara

Red sugar

Brown sugar

Palm sugar

Peanut candy

Sugared melon sticks

Dried longans

Chinese red dates

Kamchor

Yeast

Salt fish

Poppadom

INDEX